We Must Not Be Enemies

We Must Not
Be Enemies

Restoring America's
Civic Tradition

Michael Austin

ROWMAN & LITTLEFIELD
Lanham • Boulder • New York • London

Published by Rowman & Littlefield
An imprint of The Rowman & Littlefield Publishing Group, Inc.
4501 Forbes Boulevard, Suite 200, Lanham, Maryland 20706
www.rowman.com

6 Tinworth Street, London SE11 5AL, United Kingdom

British Library Cataloguing in Publication Information Available

Library of Congress Cataloging-in-Publication Data
Names: Austin, Michael, 1966– author.
Title: We must not be enemies : restoring America's civic tradition / Michael
    Austin.
Description: Lanham, Maryland : Rowman & Littlefield, [2019] | Includes
    bibliographical references and index.
Identifiers: LCCN 2018050571 (print) | LCCN 2019000297 (ebook) | ISBN
    9781538121269 (electronic) | ISBN 9781538121252 (cloth : alk. paper)
Subjects: LCSH: Political culture—United States. | Democracy—United States.
    | Civics. | Polarization (Social sciences)—Political aspects—United
    States.
Classification: LCC JK1726 (ebook) | LCC JK1726 .A87 2019 (print) | DDC
    323.6/50973—dc23
LC record available at https://lccn.loc.gov/2018050571

∞™ The paper used in this publication meets the minimum requirements of American
National Standard for Information Sciences—Permanence of Paper for Printed Library
Materials, ANSI/NISO Z39.48-1992.

Printed in the United States of America

For Russel Arben Fox, one of the best arguers I know.
And also the best friend.

The spirit of liberty is the spirit which is not too sure that it is right; the spirit of liberty is the spirit which seeks to understand the minds of other men and women; the spirit of liberty is the spirit which weighs their interest alongside its own without bias; the spirit of liberty remembers that not even a sparrow falls to earth unheeded; the spirit of liberty is the spirit of him who, near two thousand years ago, taught mankind that lesson it has never learned, but has never quite forgotten—that there may be a kingdom where the least shall be heard and considered side-by-side with the greatest.

—Learned Hand, "The Spirit of Liberty"

We must love one another or die.

—W. H. Auden, "September 1, 1939"

Contents

Preface

*W*hen I first began thinking about this book, I gave it a much simpler title than it has now: *Arguing as Friends*. This, it seemed to me, was the essence of what I wanted to talk about. Citizens of a democracy need to argue with each other more and shout at each other less. We need to stop dividing the world into people we disagree with, and must therefore hate, and people we like, and must therefore agree with. This way of thinking, while perfectly in line with our natural impulses, is contrary to the idea of democracy.

When I tested these ideas on some of my own friends, I got two overwhelming responses. First, they told me that the world needed such a book. They, too, perceived the need to address our polarized political culture in a way that did not undermine the value of intense (and not always polite) disagreement and debate. Second, they told me that *Arguing as Friends* was a really dumb title.

So, I present *We Must Not Be Enemies* as a book about arguing as friends. The title comes from Abraham Lincoln's First Inaugural Address. Lincoln likely thought more than any American ever has about the things that hold us together—the traditions, institutions, and relationships that make us a nation. His writings and speeches during America's darkest hour created a template that we can use to become more united in a time that is nowhere near as perilous.

When I have needed examples of arguments and debates, I have drawn them from important points in America's history, or from the great literature of the past, or from the surviving classic texts of democratic Athens and republican Rome. I have quite intentionally used few contemporary examples, not because I don't think that what I have to say applies to the current historical moment, but because I know that much of it applies extremely well and must therefore be handled with care. I want to use the distance afforded by history and literature to avoid the reflexive responses that come when we have too much skin in the game.

But that is not the only reason. I have chosen examples and relevant commentary from a broad spectrum of what we usually call the "liberal arts": philosophy (Aristotle, Cicero, Francis Bacon), history (Thucydides, Plutarch), sociology and political science (Alexis de Tocqueville, James Madison), poetry (Walt Whitman, Ralph Waldo Emerson), drama (Aeschylus, Shakespeare), and fiction (Sinclair Lewis). These authors are the figures who have contributed the most to my own thinking about democracy, debate, and friendship. I believe that they still have much to teach the world. The guiding belief of my career as an educator has been that ideas matter. A solid grounding in the liberal arts—where we encounter many of humanity's greatest and most influential ideas—can make us better friends, better arguers, and better citizens. I hope that this book will demonstrate why this is so.

We Must Not Be Enemies includes ten chapters. Chapters 1 and 2 deal with the responsibilities of citizens in a democracy and develop the argument that democracy can only work if citizens accept the obligations of self-government. Chapters 3–6 deal, in different ways, with the concept of "civic friendship," or the relationship that citizens need to develop with each other in order to govern themselves in a meaningful way. And chapters 7–10 explore strategies for disagreement and debate that allow for vigorous argument about ideas within the context of civic friendship.

I have also included a series of appendices reprinting some of the most important texts that I refer to in these chapters to allow readers to quickly find and read the primary texts themselves rather than relying on my interpretations. The appendices likewise serve as a brief reader of some of the most important things ever thought or said about American democracy.

A lot of people have argued with me—in good ways—about parts of the book that I persisted in sending out through the Interwebs two or three sentences at a time. Among those who allowed me to test my ideas on them, and who provided valuable feedback, were Peter de Schweinitz, Chris Kimball, Ardis Parshall, Russell Fox, Twila Newey, Marianne Eileen Wardle, Jim Fleetwood, David Pace, Jen Black, Arnie Trefflich, Darryl Dickson-Carr, Steven Peck, Emily Hess-Flinders, Heather Harris-Bergevin, Emily Huff Burley, Kevin Payne, Patricia Gunter Karamesines, Kelly McFall, Laura Holliday, Paul Bone, Rachel Mabey Whipple, Katie Mullins, Rebecca Robinson, Lindy Maxwell, Mitch Jarvis, Sally Rideout, Cynthia Bailey Lee, Steve Dunn, and Kristine Haglund. These friends were willing to argue with me, sometimes quite vigorously, and in doing so they allowed me to refine and hone my own arguments—a case in point as to the importance of arguing with friends.

Other colleagues have read large portions of the manuscript and provided feedback, including Tom Kazee, Omer Bayer, and Tony Beavers. Three people—my father, Roger Austin; my good friend Kathryn Duncan; and my new friend Regina Layton—read the entire manuscript and offered detailed, and excellent, recommendations, without which this would be a very different (and substantially inferior) book. My wife, Karen Austin, read the typeset proofs and caught many of my errors. The generosity of these friends and colleagues continues to amaze me.

Finally, I must acknowledge, before anybody beats me to it, that I am not particularly good at doing most of the things that I recommend in this book. I am often outraged, I rarely resist flattery, I frequently argue in ways that are unnecessarily critical and hurtful, and I have a genuinely difficult time displaying charity or kindness. The figure I refer to as "me" in these pages is an aspirational me and not the real thing, and anything I have learned, I have learned by doing things badly. As Robert Browning's Andrea del Sarto mused, "Ah, but a man's reach should exceed his grasp, Or what's a heaven for?"

"The Height to Be Superb Humanity"

*Democracy is hard work that demands our
attention and engagement.*

> If American democracy fails, the ultimate cause will not be a
> foreign invasion or the power of big money or the greed and
> dishonesty of some elected officials or a military coup or the
> internal communist/socialist/fascist takeover that keeps some
> Americans up at night. It will happen because we—you and
> I—became so fearful of each other, of our differences and of
> the future, that we unraveled the civic community on which
> democracy depends.
>
> —Parker J. Palmer, *Healing the Heart of Democracy*

> Remember Democracy never lasts long. It soon wastes exhausts
> and murders itself. There never was a Democracy Yet, that did
> not commit suicide.
>
> —John Adams, letter to John Taylor, December 17, 1814

$\mathcal{A}$mericans do a bad job of talking to each other about politics, and we
need to find ways to do better or we will lose our democracy.

That's the one-sentence version of this book—the quick-and-dirty
elevator pitch designed to grab your attention and make you want to read
more. Like any one-sentence summary, it simplifies relentlessly as it forces
complicated thoughts into a neat little rhetorical package. In the pages that
follow, I will extend, contextualize, historicize, clarify, qualify, and support
this statement, hopefully transforming it from a simple assertion into a persuasive argument.

More than anything else, I want to convince you that we can do it. We can save our democracy. As a nation, we already know how we should talk to each other. Meaningful civic engagement is part of our national DNA. The United States began when fifty-five people who disagreed with each other about almost everything came together at the Constitutional Convention and discussed, debated, negotiated, and compromised until they had created the modern world's first democracy.[1]

Americans have been disagreeing with each other ever since—but this has not stopped us from moving forward. As of 2018, we have gone through fifty-six presidential elections, twenty-four peaceful transfers of power between parties, four presidential assassinations, two presidential impeachments, multiple scandals, and a civil war that almost destroyed the Union. In the process, we have become a much more inclusive democracy than we were when we started out.

We have realized the true potential of words like "created equal" and "we the people" by expanding political rights and civil protections to millions of people who were not considered part of the initial social compact, including women, Native Americans, and people of African descent—all of whom were present when America was founded but excluded from the political body created by the Constitution.

None of this has been easy. We did not end slavery, enfranchise African Americans and women, integrate our society, or outlaw discrimination simply by snapping our fingers and wishing it so. Nor did we accomplish these things by conducting polite debates and vigorous, good-natured discussions. These changes took marches and demonstrations, sustained campaigns of civil disobedience, many contentious elections, more than a few armed soldiers, and an unimaginably horrible war. The civic tradition forged in these furnaces can still serve us today.

The first rule of America's civic tradition is that we will always disagree with each other about important things. Disagreement is the machine that makes our system move forward. If we all woke up one morning and agreed with each other, our entire system would stop working. We are supposed to argue. We are supposed to think that our side is right and the other is wrong and do everything possible to win elections. But we are not supposed to be enemies, as DC Circuit judge Thomas B. Griffith made clear in a 2012 address titled "The Hard Work of Understanding the Constitution":

> Disagreement is critical to the well-being of our nation. But we must carry on our arguments with the realization that those with whom we disagree are not our enemies; rather, they are our colleagues in a great enterprise. When we respect each other enough to respond carefully to argument, we are filling roles necessary in a republic.[2]

This is what democracy looks like when it is working. When it breaks, people treat each other as enemies who do not have a right to exist. They divide into factions that require absolute loyalty from members and intractable opposition to the other side. Factions in power do everything they can to change the rules so they can stay in power. Factions out of power have no agenda beyond getting into power so they can change the rules to favor their side. Social contact between members of different parties becomes increasingly difficult as partisans develop their own vocabularies, historical interpretations, and purported facts. Elections go on as before, but their goal is not to advance policy agendas or select qualified candidates for public service. In a democracy that has stopped working, the only goal of elections is to vanquish the enemy.

When opposition becomes enmity, and the political body descends into factions that do not acknowledge each other's right to exist, and the most basic mechanism of democratic choice—the majority vote—becomes a weapon of mass destruction, democracy dies. People who see those on the other side as enemies who must be destroyed will vote for the candidate who promises to do so—even if it costs them their democracy (spoiler alert: it usually does).

Happily, we are not quite there. But we are getting much too close. A shocking number of books published each year announce that one party or ideological position is destroying America and that the only way to get our country back is to defeat that group (usually about half the country) decisively and forever. The same messages dominate our broadcast stations and our political blogs. Every day we get dozens of messages that encourage us to isolate ourselves in political tribes and treat our political opponents as enemies who cannot be reasoned with and must therefore be vanquished forever.

In the summer of 2016, the Pew Research Center published the results of its most recent survey of partisan animosity among American voters. The results show disturbing shifts from similar surveys conducted in 2008 and 2014. As a nation, we are rapidly becoming much more hostile to, and much less willing to engage with, people who disagree with us on political issues. The survey found, for instance, that

- "58% of Republicans have a very unfavorable impression of the Democratic Party, up from 46% in 2014 and just 32% during the 2008 election year. Among Democrats, highly negative views of the GOP have followed a similar trajectory—from 37% in 2008 to 43% in 2014 and 55% currently."
- 45 percent of Republicans consider Democrats "so misguided that they threaten the nation's well-being," compared to 37 percent in 2014. And "41% of Democrats say the same about the Republican

Party's policies, an increase of 10 percentage points from two years ago."

- 68 percent of Republicans "say a major reason they identify with the GOP is that 'the Democratic Party's policies are harmful to the country,' while 64% say it is because they think 'the Republican Party's policies are good for the country.'" Among Democrats, "68% say a major reason they are a Democrat is that the Democratic Party's policies are beneficial for the country, while 62% say a major reason is because Republican policies harm the country."
- 50 percent of Republicans and 46 percent of Democrats report that they find political discussions with people they disagree with "stressful and frustrating."
- 55 percent of Democrats and 49 percent of Republicans say that the other party "makes them feel afraid"; 47 percent of Democrats and 46 percent of Republicans say that the other party "makes them feel angry."[3]

Results like these do not bode well for the health of our democracy, but neither do they sound the death knell. We shouldn't get swept up by a narrative that sees our society as the endpoint of a long decline in civility from the glories of the founding era down to the slime and corruption of the current day. Such narratives are common enough across the political spectrum because they don't take much effort to create—and they tap into a quirk of the human psyche that causes us to filter out the bad things of the past and the good things of the present in almost equal measure.

But the Americans of the past fought about politics a lot—sometimes with lethal results. Three of our founding fathers died in political duels with other founding fathers, including Alexander Hamilton, who was shot by the sitting vice president of the United States. The elections of 1800 (John Adams versus Thomas Jefferson) and 1828 (John Quincy Adams versus Andrew Jackson) were as nasty and polarized as anything we have seen in our recent history. Duels between politicians continued well into the 1850s. And political dysfunction today does not approach what the country experienced in the years leading up to the Civil War. When Abraham Lincoln won the presidency in 1860, he was not even on the ballot in ten southern states, and the mere fact of his election caused seven of those states to secede from the Union before his first day in office.

The American Civil War will loom large in these pages as the one time in our history when the mechanisms of democracy failed. In retrospect, though, we can see that these mechanisms had never really been democratic in the first place. The institution of slavery was never compatible with democracy.

America could not be a truly democratic nation until it had ended this perni-
cious practice and fully enfranchised its population. And because slavery was
built into the Constitution in a fundamentally undemocratic way—without
any input from the people who suffered the most from it—it could not be
addressed with the mechanisms created by that Constitution.

But the Civil War also encouraged people to think more about things
like unity, friendship, and democracy than they had ever done before. As
Americans sacrificed enormous blood and treasure preserving the Union,
some of them tried hard to understand the value of what they were trying to
save. The phrase "We must not be enemies" comes from the inaugural address that Abraham Lincoln gave after seven states had already seceded—part
of his last-ditch effort to keep the rest of the Union together. Lincoln thought
deeply about America and democracy—and he did more than anybody else
ever has to articulate the shape that democracy must take to succeed in the
future. "We must not be enemies," I believe, is the best summary that we have
of Lincoln's political thought.

Another American from the Civil War era who thought deeply about
democracy was the great American poet Walt Whitman. Whitman was democracy's number one fan for more than forty years, and during the period
leading up to the Civil War, he published poem after poem appealing to his
fellow citizens to embrace each other. Among the many pleas for unity in
the 1860 edition of *Leaves of Grass* we find the lengthy "Calamus" sequence,
which includes the following passage:

> STATES!
> Were you looking to be held together by the lawyers?
> By an agreement on a paper? Or by arms?
> Away!
> I arrive, bringing these, beyond all the forces of courts and arms,
> These! to hold you together as firmly as the earth itself is held together.
> . . .
> There shall from me be a new friendship—It shall be called after my name,
> It shall circulate through The States, indifferent of place,
> It shall twist and intertwist them through and around each other—Compact
>   shall they be,
> showing new signs,
> Affection shall solve every one of the problems of freedom,
> Those who love each other shall be invincible,
> They shall finally make America completely victorious, in my name.[4]

Whitman makes some big claims here. Can affection really "solve every
one of the problems of freedom" in a democratic society? Probably not. But

it can solve some of them. In democracies, the "problems of freedom" usually have a lot to do with divisions between free people: majorities can enact legislation hostile to minorities, social stratification can produce intractable class differences, and people who do not feel well served by large populations can withdraw from the body politic and cause it to collapse. These are all problems that affection—or the ability of citizens to see each other as friends rather than enemies—can solve.

"Friendship," of course, can mean many different things. Both Lincoln and Whitman were talking about a very specific kind of friendship, what the ancient Greek philosopher Aristotle called *philia politikē*, or "civic friendship." Civic friendship is not the same as the personal intimacy that we can only have with a handful of people throughout our lives. It isn't even the same as the general goodwill that we (hopefully) feel for the people we know from work, school, or Facebook. Civic friendship is a posture that we take toward our fellow citizens that grows out of the realization that we are not playing a zero-sum game with each other. It proceeds from the assumption that our lives are connected in ways that matter and that we stand to benefit jointly when our nation does well—and suffer jointly when it does not.

Civic friendship also means that we must argue with each other without becoming enemies, which might be the hardest thing that democracy requires. It goes against much of our evolutionary programming. We evolved in a tribal environment, and through millions of years of natural selection, our brains have been hard-wired to want to cooperate with our friends and destroy our enemies. Arguing with friends is unnatural. But so are committee meetings, waking up early, loving our neighbors as ourselves, and just about everything else that makes civilization possible. As Katharine Hepburn tells Humphrey Bogart in *The African Queen*, "Nature, Mr. Allnut, is what we are put in this world to rise above."

Democracy has always required people to overcome their tribal instincts. In fact, the world's first democracy began as a response to the tribalism that dominated Athens before the fifth century BCE. The founder of Athenian democracy, a man named Cleisthenes, knew that old divisions would eventually swamp his new form of government unless he did something to break the power of the tribes. So he disbanded them and created ten new ones named after mythical heroes instead of existing clans.

The basic units of these new tribes were 139 *demes*, or organized communities with their own councils and elected officials. Cleisthenes took great pains to combine *demes* from different parts of Athens into the same tribe so that "members of the same tribe came from different parts of the country" and "old local and territorial loyalties were dissolved."[5] The rule of the demos, or the people of the *demes*, replaced the rule of the *aristoi*, or the tribal nobility. The very word "democracy," then, literally means something like "self-government by people organized in a way specifically designed to override their tribal nature."

For much of Athens's history, the principles of democracy warred with the principles of tribalism—just as they do in every democracy, including ours. Tribalism—with its clear-cut lines between "us" and "them" and its appeals to our deepest fears and resentments—permits the mind to travel along its most comfortable and well-worn neural paths. Civic friendship means that we have to be friends with people who aren't like us at all, and we have to disagree with them without casting them in the role of "other." It means that we have to work diligently for the benefit of people we don't like. And it means that we have to respond gracefully (or at least nonviolently) when we lose contests about things that we consider important.

Democracy, in other words, asks us to do hard things. This was Whitman's last word on the subject. In 1889, three years before his death, Whitman wrote his final poem about democracy—not to his fellow US citizens but to the people of Brazil, who had just thrown off their hereditary monarch and proclaimed their country a republic. On December 25, Whitman wrote the poem "A Christmas Greeting" to welcome Brazil into the family of democratic nations. In the process, he distilled a lifetime of thought about democracy into a final letter to the world:

> WELCOME, Brazilian brother—thy ample place is ready;
> A loving hand—a smile from the north—a sunny instant hail!
> (Let the future care for itself, where it reveals its troubles, impedimentas,
> Ours, ours the present throe, the democratic aim, the acceptance and the faith;)
> To thee to-day our reaching arm, our turning neck—to thee from us the
>   expectant eye,
> Thou cluster free! thou brilliant lustrous one! thou, learning well,
> The true lesson of a nation's light in the sky,
> (More shining than the Cross, more than the Crown,)
> The height to be superb humanity.[6]

The final lines of this poem explain, as well as anybody ever has, what it takes to have a successful democracy. We can't do it by appealing to a divine force or by changing the structure of government (the Cross and the Crown). Good governments are created not by certain kinds of constitutions but by certain kinds of people. Democracy requires "the height to be superb humanity." Ordinary humanity just won't do.

Superb humans do the hard things necessary to create good societies: they study issues, they reach across political divides, they try to understand people on their own terms, and they spend time crafting careful arguments rather than simply shouting at people they disagree with. This all takes time and requires that we do things that make us uncomfortable. It is much easier to stay in our echo chambers, flatter our friends, let them flatter us, and indulge in recreational outrage on social media. This is the path of least resistance. It is familiar and comfortable, but it does not lead to democracy.

THREE THINGS THIS BOOK IS NOT

I usually don't like negative definitions—especially in introductory chapters. I much prefer introductory chapters that tell me what a book is rather than what it is not, and I have tried to do exactly that in this chapter so far. In my experience of writing and talking about some of the topics in this book, however, I have found that audiences often hear three arguments that I am not making—but that have been made so often, and in so many books about contemporary politics, that people naturally expect them to be part of my argument too. I present these three arguments here briefly as a way to distance myself from them before I start in earnest to make my own.

This Book Is Not a Call for Politeness

This book will have little to say about what people normally call "civility." If we could use the word the way that the Romans once did—as something like "citizencraft" or "civic engagement"—it would be exactly the right word to describe what I think we need more of. But in contemporary usage, "civility" usually gets reduced to "politeness." This is not merely wrong; it is exactly wrong. Civic engagement is necessary to democracy. Politeness is not even particularly helpful. Meaningful civic discussion can aspire to be respectful, but it must never try to be polite.

I am not suggesting that we try to be rude or hurtful. But the essence of good manners is to make sure that everybody feels comfortable, while any political discussion worth having requires us to make sure that everybody feels uncomfortable. Discomfort produces tension, and tension is essential to growth, persuasion, compromise, and forward movement. And while it might be nice to manage the necessary levels of tension with grace and good humor—focusing only on arguments without criticizing or becoming defensive—this probably isn't going to happen because human beings just don't work that way.

The desire to be polite will often push us away from precisely the uncomfortable discussions that we need to have. And this is just when we are talking to our friends. When we worry about being polite with political opponents, we will often discover that everybody is a lot more comfortable just not talking at all. And this is the fatal shift. When we choose to be comfortable instead of having hard conversations, we stop doing democracy.

We have centuries of proof that democracy can survive impoliteness. The republic can withstand people insulting each other, blaming each other, and being mean to each other. It can even withstand the occasional shouting match (though there are a lot of very good reasons to move past this stage). But democracy cannot long endure when we refuse to engage with each other at all—when we divide into self-contained tribes, each with its own values, perspectives, definitions, and facts. This, too, has happened in our country—with an issue that really could not be solved with the existing democratic institutions—and it led to the bloodiest war of our history.

When we reach the point that we are not willing to be in each other's presence anymore, and we refuse to engage because we would rather be comfortable, then our institutions aren't going to keep working for very long. The echo chamber, not the shouting match, is the greatest threat to our republic. The greatest fear I have is that we will once again become two nonoverlapping nations within a nation who separate themselves because they don't want to be uncomfortable. That will mean that democracy really is over, and war will not be far behind.

This Book Does Not Argue That We Need to Change the Structure of Our Government

There are all sorts of structural changes we could make to try to fix our government. Depending on whom you ask, the big contenders include abolishing the electoral college, limiting congressional terms, revoking lifetime tenure for Supreme Court justices, eliminating gerrymandering, limiting campaign contributions, requiring a balanced budget, and instituting a European-style parliamentary system that encourages multiparty voting. Lots of people have written books—some of them excellent—advocating all these changes and many more.

I am not going to talk about any of these proposals because I do not think any of them has much chance of happening. Nearly all of them would require amending the Constitution, which would in turn require a two-thirds vote in both houses of Congress and approval of three-quarters of the states. This can only happen when people in the country trust each other and are willing to set aside differences and work for the common good. We can't even convince our representatives to keep the government open on a regular basis. We don't have anywhere near the level of consensus necessary to amend the Constitution—especially in ways likely to benefit one party more than another (as all the examples above would do).

This does not mean that I don't agree with these proposals. Some of them would be wonderful changes to our system. Our constitution is 240 years old and was designed for a very different country and world than we now live in. If we set out to design a country from the ground up today, we would do a lot of things differently. But that is not the task before us. We have to focus on things that we actually control, and one of these things, no matter who we are, is the way we talk to other people. And if we get better at talking to each other, we might create a political environment capable of amending the Constitution and working for the public good.

This Book Does Not Describe All the Other People Who Are Destroying Democracy

If you want to know who is destroying democracy, just do a quick Google search. It will give you a comprehensive list that includes conservatives, white people, the elite, millennials, illegal immigrants, liberals, political parties, stupid people, socialism, rich people, and David Brooks—and that's just the first two screens. There is no shortage of Internet opinions about just who is responsible for our ills, and more than a few have found their way into best-selling books.

The world doesn't need any more books like that. Hundreds of them are published every year—all with the same basic argument: "Somebody else broke America, and *we* must take it back from *them*." The identity of "them," of course, varies with the bias of the writer and the target audience, but the rhetoric rarely changes. Our side is "We, the People," the rightful owners of the country, and the other side consists of "They, Not the People," usurpers whose opinions place them outside the legitimate political body.

And this mind-set is precisely what needs fixing. Decades of bad arguments have left many of us unable to imagine a better future that does not involve the unconditional surrender of *them* (whoever they may be) and the final victory of *us*. But democracy doesn't work that way. We are all us; there is no them. The other side is us. The government is us. The liberals and the conservatives are us. And the responsibility for making our government work better lies entirely with us. Democracy does not always give us the government we want; it usually gives us the government we deserve.

Those of us who have lived all our lives in self-governing societies often fail to realize just how fragile democracy can be. We can't afford to take ours for granted. Liberal democracy—a political system that combines the mechanisms of self-government with respect for individual liberties and the rule of law—came as late as it did in human history because it requires an extraordinarily high degree of social organization, cooperation, and non-zero-sum thinking. Most of the world's people did not live under democratic governments until the end of the twentieth century, and in the twenty-first century, this number has gotten smaller. Formerly democratic nations have slipped back into authoritarianism and lost many of the democratic institutions they once had.

We don't have to follow these nations. But we can if we want to—or if we don't want to do the hard work that keeping our democracy requires. Democracy means that we can have the kind of government that we want, but it also means that we must accept responsibility for the kind of government we have. When we allow ourselves to be persuaded by bad arguments and despicable behavior, we get bad arguments and despicable behavior. If we required better arguments, we would get better arguments. If we demanded more cooperation between parties, we would get that too.

Most of us will never run for Congress or control a super PAC. Few of us will ever appear on national television to explain our political positions. But we all talk to each other. And most of us talk to each other about politics—at our work and family gatherings, in our places of worship, on our social media feeds. And we consume political discussions at an impressive rate: politically themed media—newspapers, blogs, websites, talk radio, TV news, and books—generate billions of dollars a year in revenues for their producers and engage millions of Americans every day. We likely talk to each other about politics more than any other society on earth. And despite years of practice, we still do it very badly.

My great hope for this book is that it will help some of us do it better.

• 2 •

"The Apprenticeship of Liberty"

Good citizens practice democracy every day.

There is nothing more prodigal of wonders than the art of being
free . . . but nothing is harder than the apprenticeship of liberty.

—Alexis de Tocqueville, *Democracy in America*

In 1976, my school, Carnegie Elementary School in Tulsa, Oklahoma,
decided to start a football team. We needed a name and a mascot, and the
principal announced that we would take a vote. Anyone who had a suggestion
could submit it to the office, and he would compile them onto a ballot that
would go out to the whole school. I didn't know much about football, but I
did know that Andrew Carnegie made his fortune in steel, and there was a
professional team in Pittsburgh called the Steelers, so I submitted the name
"Carnegie Steelers."

Over the next week or so I campaigned with vigor. I told all my friends
that we had to be the Steelers because it reflected something unique about
us. Any school in town could call themselves Lions or Grizzlies, but only
Carnegie could be the Steelers. I realize now that I could not have been
the only person to submit this name. It was such an obvious choice that it
probably occurred to half the school (and it certainly didn't hurt that the
Pittsburgh Steelers had just won back-to-back Super Bowls). Nonetheless,
when the principal announced that we would indeed be the Carnegie Steelers,
I felt that I had done something significant. And I felt like I owned the name.

Though I didn't realize it at the time, I know now that I had been
participating in what Alexis de Tocqueville called "the apprenticeship of
liberty." The American "teaches himself about the forms of government by

13

governing," Tocqueville wrote in his monumental book *Democracy in America*. "He watches the great work of society being done every day before his eyes and, in a sense, by his hand."[1] So when we students of Carnegie Elementary picked a name for our football team, we were learning how to be citizens— not by reading little fifth-grade editions of Thucydides or by memorizing the preamble to the Constitution but by actually doing democracy.

Like most Americans, I have been doing democracy on a small scale all my life—in student councils, homeowner associations, faculty committees, administrative councils, and religious congregations and in the informal company of friends, where choosing a movie to watch on a Saturday night often involves three parliamentary motions and a filibuster. We do not do these things naturally. We do them culturally, because democracy and self-government have become such an important part of our culture that we can't imagine doing things any other way. And, Tocqueville notes, Americans did these things before there was an America. The framers of the Constitution designed our republic, but our democracy arose from a culture that was already here.

WHAT TOCQUEVILLE SAW

Alexis Charles Henri Clérel, Viscount de Tocqueville (1805–1859), had a deeply personal interest in democracy. He wanted to know what made democracy work in the United States because he wanted to understand why it had failed in his native France. The French Revolution began with noble sentiments about equality, freedom, and democracy. But it soon descended into anarchy, and most of Tocqueville's relatives were guillotined during the Reign of Terror. His own parents were spared only at the last minute, by the fall of Robespierre three days before their scheduled execution. Twelve years later, Alexis de Tocqueville was born into a very different France ruled by the emperor Napoleon I, who exploited the chaos of the Revolution to make himself a dictator.

Throughout his life, Tocqueville watched France lurch from one extreme form of government to another—never quite able to give up the democratic ideals of the Revolution but never able to use those ideals to create a stable democracy.[2] Both a liberal and an optimist, Tocqueville wanted to help his country find the path to functioning self-government, but he knew that just getting rid of tyrants wouldn't do the trick. The Revolution had made it clear that democracy is not the default position for human societies. It does not spring up automatically wherever people are not being actively oppressed by emperors and kings. It takes something else.

If he wanted to find out what it really took to create a democracy, Tocqueville understood, he would have to study one up close. So in 1831, at age twenty-five, he set out with his friend Francis Beaumont on a nine-month tour of the United States. Officially they were on a mission to study prisons and penitentiaries on behalf of the new French king. But really Tocqueville wanted to get to know the world's only large democracy to see what made it work. After his travels, Tocqueville returned to France and wrote *Democracy in America*, which many people (and I am one of them) consider the best book ever written about either democracy or America.

Democracy in America is a big book that tries to answer a big question: Why can democracy work in the United States but not in Europe? Tocqueville offers a lot of answers. American democracy works because it was incorporated into a well-designed republic with a written constitution. It works because the branches of government constantly monitor and check each other. It works because it protects certain freedoms—expression, press, religion, and assembly—from the caprices of the majority. Tocqueville determined, however, that these things were the consequences of democracy in America, not its causes.

The true secret of America's successful democracy, Tocqueville determined, lay in what he referred to as the mores of its people. "By *mores*," Tocqueville explains, "I mean here what the Ancients meant by the term: I apply it not only to mores in the strictest sense, what one might call habits of the heart, but also to . . . the whole range of ideas that shape habits of mind." Mores can refer to beliefs, values, biases, rhetorical styles, and just about anything else that shapes how we evaluate and interact with our environments. "I use the word to refer to the whole moral and intellectual state of a people."[3]

Democratic mores produced a population that enacted democracy in everything it did. Americans liked to talk to each other about politics, and they did so exuberantly. Tocqueville saw political conversations happening everywhere in the United States—not just about the big national issues that showed up in presidential elections but also about local and community issues that most Europeans would not even consider political:

> To set foot on American soil is to find oneself in tumultuous surroundings. A confused clamor proceeds from every quarter. A thousand voices assail the ear simultaneously, each giving expression to some social need. Everywhere things are in an uproar; the people of one neighborhood decide whether they should build a church; in another they are busy choosing a representative; elsewhere delegates from the country rush to the city to offer their views on certain local improvements. In yet another village, farmers abandon their fields to discuss plans for a highway or school. Citizens meet for the sole purpose of announcing that they disapprove of the government,

while others hail the men now in office as the fathers of their country. Still others, being of the opinion that drunkenness is the principal cause of the state's woes, solemnly pledge to set an example of temperance.[4]

It is hard for modern Americans to understand the bewilderment that Tocqueville felt when he saw Americans having political discussions as though they were a form of entertainment. For Americans, political meetings were social occasions, and political rallies were a night on the town. "Even women often attend public meetings and find relaxation from the cares of the household in listening to political speeches."[5] These sorts of things just didn't happen in the Old World, where one might secretly pledge one's life and honor to a set of political ideals but would never argue about those ideals casually while getting a haircut.

In America, Tocqueville experienced comprehensive political conversations that actually made a difference. Americans voted for things in their communities and neighborhoods, and they saw the tangible results of their participation every day. Tocqueville marveled, "Americans almost always carry the habits of public life over into private life. With them, the idea of the jury turns up in games played in school, and parliamentary forms influence even banquet arrangements."[6] Americans succeeded where France failed because they had developed a culture of discussing politics, and even disagreeing about important political issues, without feeling the need to kill each other. They got good at democracy the same way that anybody gets good at anything: they practiced.

Tocqueville never made a list of the mores that support democracy. From his writings, though, combined with the work of other philosophers and political scientists who have studied successful democracies, we can distill some of the most important attitudes and assumptions that make democracy work. None of these are universal, of course, but they can all be reasonably described as social mores that have been common throughout American history and continue to influence us today. Collectively, these represent what Tocqueville called "the apprenticeship of liberty."

We Accept the Right of Other Points of View to Exist

In 1978, the American Civil Liberties Union (ACLU) made national headlines when it chose to defend the right of a group of avowed neo-Nazis to march through the Chicago suburb of Skokie, Illinois, carrying swastikas. The city of Skokie, home to a large number of Holocaust survivors, denied the group's request to march on the grounds that a display of swastikas would likely incite violence. The ACLU took the case all the way to the Supreme Court and won, arguing that the conflict "tests the very foundations of democracy" and that the city's order, "whatever we might feel about the content of the speech, violates the very essence of the First Amendment."[7]

The Skokie case became famous for the sharp contrast between the ACLU and its clients. The core principle involved in the dispute—that people have the right to believe and say things that other people find extremely offensive—is fundamental to American democracy. Americans may pass laws against actions that stem from certain opinions, but we do not criminalize the expression of those opinions, no matter how offensive we find them.

Nothing is more deeply ingrained in American democracy than the principle of free speech—and nothing will bring Americans together more quickly than the perception that some government entity wants to punish people for having or expressing an opinion. This is not universally true of the world's established democracies. In 2010, for example, France made it a crime to publicly disrespect the French flag or to boo during a public playing of "La Marseillaise."[8] Germany has long banned Holocaust denial and the display of Nazi symbols and, in 2017, passed Europe's toughest laws against hate speech in online forums.[9] And a number of European democracies ban or restrict various types of face and head coverings worn by Muslim women.[10]

American courts have consistently rejected attempts to impose these kinds of regulations on free speech, as they did in 1989 in the *Texas v. Johnson* decision invalidating state laws against desecrating the American flag and a year later when they overturned legislation that made flag burning a federal crime.[11] But institutions have not usually had to force a broad interpretation of the right to free speech on the American public. It has long been, and remains, a core part of our national identity.

In 2015, the Pew Research Center interviewed more than forty thousand people in thirty-eight countries and asked a series of questions about free speech, free press, and free assembly. Table 2.1 reports the answers of people in established democracies to two crucial questions: (1) Should people be able to make statements that publicly criticize the government? (2) Should people be able to make public statements that are offensive to your religion or beliefs?[12] The results tell an important story about the way that Americans think.

Like people in most modern democracies, Americans believe that they should be allowed to criticize the government. Americans score high in this belief, but not remarkably so. On the second question, however, America is the extreme outlier. In many of the world's established democracies, fewer than half the people believe that the government should protect speech that personally offends them. Among Americans, 77 percent believe it should—a figure thirteen points higher than that for the second-ranking Canadians and thirty-three points higher than the international mean.

Table 2.1. Views on Critical and Offensive Speech by Country

Country	People Should Be Free to Criticize the Government	People Should Be Free to Say Things Offensive to Your Religion or Beliefs
Australia	95	62
Brazil	90	43
Canada	93	64
Chile	94	26
France	89	53
Germany	93	38
India	72	28
Israel	93	32
Italy	88	29
Japan	67	24
Mexico	84	56
Nigeria	71	33
South Africa	64	50
Spain	96	54
Turkey	52	24
United Kingdom	94	57
United States	95	77
Average	**84.12 percent**	**44.12 percent**

Defending speech that we disagree with—and even speech that profoundly offends us—is an important part of the American character. This does not mean that every single American does it, or that nobody else does it, or that there aren't limits to our willingness to suffer insult in the name of free speech. But freedom of speech plays an important role in the way that we define ourselves to ourselves—and to others. As a result, we are more inclined than the citizens of most other nations to fight for other people's right to offend us. *That's a more!*

We Feel Ownership in Our Government

When I chaired a large department at a public university, one of my least favorite duties was responding to complaints from students and, more frequently, their parents. Nearly every parent I spoke with on these occasions eventually got around to reminding me that he or she paid taxes and was therefore my employer. As annoying as I found this line of reasoning at the time (and I usually found it *very* annoying), it says something important about the way Americans think: we see ourselves as the rightful owners of our government.

Tocqueville noticed the same thing when he visited in 1831. The Americans he met felt ownership in their government. They complained about their elected officials, of course, but they complained in a way that one complains about employees, not kings. And the fact that ordinary citizens felt that they owned the government created strong incentive for public virtue:

> In the United States, the common man understands how the general prosperity affects his own happiness—a very simple idea, yet one of which the people in most countries have only a very limited grasp. What is more, he has become accustomed to looking at that prosperity as his own handiwork. He therefore identifies the public fortune with his own, and he works for the good of the state not only out of duty or pride, but, I would almost venture to say, out of greed.[13]

We need to remember that Tocqueville visited the United States during one of the most politically divided times in the nation's history. Andrew Jackson had just won one of the nastiest election contests ever. Most of the political elites in the country considered the new president both an illegitimate dictator and an utter barbarian, while a large portion of the common people saw him as a political savior. Nearly every newspaper in the country was affiliated with either the Whigs or the Democrats and regularly published damaging (and often false) information about the other party. And a lot of people couldn't even imagine being friends with somebody on the other side.

It was, in other words, a time very much like our own.

Tocqueville's observations about the sense of ownership that people feel in a democratic society transcend any specific time and get to the core of what democracy means. It is a mechanism for self-government, not just a way to select rulers. This means that, for a nation to function democratically, its people must believe (to paraphrase the famous words attributed to Louis XIV) that they are the state. They must have a sense of their own power to control—through their collective action—the business of their community, their state, and their nation. For a free and democratic people, the government should always be an "us" and not a "them."

We Believe That Persuasion Is Possible

In the world that Tocqueville knew, someone who wanted to change society had to follow a time-honored set of procedures: start a secret society, swear oaths of fidelity, throw up barricades, riot in the streets, and then hope that people came in from the countryside to join the cause. These strategies produced major revolutions in 1789, 1830, and 1848. But France never managed to produce a stable democracy because force alone cannot produce a culture that values persuasion more highly than force.

Tocqueville believed that America succeeded where France failed because Americans had developed a culture of persuasion, whereas the French saw political action as "nothing more than the right to make war on the government." He argued that "with consciousness of strength comes violence as the first idea to come to a party or individual" and that "the idea of persuasion comes only later; it is born of experience." Whereas European nations in the nineteenth century saw political association as "a weapon of war," Americans saw it as a way to "promote competition among ideas in order to discover which arguments are most likely to make an impression on the majority."[14] This made the difference between a nation that transferred power peacefully and one that had six violent changes of government in just over sixty years.

With the exception of the Civil War, Americans have resolved most of their internal disputes either by voting or by accepting, however grudgingly, the decisions of courts and other democratic institutions. Given the history of most of the world in the last 250 years or so, this has not been a minor accomplishment. But even in moments like the present one—when partisan divisions are deep and public discourse is shallow—advocacy of violent overthrow or civil war remains a fringe position. Most Americans still believe, as we have always believed, that the best way to change society is to argue, persuade people to our side, hold elections, and live with the results until the next election season.

In the landmark 1996 book *Democracy and Disagreement*, Amy Gutmann and Dennis Thompson argued that serious moral disagreements are both inevitable and desirable in a democracy. Such disagreements will always be difficult, as they deal with the values that most define us as individuals. We rarely resolve serious moral conflicts once and for all, but we do find temporary solutions that allow us to keep living together. Yet democracy requires that we keep having the discussions and that we come to them with reasons and positions capable of persuading other people to accept (even if they don't completely adopt) our views. Gutmann and Thompson call this "reciprocity," in which "citizens try to offer reasons that other similarly motivated citizens can accept even though they recognize that they share only some of one another's values. When our deliberations about moral disagreements in politics are guided by reciprocity, citizens recognize and respect one another as moral agents, not merely as abstract objects of others' moral reasoning."[15] Persuasion, in other words, can only occur when people consider each other competent moral agents who have compelling reasons for their beliefs—even if we do not share, and even if we fundamentally disagree with, those reasons. And somewhere behind our disagreements there have to be values that we share and can appeal to as part of our attempt to persuade. As Gutmann and Thompson explain, "Disagreements often run deep. If they did not, there would be no need for argument. But if they ran too deep, there would be no point in argument. Deliberative disagreements lie in the depths between simple misunderstanding and immutable irreconcilability."[16]

We persuade other people by appealing to the values that we share with them. If we have no shared values or we become so blinded by partisan hatred that we can no longer acknowledge the values we share, then argument becomes irrelevant. When that happens, violence becomes inevitable. This, Tocqueville noted, was the case in Europe, where "there exist parties so different from the majority that they can never hope to gain its support, yet they believe themselves strong enough to take it on in battle. When a party of this kind forms an association, its aim is not to convince but to combat."[17]

One of the American mores most responsible for democracy, Tocqueville believed, is the fact that we believe that we share enough with our fellow citizens that we can persuade them into acceptable positions and compromises without resorting to force.

We Accept the Results of Elections

On March 4, 1801, something happened in the United States that had never before happened in the history of human beings: an elected head of state gave up his power voluntarily after losing a bitterly disputed election to a political opponent. John Adams retired quietly to his home in Massachusetts and allowed Thomas Jefferson to be sworn in as his successor.

To the watching world, it had been by no means clear that Adams would step aside. Executive transitions caused great anxiety in most of the world. Kings and emperors went to great lengths to secure male heirs so that their states would not be thrown into chaos when they died. Childless monarchs produced extreme uneasiness throughout their kingdoms, since their deaths often resulted in secession crises and civil wars. And the postelection dustup between Jefferson and Aaron Burr did little to convince the international community that the Republicans were ready to govern. Few Europeans could have imagined a tumultuous period like the election of 1800 ending with anything other than a civil war.

Despite what the Jeffersonians said, though, Adams had no intention of starting a monarchy. Adams was impeccably ethical and constitutionally incapable of subterfuge. He was also one of the nation's foremost constitutional theorists and a true believer in democracy. There was never any question that he would step aside after losing the election. But when he did, he set a precedent that has held for our entire history: people step aside when they lose elections. This did not happen with a head of state anywhere but in the United States until the twentieth century.[18]

As Americans, we expect each other to accept the results of elections too, which is not the same thing as being happy about those results or not wanting to change them in the next election. But we don't try to change them through violent insurrections that would destroy the democratic process. As Tocqueville explains, this is one of the mores most deeply rooted in the American mind:

> There is also a second reason, more direct and more powerful than the first: in the United States each individual has in a sense a personal interest in seeing to it that everyone obeys the law. For a person who is not in the majority today may find himself in it tomorrow, and the respect that he professes for the will of the legislature now he may later have occasion to demand for himself. No matter how irksome a law may be, the resident of the United States therefore submits to it without protest, not simply because it is the work of the majority but also because he had a hand in making it himself. He looks upon it as a contract to which he is a party.

This aspect of our national character, without which democracy could not exist, seeps into almost every aspect of our lives. We vote on everything: what movie to see, where to go on vacation, who the new "American Idol" will be, and even what mascot our elementary school football team will have. These things teach us the skills not only of discussion and debate but also of accepting the results of an election that we have had a fair chance to participate in. And when we incorporate these skills into the fabric of our lives every day, they seem perfectly normal to us every four years when we use them to select a president.[19]

We Let Our Institutions Do Their Work

In September 1957, the United States passed one of the most significant tests of its democratic institutions since the Civil War. Three years earlier, the Supreme Court had unanimously decided in the *Brown v. Board of Education* decision that segregation of public schools was unconstitutional. The Little Rock, Arkansas, school board had voluntarily complied with the order by submitting a plan to integrate its schools gradually beginning in 1957, when nine handpicked African American students would be invited to enroll at Little Rock Central High School.

When the first day of school came, large crowds materialized to protest the school board's decision, and Governor Orval Faubus deployed the Arkansas National Guard with instructions to prevent the students from enrolling. Woodrow Wilson Mann, the pro-integration mayor of Little Rock, sent a telegram to President Dwight D. Eisenhower asking him to intervene, and the federal court in Arkansas directed the governor to stand down. The state's most influential newspapers—the *Arkansas Democrat* and the *Arkansas Gazette*—ran a series of editorials criticizing the governor for his stance and urging citizens to support the decision of the courts and the school board.[20]

After a twenty-one-day standoff, President Eisenhower responded decisively. He federalized all National Guard troops in Arkansas and ordered them to protect the African American students and ensure their enrollment. On September 24, 1957, Eisenhower addressed the nation in a televised speech that set forth a forceful argument, not for integration per se but for the importance of supporting the institutions of democracy:

> It is important that the reasons for my action be understood by all our citizens. As you know, the Supreme Court of the United States has decided that separate public educational facilities for the races are inherently unequal and therefore compulsory school segregation laws are unconstitutional. Our personal opinions about the decision have no bearing on the matter of enforcement; the responsibility and authority of the Supreme Court to interpret the Constitution are very clear. Local Federal courts were instructed by the Supreme Court to issue such orders and decrees as might be necessary to achieve admission to public schools without regard to race—and with all deliberate speed. . . .
>
> The very basis of our individual rights and freedoms rests upon the certainty that the President and the Executive Branch of Government will support and insure the carrying out of the decisions of the Federal Courts, even, when necessary, with all the means at the President's command. Unless the President did so, anarchy would result. There would be no security for any except that which each one of us could provide for himself. The interest of the nation in the proper fulfillment of the law's requirements cannot yield to opposition and demonstrations by some few persons. Mob rule cannot be allowed to override the decisions of our courts.[21]

Eisenhower was speaking to a nation deeply divided over the Supreme Court's decision. A NORC survey conducted in June 1956 reported an even split—49 percent to 49 percent, with 2 percent undecided—on the question "Do you think white students and Negro/black students should go to the same schools or to separate schools?"[22] After Eisenhower's speech, however,

68.4 percent of the nation supported his actions—nearly 20 percent more than supported integration itself at the time.[23]

The Little Rock standoff involved many of the laws, policies, and governing bodies that Tocqueville considered our "democratic institutions": the Constitution, the federal courts, separation of powers, civilian control of the military, state and local governments, and a free press. It was an ugly and frightening time, but it did not end in an insurrection or a bloodbath because the institutions empowered to protect democracy held firmly in place.

Our institutions don't get stretched to the breaking point every day, but when they have been, they have held the nation together—at least since the Civil War. This does not mean that Americans like or agree with the way that these institutions decide controversial questions. Both citizens and politicians regularly criticize federal court decisions as "judicial activism" and "gross abuses of power." But they usually accept them and abide by them anyway. Disputed presidential elections in 1876 and 2000 made a lot of people very angry, but they didn't break the nation. When things like this happen, people channel their anger into trying to win the next election. They do not employ violence to overthrow the government to get what they want because respect for these institutions is an important part of our national character.

We Are Suspicious of Power

Vast ambition has never fit well with democracy. One of the first people to find this out was the Athenian general Themistocles, whose long-term vision and tactical brilliance saved the Greek world from a Persian invasion in 480 BCE. Nine years later, Themistocles was kicked out of Athens and forced to live the rest of his life in exile. He committed no crime; he was just too ambitious.

The Athenians guarded their democracy fiercely. To make sure that nobody ever became a tyrant, they instituted a procedure called "ostracism" by which the assembly could choose one man who seemed to be getting too popular or who had too much ambition and exile him for ten years. No reason had to be given. Ostracism was a preventative measure, not a punitive one— and, by design, it could happen to anyone. Themistocles had frequently used ostracism himself against those who opposed his plans to build Athens's naval power in preparation for a Persian invasion. Savior of Western civilization though he was, few of his contemporaries cried when he had to leave.

Americans have never been quite as proactive as the Athenians were in guarding against tyranny. We don't practice ostracism, but we have devoted a lot of our national energy to balancing the need for a strong executive with the desire to prevent the establishment of a European-style monarchy. Our founders loaded the Constitution with a dizzying array of checks and balances. They didn't just separate government power; they chopped it up into little pieces and buried them all over the country—in three branches, two legislative bodies, and the various state governments, with specifically enumerated limits on what could even be considered the responsibility of government.

One thing that the Constitution did not originally do was limit the number of terms a president could serve, though it did place strong checks on presidential powers and provide Congress with a mechanism to impeach a president for almost any reason. An expectation that presidents would limit themselves to two terms evolved very quickly when George Washington declined to accept a nomination to a third—a precedent that Thomas Jefferson explicitly invoked in a letter to the Vermont state legislature when it urged him to seek a third term:

> That I should lay down my charge at a proper period is as much a duty as to have borne it faithfully. If some termination to the services of the Chief Magistrate be not fixed by the Constitution, or supplied by practice, his office, nominally four years, will in fact become for life, and history shows how easily that degenerates into an inheritance. Believing that a representative government, responsible at short periods of election is that which produces the greatest sum of happiness to mankind, I feel it a duty to do no act which shall essentially impair that principle, and I should unwillingly be the person who, disregarding the sound precedent set by an illustrious predecessor, should furnish the first example of prolongation beyond a second term of office.[24]

The Washington-Jefferson precedent held informally until 1940, when Franklin Delano Roosevelt won a third term, and then, in 1944, a fourth. Once it became clear that the two-term precedent could not prevent someone from becoming president for life, America's distrust of excessive ambition kicked into high gear. In 1947, Congress approved by the requisite two-thirds majority the Twenty-Second Amendment, which limited future presidents to two terms, consecutive or nonconsecutive. By 1951, three-quarters of the states had also approved the measure, and the amendment became part of the Constitution.

We Can Take a Joke

In 1972, Republican Richard Nixon won reelection in one of the biggest landslide elections in our nation's history, capturing more than 60 percent of the popular vote and every state but Massachusetts and the District of Columbia. That same year, the most popular television program in the country was *All in the Family*, a show that relentlessly satirized the sorts of people who voted for Richard Nixon.

Eight years later, in 1980, Ronald Reagan scored the biggest electoral victory over an incumbent president in American history, beating President Jimmy Carter in forty-four states and winning more than 90 percent of the electoral college. That year, the top-rated comedy on television (and fourth-highest-rated show overall) was the Korean War sitcom *M*A*S*H*, another notoriously liberal satirical show that skewered the militarism and national-ism often associated with Reagan.

It would be hard to imagine two television programs more out of sync with the larger political movements of their times. I remember watching both shows with members of my family who complained bitterly about their liberal slants but tuned in faithfully every week, laughed at the jokes, and fell in love with the characters anyway. These shows were funny. They had moments of touching human connection. And liberal viewers did not get a free pass. Archie Bunker was a lovable conservative curmudgeon who didn't always get it wrong, and Hawkeye Pierce was a self-righteous liberal scold who didn't always get it right.

Both shows required members of the audience to be able to laugh at themselves. Political scientist Jason Scorza labels this a characteristic of "re-flective political humor"—a style of satire that "reminds citizens that they need to *take* a joke, as well as laugh at jokes made about others." Like other reflective works, both *All in the Family* and *M*A*S*H* "took politics seriously by treating it irreverently" and "took their audiences seriously by provoking—rather than pandering to—them."[25]

Reflexive political humor is as old as democracy itself. Its first great practitioner was the Athenian comic playwright Aristophanes, who satirized almost everything his society held dear, including philosophy (*The Clouds*), warfare (*Lysistrata*), the tragic poets (*The Frogs*), the law courts (*The Wasps*), and the political leadership of Athens (*The Knights*). In *The Knights*, which levels sharp criticism against the Athenian demagogue Creon, Aristophanes makes it clear that Creon is a servant whose power lies in his ability to flatter his ridiculous master, whose name is *Demos*, or "The People." Here, as in most of his plays, Aristophanes targets the people watching his plays with his most intense criticism.

It is hard to be the butt of the joke, but Americans have always been reasonably good at it. From the traveling routines of Artemis Ward to the radio broadcasts of Will Rogers to *The Daily Show* and *The Colbert Report*, we have shown an ability to laugh even when the joke is on us, and we have been a better nation because of it.

But one group of people has never been able to make fun of the Amer-ican people: our politicians and elected officials. Here, our relationship is one-sided. We can make fun of them relentlessly and laugh at the most outlandish portrayals of them that our satirists can dream up, while they must treat their constituents with respect and deference lest they incur our wrath and lose their positions. The unwritten rules about who can laugh and at whom can tell us a lot about what a society values. When a *Saturday Night Live* sketch shows Gerald Ford tripping down a flight of stairs or Bill Clinton stealing somebody's French fries at a McDonald's, we realize that we get to make fun of them while they have to treat us with respect—and we are reminded of how power actually flows in a democracy.

MAKING DEMOCRACY WORK

Perhaps the most important of Tocqueville's many important observations in *Democracy in America* is that democracies ultimately rely on mores, rather than laws or institutions, to protect the liberty of the people.

Democracy is not the same thing as liberty, and in some cases, democracy and liberty are mutually exclusive. Democracy simply requires that people be allowed to vote. Liberty has more to do with what they vote for. The majoritarian impulse in a democracy must be carefully managed, or it will produce majorities that use their power to enhance their own status at the expense of everybody else.

In contemporary political parlance, the term "liberal democracy" denotes "a political system marked not only by free and fair elections but also by the rule of law, a separation of powers, and the protection of basic liberties of speech, assembly, religion, and property."[26] Governments that simply hold elections without protecting liberties are what Fareed Zakaria calls "illiberal democracies."[27] Illiberal democracies count votes, and they may even do so fairly. But they do not prevent the majority from invading the rights of everybody else, so for the minority they are no different from the worst dictatorship. As Tocqueville so aptly put it, "When I feel the hand of power weigh upon my brow, it scarcely matters who my oppressor is, and I am not more inclined to submit to the yoke because a million arms are prepared to place it around my neck."[28]

Ultimately, there is no way that laws or institutions can prevent a democracy from becoming illiberal. All our institutionalized protections can be undone, given enough time, by an unsympathetic majority. The constitution can be amended, new judges can be appointed, agencies can be dismantled, and freedoms can be curtailed. And once a democracy devolves into illiberal majoritarianism, it rarely stays democratic for long. "If America ever loses its liberty," Tocqueville prophesied, "the fault will surely lie with the omnipotence of the majority, which may drive minorities to despair and force them to resort to physical force."[29] Institutions can slow down the march toward majoritarian tyranny, but they cannot stop it.

To remain truly democratic, people have to be willing to protect each other's rights and interests even when they control enough votes to do otherwise. They have to recognize each other's right to exist, express opinions, and participate fully in the political process. And they have to preserve the laws and institutions that guarantee human rights and civil liberties for everyone, not just for the ruling majority. We must have enough regard for each other that we decline to use the mechanisms of democracy to treat our fellow citizens unjustly.

Another way to say this is that we must not be enemies. We must be friends.

• 3 •

"We Are Not Enemies, but Friends"

Democracy requires us to listen to the
better angels of our nature.

I am loath to close. We are not enemies, but friends. We must
not be enemies. Though passion may have strained, it must not
break our bonds of affection. The mystic chords of memory,
stretching from every battlefield and patriot grave to every living
heart and hearthstone all over this broad land, will yet swell the
chorus of the Union, when again touched, as surely they will be,
by the better angels of our nature.

—Abraham Lincoln, First Inaugural Address, March 4, 1861

In his 1861 inaugural address, Abraham Lincoln made one last appeal to
keep the Union together. It was beyond a hard sell. Between the election in
November and the inauguration in March, seven southern states had seceded
and formed a new government. Over the next three months, four more states
would secede, and the most destructive war in American history would begin. To most observers, the bonds of affection had already been severed, and
the mystic chords of memory were permanently out of the chorus-swelling
business.

There were not multiple issues separating the two regions of the country.
There was one issue, slavery, which had divided Americans from the very
beginning. From the Constitutional Convention on, every attempt to deal
with this issue had failed. For most of the nineteenth century, the Union had
been held together by compromises and negotiations that tried mightily to
placate the two sides as they moved further and further apart. Northerners

29

increasingly resented having to make concessions to slavery to keep the South from leaving the Union. Southerners feared that growing northern political and economic power would eventually make slavery impossible to sustain—a fear confirmed when Abraham Lincoln, who had not even been on the ballot in most southern states, won the presidency.[1]

But Lincoln was no abolitionist—at least not in 1861. He began his inaugural address by stating, "I have no purpose, directly or indirectly, to interfere with the institution of slavery in the States where it exists. I believe I have no lawful right to do so, and I have no inclination to do so."[2] He did not believe that he had the authority to make slavery illegal, nor did he believe (at the time) that the United States was prepared to absorb four million freed slaves into its social fabric. He insisted, though, on the right to call slavery immoral, and he did so consistently, unapologetically, and in no uncertain terms.

And then he said that we must be friends.

This was a bold statement, but it had to be; Lincoln had a lot of ground to cover. In addition to making one last attempt to bring the seven secessionist states back into the Union without a civil war, he had to convince at least some of the slave states that had not seceded to remain.[3] He also had to convince northerners that he was doing everything in his power to preserve the Union. If there was going to be a war, he had to assure people that it was truly a last resort and that he had done everything possible to preserve the Union without violence.

This excruciatingly complex rhetorical calculus played directly to Lincoln's strengths. More than any other politician in American history, he had the ability to size up his various audiences, isolate his opponents' most important arguments, understand the assumptions behind those arguments, and respond with the kinds of counterarguments that addressed the real issues at stake. And he knew how to add moral force and urgency to his arguments by using simple words to invoke big ideas. Lincoln's call for friendship was one of the biggest ideas that any American president has ever tried to communicate to the nation.

But there are some important things that Lincoln didn't say. He did not say that people should abandon their principles for the sake of friendship—and he certainly didn't offer to abandon his. He laid those principles out clearly and effectively before the election, and he repeated them in his inaugural address: that slavery was immoral, that it should not be allowed to expand into new territories, and that secession was illegal. Lincoln refused to give an inch on these points, and he went to greater extremes to defend them than anyone thought possible at the time.

He also did not say that the North and the South should work out their differences and find a mutually acceptable compromise. Americans had been compromising over slavery since the Constitutional Convention in 1787. The history of the United States before 1860 could have been written almost entirely as the consequence of these compromises: the Three-Fifths Compromise, the Missouri Compromise, the Compromise of 1850, and the Kansas-Nebraska Act. In both 1858 and 1860, Stephen A. Douglas campaigned almost entirely on the compromise he called "popular sovereignty." If a willingness to compromise could have resolved the issue of slavery, Americans would have resolved it without a war.

Finally, Lincoln did not say that Americans should stop being so extreme in their positions and move to the center. Both parties included moderate and extreme positions on slavery. Lincoln did not suggest that the moderate positions were objectively better than extreme ones. And by the end of the war, he had moved to embrace the most extreme anti-slavery position on the spectrum: universal abolition and the integration of former slaves into the political body. But he did not make his offer of friendship contingent on holding any position about slavery. He simply said that we must be friends.

Even the violence of civil war was, for Lincoln, a requirement of civic friendship—because any meaningful civic relationship must assume perpetuity. Unlike personal friendships, which can last no longer than the lives of the people involved, civic unions must outlast the individuals who participate in them. This is especially crucial in a democracy, where the most basic mechanism of self-government—free elections—can only work if people are willing to stay together after the votes are counted. The "idea of secession, is the essence of anarchy," as Lincoln argued, because "the rule of a minority, as a permanent arrangement, is wholly inadmissible; so that, rejecting the majority principle, anarchy or despotism in some form is all that is left."[4]

As citizens of a democracy, we hold the political body in trust for the next generation, to whom we should deliver it in at least as good a shape as it was in when we inherited it. At a bare minimum, we have a duty not to kill the body ourselves or to allow it to die of neglect on our watch. Lincoln's drive to preserve the Union grew out of his belief that the United States was a unified community whose citizens had sacred responsibilities to each other and to its future members. "You have no oath registered in Heaven to destroy the government," he told the people of the South, "while I shall have the most solemn one to 'preserve, protect, and defend it.'"[5]

The closing lines of the First Inaugural Address, quoted at the beginning of this chapter, rise to the level of great poetry. They also constitute the most important argument of Lincoln's speech—that friendship among the citizens of a large democracy is possible only when we allow ourselves to be governed by our "better angels." Lincoln understood intuitively something that contemporary psychologists are just beginning to explore experimentally: that human nature is complex and inconsistent. It contains some elements that promote selfishness, aggression, and division and other elements that promote altruism, compassion, and unity. The kind of society we have depends on which group of angels we listen to.

GETTING TO KNOW THE GOOD ANGELS

Abraham Lincoln knew plenty about our bad angels—the ones that sit on one shoulder and stir up fear, rage, aggression, tribalism, and insecurity. He spent, and ultimately gave, his life dealing with these angels and their effects on the country he loved. He also knew that we all have good angels that sit on our shoulders and quietly encourage us to have empathy and compassion. And he knew that the bad angels scream much more loudly and are therefore much easier targets for those who want to control our behavior. And he understood that social progress only happens when we listen to the good angels.

What do our good angels look like? How will we know them when we meet them? Another book with a title borrowed from Lincoln's First Inaugural Address—Steven Pinker's best-selling *The Better Angels of Our Nature: Why Violence Has Declined*—identifies four of these angels and devotes a full chapter to each: empathy, self-control, morality, and reason. These angels play an important role in Pinker's remarkable story, which stretches across seven hundred pages, includes hundreds of graphs and charts, and frames the arc of human history as the gradual victory of our better angels.[6]

In addition to Pinker's angels—all of which have played an important role in the development of democratic societies—I offer a few of my own. These angels are human instincts and characteristics that help explain the rise of what we might call the "civic tradition" in the United States and in many other countries. These are the aspects of human nature that promote friendship, civic discussion, meaningful debate, and democracy.

We Derive Genuine Pleasure from Friendship

Humans have always been social animals. We evolved to be part of groups, and we owe our big brains to the fact that our ancestors needed to understand and keep track of the people they interacted with. We are adapted to other people in the same way that dolphins and whales are adapted to the ocean: they sustain us, support us, and help us make sense of our experiences. Friendship is generally not difficult for us. We want and need people to share our experiences with us. We enjoy the company of others, and we often become depressed when we are deprived of human contact and affection. Most of us cannot imagine living a meaningful life without close friends to share it with.

We Like to Know What People Are Thinking

Understanding that other people have thoughts that differ from our own is one of the most difficult things that human beings know how to do. I don't mean the moral effort it takes to value other people's emotional states and mental perspectives. Just keeping track of other people's versions of reality and separating them from our own requires enormous cognitive processing power. Take a sentence like "Jack thinks that Mary doesn't know what his ex-wife told Jim." To understand the basic meaning of this sentence, we have to keep track of five different perspectives: our own, Jack's, Mary's, Jack's ex-wife's, and Jim's. No other animal can even keep track of a second perspective, but we can maneuver through five of them effortlessly. And we spend a lot of our time and money consuming fictional narratives (e.g., books, movies, TV shows) that give us more minds to keep track of—and we do this for fun.

The entertainment choices that we make today have deep roots in the evolutionary choices that our ancestors made in very different environments. Other people's minds have always been an extremely important source of information for humans. If we know how other people think, we can better predict their actions. This makes us safer from any designs that they may have on us, and it helps us create mutually beneficial alliances. Meaningful conversations with other people about what they think and believe are not just satisfying because they improve our friendships. They give us exactly the kind of information that we crave because our ancestors needed it to survive.

We Can Play the Long Game

Many species have evolved the ability to reciprocate altruistic behaviors. Vampire bats learn how to share blood with other vampire bats who have had a bad night, and chimpanzees will pick and eat the lice off other chimps, who are willing to do the same for them. Tit for tat is an important phenomenon in nature. But only human beings can play the long game. We can remember how people treated us for decades and may reward or punish them accordingly; they can do the same with regard to us. This means that when we know our interactions with other people will recur over time, we have much less to gain by treating them with suspicion and hostility. The likelihood of future reciprocity makes friendship in the present a good bet.

We Have an Innate Sense of Fairness

Though we tend to be very bad judges when our own interests are on the line, we do appear to have an inborn sense of fairness and an instinctive desire to remedy obvious injustices. A large body of research into a phenomenon called "altruistic punishment" suggests that most people will forego their own advantage and even make tangible sacrifices to punish actions they perceive as unfair. This is why we root for underdogs, intervene when we see someone being bullied, and feel a great sense of satisfaction at the end of a movie when characters—both good and bad—get what is coming to them.[7] There are all sorts of ways to override this instinct. We can be convinced that certain people do not deserve the same consideration as others or that seemingly unfair actions really aren't. But most of us have an innate balancing instinct that causes us to prefer just societies to unjust ones—and this is enough to make democracy a worthwhile goal.

We Can Change Our Minds

We are not locked into any set of beliefs, opinions, or values. At any stage of our development, we can change our religion, our political affiliation, our favorite color, or anything else that we once believed. We have all changed our minds about something in our lives—often about something very important. This simple fact has profound implications for the way we engage our opponents. The fact that people can change their minds means that they can be persuaded. This means that we can use discussion and debate to try to bring others around to our point of view. And if we feel strongly about an issue, I argue, we have a moral responsibility to present it in a way capable of persuading others—which, in most cases, does not include shouting at the top of our lungs and calling anyone who disagrees with us stupid.

We Crave Community and Security

Because we can imagine life in the future, we care deeply about long-term security. We want to live in stable societies that will allow us to prosper. We want these societies to be there when we are old and need help, and we want them to be there for our loved ones when we are gone. We also know from our own history that civic enmity leads to civic conflict and that civic conflict places our survival in great jeopardy. Rationally, at least, we can see a problem with living in a society with two opposing factions who treat each other as perpetual enemies. Such a society works against our long-term interest in a secure home for ourselves and our families.

These better angels are just as much a part of our genetic makeup as aggression and tribalism are. But they will rarely be our first reaction. For a host of reasons both biological and sociological, fear is the easiest emotion to feel and the first one to come to our minds. When an organism feels threatened, its limbic response activates immediately, before hope or compassion or long-term thinking can even get started. This protects us. It makes escape with our lives much more likely when a rampaging tiger threatens.

But most things aren't rampaging tigers. We have been hard-wired to overestimate any threat to our survival, lest we ignore the one time that it really is a tiger.[8] This means that our fear-based responses will frequently activate in situations that don't really require a fight-or-flight response. Politicians and advertisers know this, and they also know that stoking our fears is good for business. For our better angels to emerge, we need to count to ten and give our rational facilities the opportunity to override our limbic responses. Otherwise, we end up with a zero-sum politics based on fear and perpetual outrage.

To have nice things, we need to learn how to filter out the voices that constantly urge us to be outraged and afraid (reserving the right to act appropriately on the few occasions when it really is a tiger). When we use our reason to override our initial fear—even imperfectly—we get things like civilization and science and trade and democracy. These are all things that require non-zero-sum relationships with other human beings—or what philosophers have long called "civic friendship." To understand the depth of Lincoln's address—and his famous statement that "we must not be enemies"—we must travel back to ancient Athens, the cradle of democracy, and to the writings of Aristotle, whose understanding of civic friendship has influenced the way that the world has understood citizenship for nearly twenty-five hundred years.

THE ANCIENT ROOTS OF CIVIC FRIENDSHIP

Aristotle's notion of civic friendship, or *philia politikē*, comes not from the *Politics*, as we might expect, but from the *Nicomachean Ethics*, a work of practical philosophy that devotes two of its ten chapters to friendship. This discussion of friendship as an ethical principle makes sense if we define ethics, as Aristotle does, as a set of behavioral principles that allow human beings to live well. Aristotle wanted to isolate the principles that produce what the ancient Greeks called *eudaimonia*, which has been translated variously as "happiness," "well-being," "human flourishing," and "the good life." Aristotle saw friendship is essential to this end because, as social animals, human beings can only live well in relationships with other people.

The bare-bones definition of friendship for Aristotle is a relationship between two people who desire each other's happiness for its own sake. The "for its own sake" here is important. I can desire another's success for all sorts of selfish reasons—because he might give me money, perhaps, or because her promotion might give me a corner office. But this is not quite friendship, though people who begin associating with each other for instrumental reasons can become friends with the addition of some degree of mutual affection.

This is not to discount the importance of strategic alliances. To survive, humans must have allies: people who hunt and gather with us, share food with us, take turns staying up to watch for bears—that sort of thing. We can say the same for many animal species. But humans have the unique ability to form deep intellectual and emotional connections with each other. When we create these kinds of bonds with our natural allies, they become our friends.

Civic friendship is a subcategory of friendship that we create with our fellow citizens (literally, people who live in our city). Citizens inherently have an alliance with other citizens. In any political unit, people will work together in areas of clear mutual benefit. My desire not to see my neighbor impaled by invading Vikings coordinates strongly with my own desire not to be impaled by the same Vikings, so joining together to build a Viking-proof wall does not require affection—just enlightened self-interest.

Civic friendship builds on this mutual interest but transcends it by combining it with goodwill. As contemporary philosopher John M. Cooper explains, "In a city animated by civic friendship each citizen has a certain measure of interest in and concern for the well-being of each other citizen just because the other *is* a fellow citizen. Civic friendship makes fellow-citizens' well-being matter to one another, simply as such."[9] The civic relationship moves from alliance to friendship when people desire the happiness and well-being of their fellow citizens for its own sake.

For Aristotle, civic friendship and justice require each other because they both produce the same type of behavior toward other people. Laws alone cannot guarantee a just society, because laws are passed and administered by human beings. Justice is a consequence of a kind of human relationship that looks a lot like friendship:

> Friendship and justice seem . . . to be exhibited in the same sphere of conduct and between the same persons; because in every community there is supposed to be some kind of justice and also some friendly feeling. At any rate people address those who are on the same ship or serving in the same force with them as friends; and similarly those with whom they are otherwise associated. But the term of the friendship is that of the association, for so also is the term of their form of justice. And the proverb

"friends have all things in common" is quite right, because friendship is based on community.[10]

Aristotle does not confine himself to discussing democracies in this analysis. In fact, Aristotle didn't have a high opinion of Athenian democracy, which had very few safeguards against demagoguery or majoritarianism. A much better form of government, he thought, was what he called a *politeia*, or a "constitutional government." (Roman writers translated *politeia* as "affairs of the state," or *res publica*, which gave us our word "republic.") In this kind of society, people govern themselves through deliberations and elections, but they do so in a framework constrained by written constitutions and protections of individual rights.

The constitutional government was one of three natural forms of government, along with aristocracy (rule by the *aristoi*, or "best people" in a society) and monarchy (rule by a single king). Aristotle believed that each of these types of state can produce good government and human flourishing as long as they meet one important criteria: the sovereign power must display natural affection for everybody in the society. There is no structural way to guarantee that any form of government will remain conducive to human flourishing. Only *philia politikē* can do that.

The absence of civic friendship turns each of the natural forms of government into a corresponding perversion. A tyranny is a monarchy in which the king feels no concern for the people. An oligarchy is an aristocracy in which the ruling class oppresses the people to serve its own interests. And a democracy is a *politeia* in which people come together to form majorities that impose their will on minorities for selfish ends. The presence of civic friendship is more important to the creation of a just society than the form of government. Any state in which the leaders and the people take civic friendship seriously can produce justice. Any state in which people treat each other as enemies will ultimately become unjust.

In other words, good government requires justice, and justice ultimately requires that people be governed by their friends. In a democracy, where we govern each other, we must all be friends, or the system will become oppressive. That doesn't mean we have to like or socialize or even agree with each other. Sybil Schwarzenbach, a philosopher at the City University of New York who has written broadly on Aristotle, explains that civic friendship is institutional rather than personal. It manifests in the kind of society we choose to work toward:

> Aristotle is not saying that in the just *polis* all members know each other, are emotionally close, and personally like each other. Such is as impossible given the forty thousand inhabitants (not including their

families) which make up his ideal polis as it is today with 250 million. In Aristotle's view, political friendship is evidenced, rather, by a general concern and attitude in the everyday lives of its citizens and works via the constitution; it is recognized in legal and social norms regarding the treatment of persons in that society, as well as in the willingness of fellow citizens to uphold them.[11]

The "legal and social norms" that Schwarzenbach refers to define what civic friendship means in a modern democracy. Both justice and friendship require that our laws treat people fairly and with dignity. But laws alone do not make a society just, because so much of what constitutes any meaningful definition of "justice" takes place outside the purview of the law. Real justice requires that people treat each other fairly when they don't have to. This, in turn, requires behavioral norms that we all agree to adopt and enforce.

For example, consider the way that society treats people with physical disabilities. Like many countries, the United States has laws that prohibit employment or housing discrimination based on physical disability. Laws also require reasonable accommodations in education, employment, and public services. Once passed, these laws make it much easier for people with disabilities to participate fully in public life.

But society has also adopted social norms that influence how we treat people with disabilities. We consider it cruel and irresponsible to mock disabled people or to humiliate them in public—or berate them in private—for things beyond their control. No law prohibits this kind of crude behavior, but most people avoid it because society considers it unacceptable and enforces that opinion through powerful social mechanisms. Those who violate social norms face real social consequences, ranging from widespread disapproval and ostracism to a loss of employment, opportunities, or privileges.

Social norms evolve over time; they cannot simply be enacted by a governing body or vetoed by an executive authority. But they have great power to shape our behavior as a society because they become part of most people's internal moral code. Parents enforce them with young children; schools teach them to students; movies, television programs, and books build them into popular narratives. Eventually laws become unnecessary because we learn to police ourselves and those within our sphere of influence.

We exercise civic friendship, or fail to exercise it, when we decide what kind of society we want to be. We vote on this question every day—occasionally in a formal election but more often through the purchases we make, the people and institutions we choose to associate with, and the things that we give our attention to. No law can force us, and no syllogism can persuade us, to care about other people; only friendship can do that. When animated by a genuine concern for the well-being of others, we will find ways to make our society more just. When animated by civic enmity or the desire to injure or defeat some group of people, we will find ways to make our society less just.

"THAT WHICH UNITES US . . . IS FAR GREATER THAN THAT WHICH DIVIDES US"

Gracious concession speeches are a staple of American politics. We expect unsuccessful candidates to do their part in rebuilding national unity and assuring everyone that we really are all on the same team. Concession speeches assure the general population that power will transfer peacefully from one official to the next—that there will be no civil war or rioting in the streets and that we can continue with our lives knowing that, even if our candidate lost, we will not be dragged out of our beds at night and shipped off to a penal colony without a trial. These sorts of things still happen in many places when one regime replaces another.

In 1952, Illinois governor Adlai Stevenson gave one of the best-known concession speeches in American history. Stevenson had just lost the presidential election to Dwight D. Eisenhower in a landslide. When he spoke to his supporters on election night, he rallied them not to a lost cause but to the idea of national unity:

> That which unites us as American citizens is far greater than that which divides us as political parties. I urge you all to give General Eisenhower the support he will need to carry out the great tasks that lie before him. I pledge him mine. We vote as many, but we pray as one. With a united people, with faith in democracy, with common concern for others less fortunate around the globe, we shall move forward with God's guidance toward the time when his children shall grow in freedom and dignity in a world at peace.[12]

The key topics in Stevenson's speech—country over party, common goals, shared faith in democracy, a special relationship with divine providence—constitute the core of what some have called the American civil religion. According to this idea, first articulated by sociologist Robert Bellah in 1967, Americans from different religious traditions (and no religion at all) share a set of quasi-religious values enshrined in the Declaration of Independence, the Constitution, and images from secular history that have taken on an air of sacredness. Throughout American history, Bellah writes, these images have mingled freely with concepts drawn directly from religious sources to produce "powerful symbols of national solidarity and to mobilize deep levels of personal motivation for the attainment of national goals."[13]

In his description of this phenomenon, Bellah draws heavily on Alexis de Tocqueville, who wrote that "in the United States the religion of the majority is itself republican" and averred that religious and republican principles are so comingled in our national consciousness that politics "allows each man free choice of the path that is to lead him to heaven, just as the law grants each citizen the right to choose his government."[14]

At the center of the civil religion, then, is the notion that Americans hold enough beliefs in common to build a political process based on persuasion rather than force. We are close enough together for civic friendship to work. This sounds absurd to us now, when the political divide seems so wide that nearly 60 percent of us are afraid to talk to members of our own family at Thanksgiving.[15] Is it possible that Tocqueville is no longer right and that Americans no longer share the symbols, traditions, and values that make meaningful democracy possible?

No. We are not more divided today than we were when Tocqueville visited in 1831. At that time, Americans could barely conceive of political opponents more diametrically opposed than Andrew Jackson and John Quincy Adams, who had just concluded one of the most personally and ideologically vicious elections in our history. Opposition to the ruling faction was just beginning to coalesce into a new political party, the Whig Party, whose organizing principle was a hatred for Jackson. Americans in 1831 would have considered themselves every bit as divided as do Americans today. But Tocqueville knew better. Jackson and Adams would have been almost indistinguishable in France, which, in the ten years before he was born, had experienced the reigns of King Louis XVI, Robespierre, and Napoleon.

A lot of people today want to sell us the notion that Americans are "hopelessly divided" and that we have reached "unprecedented levels of partisanship." We haven't. Not even close. It has been 150 years since anybody was beaten to a pulp on the Senate floor and more than 200 years since a sitting vice president killed a political rival. It has even been more than sixty years since a president has had to call in the National Guard to escort children to school past throngs of adults shouting out death threats. We tend to see our own dysfunction in superlative terms precisely because it is ours and we know about all the warts.

The "hopelessly divided" narrative creates its own blind spots. Because so many of us have bought into it, we often overestimate the differences. In a study conducted in 2015, researchers asked members of each party to estimate certain facts about the composition of the other party. The results display a startling lack of understanding between the parties. Republicans, for example, estimated that

Table 3.1. How Democrats and Republicans View Each Other

Democrats Who Are	Actual (%)	Estimated by Republicans (%)
Agnostics or atheists	9	36
Black	24	46
Lesbian/gay/bisexual	6	38
Union members	11	44

Republicans Who Are	Actual (%)	Estimated by Democrats (%)
65 or older	21	44
Evangelicals	34	44
Southerners	36	44
Make $250,000 or more per year	2	44

38 percent of Democrats were lesbian, gay, or bisexual—more than six times higher than the correct figure of 6 percent. Democrats estimated that 44 percent of Republicans earned more than $250,000 a year—a whopping twenty-four times more than the 2 percent of Republicans in this income bracket.[16]

This study gives us just a taste of the problem we now face—not hopeless division but a near-universal perception of hopeless division that obscures the profound similarities that Americans still share. Most Democrats are not communists or anarchists bent on destroying the social order. Most Republicans are not fiery racists or wealthy investment bankers bent on bringing back debtors' prisons and company scrip. These are caricatures. Most of us want exactly the same things for ourselves and our families: good jobs, good schools, safe cities, strong communities, and a peaceful world. These common dreams give us more than enough common ground on which to build meaningful civic friendships and a strong democracy.

LINCOLN AND DOUGLAS: CIVIC FRIENDSHIP IN THE DARKEST HOUR

Ideally, political conversations animated by civic friendship would be calm, rational, and good-natured. Participants would entirely separate their arguments from their egos and never confuse being contradicted with being criticized. They would never raise their voices at any time, and everybody would assiduously avoid sarcasm, personal insults, and humor at another's expense. And, most important, political discussions would be based on reason and solid evidence and not on emotion.

Unfortunately, however, these conversations have to take place among human beings and not computer programs, and human beings aren't good at calm, rational discussion. We are emotional. We care what other people think about us, and we take almost everything anybody says to us personally. We always protect what we see as our territory, both physical and rhetorical, and very few of us can manage calm discussions about controversial issues with our closest friends and family members. Telling us to have such discussions in public discourse is like telling us to stop liking chocolate or being afraid of bears.

Like all human relationships, civic friendships run hot and cold. At our best, we can be charitable and magnanimous to our opponents, but more often we are angry, sarcastic, demeaning, and emotional when we talk about issues that we consider important. What makes these discussions friendly is that, despite all the anger and sarcasm, we acknowledge that our fellow citizens and their opinions have a right to exist and that it would be incompatible with our understanding of a just society to silence them, disenfranchise them, or wish them harm.

Civic friendship, in other words, means that we must not be enemies. When Abraham Lincoln spoke these words to the nation on the eve of the Civil War, he knew perfectly well that he was tapping into an ancient understanding of democracy. But he also spoke as someone who had been participating in politics for nearly thirty years and whose civic life consistently modeled the ideals that he valued—as did the political life of his lifelong rival, Stephen A. Douglas. The extensive interactions between Lincoln and Douglas over their careers illustrate the principle of civic friendship as well as any relationship ever has. We could do much worse for models today, and we would have a hard time doing better.

Lincoln and Douglas shadowed each other for twenty-five years. They first met in 1834 in Vandalia, then the capital of Illinois. Lincoln was twenty-five years old and serving his first term as a Whig representative in the Illinois legislature. Douglas, twenty-one, had not yet been elected to public office but was lobbying the legislature on behalf of the Democratic Party. Both believed passionately in the political ideas they espoused. Douglas grew up idolizing Andrew Jackson and the idea of a nation governed by a coalition of common people. Lincoln's political hero was Henry Clay, the pragmatic compromiser from Kentucky who saw government, properly managed, as a potential force for great good in people's lives.

Over the course of their professional lives, Lincoln and Douglas worked together in the state legislature, served in the national Congress at the same time, competed for the same woman, met as opposing counsels in a murder trial, and eventually faced each other in elections for both the Senate and the US presidency. Douglas was the indispensable figure in Lincoln's political ascent. "Had it not been for Douglas," writes one biographer, "Lincoln would have remained merely a good trial lawyer in Springfield, Illinois, known locally for his droll sense of humor, bad jokes, and slightly nutty wife."[17]

For most of their careers, Douglas's star shone much more brightly than Lincoln's. The one exception was Mary Todd, who rejected Douglas and married Lincoln because, as a devout Whig herself and the daughter of one of Henry Clay's closest friends, she could not imagine being married to a Democrat.[18] In almost every other contest in the heavily Democratic state of Illinois, Douglas's political affiliation served him well. A Democratic governor made him the state's youngest supreme court justice. The Democratic voters sent him to the US House of Representatives, and the Democratic state legislature sent him to the US Senate.

Lincoln was just as popular among Whigs as Douglas was among Democrats, and he had as much talent and ambition as Douglas did, but he spent most of his life in a minority party. As an opposition leader, though, Lincoln had a lot of opportunities to argue with Douglas—starting with the presidential election of 1840, when the two men stumped through Illinois arguing the merits of, respectively, William Henry Harrison (who won by a landslide) and the incumbent, Martin Van Buren (who won Illinois).

In 1846, Lincoln won his only term in the US House of Representatives, Douglas won his first term as a US Senator, and the two became rivals in the Illinois delegation to Congress. When Senator Douglas engineered the Kansas-Nebraska Act in 1854, Lincoln, who had all but resigned from public life, felt compelled to reenter the fray and attack his rival's signature legislation throughout the state. By the time Abraham Lincoln and Stephen Douglas squared off for their famous 1858 debates, they had already faced each other dozens of times across Illinois.

When they did meet for their seven famous debates in seven Illinois cities, they produced our nation's greatest example of informed, enthusiastic political debate. They did not speak calmly or refrain from personal attacks. The debates were a form of public entertainment, and the candidates whooped and hollered and cracked jokes and did everything else that we associate with political theater today. But they also engaged with each other's ideas in a way that no political candidates have ever done since, and they left their audiences with a solid understanding of where and why they differed. In the end, they both benefited from the debates: Douglas was reelected to a third term in the Senate, and Lincoln emerged with a national reputation and became a contender for the presidency.

Two years later, when Lincoln won the most bitterly contested presidential race in US history, Douglas acted as a friend to both Lincoln and the Union. Heavy Democratic losses in Pennsylvania and Indiana convinced Douglas in early October that Lincoln's election was a "fixed fact." From October 9 through the election on November 6, Douglas became, in effect, a Lincoln surrogate in the South, crisscrossing the region to try to prevent secession. "Mr. Lincoln is the next President," he told his supporters. "We must try to save the Union. I will go south."[19] A few months later, he contracted a fatal case of typhoid fever. When he became too weak to lift his arms, he "continued to dictate letters denouncing the 'Cotton States' and calling on Democrats to 'rally to the support of our common country.'"[20]

In his final campaign, Douglas cemented his reputation as an exemplar of civic friendship. He fought as hard for his views as any person ever has, but he also believed passionately in the democratic principle. He brought his views before the public and let its members be the judges. He played by the rules, and when he lost, he accepted the legitimacy of his opponent. He also spent the last days of his life campaigning to save the Union at the side of the man he had spent twenty-five years campaigning against.

In every way but one, it would be impossible to call Abraham Lincoln and Stephen Douglas friends. They had debated and disagreed with each other on nearly every important issue of the day. And their debates were not calm and genial. They were loud and raucous and full of all the mockery and mutual recrimination necessary to hold a carnival audience's attention for three full hours. It would be hard to find any point that they agreed on— other than that people in a democracy need to have debates.

But this one point matters. Civic friendship has nothing to do with how we get along with each other and everything to do with how we go about *not* getting along with each other. It is a set of assumptions for managing the debates and disagreements that democracy requires. We should argue and defend our positions. As we do, though, we need to give some thought to the larger system that we are a part of—a system that asks us to recognize that the people we are arguing with are friends we need to persuade and not enemies we need to destroy. And when the argument ends, we need to make sure that everybody involved has the opportunity to do it all over again the next time.

· *4* ·

Parties and Political Tribes

We should see political parties as expedient fictions,
not core identities.

A party of order or stability, and a party of progress or reform, are both necessary elements of a healthy state of political
life. . . . Each of these modes of thinking derives its utility from
the deficiencies of the other; but it is in a great measure the opposition of the other that keeps each within the limits of reason
and sanity.

—John Stuart Mill, *On Liberty*

*M*odern readers have a hard time with a lot of things in Dante's *Inferno*.
But from my experience teaching it to undergraduates, they have the hardest
time with Dante's view of political parties. The ninth and final circle of hell
contains the worst sinners who ever lived—people like Judas Iscariot, who
betrayed Christ for thirty pieces of silver—buried in a frozen lake or being
perpetually eaten by a ravenous Satan. All those in this final level of hell committed an act of treachery—against a family member, a guest, their country,
or . . . their political party.

And there's the rub: Dante sees disloyalty to a political party as an evil
greater than almost any other—worse than, say, masterminding the cold-
blooded murder of entire populations. Attila the Hun, the scourge of Rome
responsible for hundreds of thousands of deaths, only managed to get cast
into the seventh circle of hell—because at least he never split his ticket in the
voting booth!

45

But political parties in Dante's world were no laughing matter. Throughout most of the twelfth century, two rival parties—the Guelphs, who supported the pope, and the Ghibellines, who supported the holy Roman emperor—battled for control of the city-states of northern Italy. The primary purpose of each party was to eliminate the other, either by killing its proponents in battle or by coming to power and exiling the opposition. The existence of the Guelphs was incompatible with the Ghibelline government of Florence. And the feeling was mutual.

A major difference between Dante's time and our own is that most political parties in modern democracies recognize that other parties are an important part of the system and should be protected. This is one of the crucial political norms that Steven Levitsky and Daniel Ziblatt define as "mutual toleration," or "the idea that as long as our rivals play by constitutional rules, we accept that they have an equal right to exist, compete for power, and govern."[1] People in healthy democracies recognize, at a very minimum, that political opposition is a necessary part of the game that we all play.

Mutual toleration, at least officially, is a nonnegotiable element of self-government. Reports such as the annual "Democracy Index" compiled by *The Economist* and the US-government-funded Freedom House organization use competitive, multiparty elections as a primary indicator of a country's democratic status.[2] Outlawing parties, or not allowing them to compete for power, is a sign that a country is slipping into authoritarianism.

Parties play a crucial role in modern democracies. Relatively few voters have the time or the inclination to research every possible candidate for every office or to master the details of complicated policy proposals. Parties filter candidates into manageable choices and distill complicated policies into proposals that one can be either for or against. And they convey as much information about candidates as most voters care to absorb. A long ballot with dozens of candidates for local, state, and federal offices would be very difficult for most voters to navigate without the minimal but crucial information about candidates' political affiliation.

But political parties are democracy's most dangerous necessity because they tap directly into our tribal instincts. The more important we consider the issues at stake in elections, the more likely we are to treat political affiliation as a core part of our identity and disagreement with our political position as a threat to our well-being. As one political scientist put it, "Parties can help citizens construct and maintain a functioning government. But if citizens use parties as a social dividing line, those same parties can keep citizens from agreeing to the compromise and cooperation that necessarily define democracy."[3]

THE BIRTH OF PARTIES

Political parties were not supposed to happen in the United States. The founders knew about them, of course. They knew that factions had been largely responsible for the fall of democratic Athens and republican Rome. They knew that political parties could replace states and nations as the primary recipients of people's civic loyalty. And they knew that deeply entrenched political affiliations could drive a country to civil war, as they had in England during the previous century.

They also knew that political parties give would-be tyrants a direct path to power. This was the essence of George Washington's strong warning against factions in his 1796 farewell address. "The alternate domination of one faction over another, sharpened by the spirit of revenge," he counseled, "is itself a frightful despotism." But it opens the door to something even worse. The chaos of perpetual division will "gradually incline the minds of men to seek security and repose in the absolute power of an individual." And when this happens, "the chief of some prevailing faction, more able or more fortunate than his competitors, turns this disposition to the purposes of his own elevation, on the ruins of Public Liberty."[4]

Of all the founders, James Madison had the most to say about factions. His best and most famous Federalist essay, #10, outlined an ingenious strategy for ensuring that parties would not emerge in the new republic. Factions, he argued, were a part of human nature. But permanent factions—which was how Madison described what we now call political parties—were a serious threat to liberty. And he understood that a permanent majority would eventually destroy democracy because it would eventually break through the Constitution's guardrails and invade the rights of the minority.

There will always be factions, Madison believed, but these factions don't have to coalesce into permanent political identities. The trick, he thought, was to multiply factions so that there are always too many of them for any one to ever form a lasting majority. In Madison's ideal republic, different issues create different coalitions of voters, and these coalitions disband and reform in new ways for every election. The way to prevent partisanship is not to limit factions but to increase them so that nobody is ever in the majority for very long: "Extend the sphere, and you take in a greater variety of parties and interests; you make it less probable that a majority of the whole will have a common motive to invade the rights of other citizens; or if such a common motive exists, it will be more difficult for all who feel it to discover their own strength, and to act in unison with each other."[5]

It was a great plan, but it didn't work. It didn't even work for Madison, who, within just a few years of writing this essay, became one of the leaders of a new political faction called the Republicans—who were dedicated to opposing the work of the other main author of the Federalist Papers, Alexander Hamilton, who became the leader of the Federalists.

The basic structure of America's first party system emerged in the first month of George Washington's presidency, as Secretary of State Thomas Jefferson and Secretary of the Treasury Alexander Hamilton battled over things like debt consolidation, a standing military, and the National Bank. People's positions on these issues coalesced into two more or less permanent ideologies, each defined by its primary representative in Washington's cabinet:

> The *Hamiltonians* favored a strong national government, robust taxation, limited immigration, a strong military, a financial infrastructure, commerce, manufacturing, and rapid industrialization. Eventually those in this group called themselves "Federalists."
>
> The *Jeffersonians* favored a weak national government, autonomous states, minimal taxation, unlimited immigration, and the preservation of an agrarian economy largely isolated from world affairs. Jefferson's allies called themselves "Republicans" and included James Madison and James Monroe, both of whom eventually followed Jefferson as president.

To understand how the first party system worked in the United States, we need to realize that neither faction saw itself as a party. Each saw itself as the nonpartisan mainstream implementing the Constitution as its framers intended. And since each side included a fair share of the Constitution's authors and original defenders, both felt entitled to represent it. But each side saw the other side as a faction—an anomalous fringe group bent on overturning the Constitution and undoing the Revolution.

The Federalists and the Republicans fought constantly during the presidencies of Washington and Adams. They fought about the military, taxes, immigration, finance, and foreign affairs. But since they didn't acknowledge themselves as political parties, they didn't fight in an organized way. They did not, for example, get together and nominate candidates or create platforms; nor did they officially organize or incorporate. Most important, they did not acknowledge each other's legitimacy or right to exist. These factional hostilities smoldered for the first eleven years of the new government before erupting spectacularly in the election of 1800 between John Adams and Thomas Jefferson.

Even by modern standards, the election of 1800 was a nasty affair from beginning to end. Supporters of the principal candidates each believed that the other candidate was cooperating with a foreign power to destroy American democracy. Republicans believed that Adams wanted to establish a monarchy and give America back to England. Jefferson wrote, in a private letter that became public before the election, "An Anglican, monarchical, and aristocratical party has sprung up whose avowed object is to draw over us the substance as they have already done the form of the British government."[6]

At the same time, Federalists were certain that Jefferson was plotting with French Jacobins to bring guillotines to the banks of the Potomac to start chopping off the heads of Christians. In the weeks before the election, a colorful editorial in the *Hartford Courant* warned that if Jefferson won the election, "murder, robbery, rape, adultery, and incest will be openly taught and practiced, the air will be rent with the cries of the distressed, the soil will be soaked with blood, and the nation black with crimes. Where is the heart that can contemplate such a scene without shivering in horror?"[7]

The flames of these competing Armageddons were fanned by a press that did not even pretend to be fair or balanced. Led by Benjamin Franklin Bache—Benjamin Franklin's grandson and publisher of the *Philadelphia Aurora*—the Republican press attacked Adams and the Federalists and caused them to commit one of the greatest blunders in American history: they passed the Alien and Sedition Acts, which, among other things, made it illegal to slander government officials and led to the imprisonment of Bache and other Republican journalists.

The response was immediate and had long-lasting implications. The Federalists ended up playing directly into the Republican narrative that portrayed them as crypto-monarchists in league with England and opposed to the liberty of the people. The Federalists lost the election and never held power at the national level again. In his sweeping history *Empire of Liberty*, Gordon S. Wood writes, "The Alien and Sedition Acts so thoroughly destroyed the Federalists' historical reputation that it is unlikely it can ever be recovered."[8]

The Federalists did not go quietly. When the Republicans took control of the New York state legislature in May—ensuring that all their electoral votes would go to Jefferson—Hamilton tried to convince Governor John Jay to change the way the state chose its electors. "The scruples of delicacy and propriety," he wrote, "ought to yield to the extraordinary nature of the crisis. They ought not to hinder the taking of a *legal* and *constitutional* step, to prevent an *Atheist* in religion and a *Fanatic* in politics from getting possession of the helm of the State."[9] Jay wisely ignored the request.

Federalists also exploited the embarrassing electoral tie between Jefferson and Aaron Burr. Since the original Constitution did not anticipate political parties or presidential tickets and gave two votes to each elector, Jefferson and Burr ended up tied. The decision then went to the House of Representatives, where the Republicans supported Jefferson for president. The Federalists, however, hated Jefferson so much that they backed Burr and dragged the election out until the middle of February, amid rumors of state militias mobilizing in Virginia and Pennsylvania to respond to a Federalist coup d'état.[10]

In the end, however, the Federalists acknowledged the results of the election. Though they hated and feared their opponents, they gave up control of the government—beginning the tradition of peaceful transfer of power that has become the norm for modern democracies. As one historian writes, "After months of plotting, they ultimately permitted the orderly, constitutional transfer of power and followed to the letter the procedures outlined in the Constitution."[11]

Gradually, Americans began to accept the legitimacy of political parties. The Twelfth Amendment—ratified in 1803 to prevent a repeat of the Jefferson-Burr fiasco—acknowledged that future presidents and vice presidents would run on party tickets. By 1832, the major parties were holding nominating conventions to choose their candidates. Every presidential election since the end of the Civil War, and every state in every presidential election since 1968, has been won by either a Democrat or a Republican—though the actual beliefs and values of these two brand names have shifted multiple times in the last 150 years. The founders' original design aside, political parties—and their arrangement in a two-party system—have become an integral part of the American electoral system.

WHY ARE THERE ALWAYS TWO PARTIES?

How did a group of intelligent, committed, forward-thinking patriots who started out with the premise that permanent factions would destroy the republic end up dividing themselves into permanent factions within the first few weeks of the new government? The likely answer can be found in a game-theory principle called "Duverger's law," introduced in 1954 by French political scientist Maurice Duverger.

Duverger's law is based on the simple premise that rational people would rather get some of the things they want than none of them. This means that certain kinds of popular elections—those that give people one vote to determine a single outcome—will almost always cause rational voters to sort themselves into two parties. Duverger explains this principle with a simple example in his book *Party Politics and Pressure Groups*:

> The brutal finality of a majority vote on a single ballot forces parties with similar tendencies to regroup their forces at the risk of being overwhelmingly defeated. Let us assume an election district in which 100,000 voters with moderate views are opposed by 80,000 communist voters. If the moderates are divided into two parties, the communist candidate may well win the election; should one of his opponents receive more than 20,000 votes, the other will be left with less than 80,000, thereby insuring the election of the communist. In the following election, the two parties with moderate views will naturally tend to unite.[12]

Duverger's law does not define a hard-and-fast principle of nature like gravity or entropy. Third parties do crop up from time to time, but they are rarely successful in the long run unless they replace one of the two major parties, as the Republican Party replaced the Whig Party in 1856. The higher the stakes in a winner-takes-all election, the greater the pressure to support the major-party candidate who comes closer than the other to your views.

Many modern democracies use proportional representation systems to create parliamentary governments that better reflect the ideological makeup of the electorate. Voters in such systems can select multiple candidates for multiple positions, and then parties form coalitions with each other after the election in order to form a government. These systems are more representative, but they also tend to be less stable than two-party systems, which build coalitions before elections rather than piecing them together afterward in ways that are not guaranteed to hold still.

But this stability comes at a price. To achieve it, the two-party structure creates a fictional narrative about our society that, if we aren't careful, we may end up actually believing. In this fiction, the American public is divided into two tribes that correspond to two logically consistent but diametrically opposed worldviews. To participate meaningfully in civic life, we must declare our eternal allegiance to one of these tribes and our undying enmity to the other. We find it pleasant when our side wins elections, but this is incidental compared to the unmitigated catastrophe that a victory by the other side would visit upon everything we hold dear.

Human nature does not naturally divide into two, and only two, sets of political opinions. Nothing about opposing abortion, for example, requires one to favor cutting the capital gains tax. Nor does supporting same-sex marriage mean that one must oppose drilling for oil in national parks. But when these positions are combined into two opposed political parties that become part of our core identity, we experience enormous pressure to align our opinions with those of the tribe. Even when we start out by affiliating with a political tribe just to oppose a common enemy, we usually end up adopting most of the tribe's opinions over time.

Evidence suggests that Americans experience politics more tribally in the first part of the twenty-first century than they have in previous generations. Consider one startling bit of comparative data: In 1960, 5 percent of Republicans and 4 percent of Democrats said they would be "displeased if their child married outside their political party." In 2010, the number stood at 49 percent of Republicans and 33 percent of Democrats.[13] These results are important because in-group endogamy has always been an important marker of tribal identity. People now feel more strongly about their children marrying outside their political party than they do about their children marrying people of a different race or nationality.[14]

Perhaps the most important thing that we need to understand about partisan animosity is that it appears to correlate only partially to people's opinions on actual issues. To try to understand this dynamic, University of Maryland political scientist Lilliana Mason surveyed twenty-five hundred people—split equally between Republicans and Democrats—to assess their opinions on a variety of controversial issues, the extent of their identification as either liberal or conservative, and their degree of willingness to (1) marry, (2) be friends with, (3) live next door to, and (4) spend occasional social time with somebody who identifies with the opposite ideology.

Mason aimed to separate out the way that people's relationships with each other were affected by "issue-based ideology," or conflicts based on different opinions, and "identity-based ideology," or conflicts based on different partisan identifications. She found that people were about twice as likely to be willing to engage in all four social interactions with people who disagreed with them about important issues as they were with people who identified with the opposite political party. "The effect of issue-based ideology," she suggests, "is less than half the size of identity-based ideology in each element of social distance."[15]

If representative, these results indicate that only about half the hostility that Americans feel toward their political opponents stems from actual political disagreement. The rest comes straight from the scared-little-mammal portion of our brain that divides the world up into "us" and "them," clings to the tribe out of a sense of desperate insecurity, and perceives anybody outside the tribe as an existential threat. When this attitude defines a population, it soon ceases to matter what anybody is for, since political engagement no longer has much to do with enacting policies that one favors. Rather, it is motivated by "defensiveness, judgment, anger, and a need to win."[16]

This appears to be the road we are traveling down. Over the summer of 2016, a Pew Research Center study asked voters whether in the November election they anticipated voting primarily *for* a candidate they preferred or *against* a candidate they opposed. Among those who intended to vote for Donald Trump, 53 percent reported that they would be voting primarily *against* Hillary Clinton, compared to 44 percent who planned to vote *for* Trump. Among those planning to vote for Clinton, 46 percent said that they would be voting primarily *against* Trump, and 53 percent would be voting *for* Clinton.[17] Thus, for the first time since Pew began asking this question in 2000, more people who voted for the eventual president saw themselves as voting against the losing candidate instead of for the winning candidate.

Political scientists call this "negative partisanship," or "the phenomenon whereby Americans largely align against one party instead of affiliating with the other."[18] Some level of negative partisanship always occurs in a two-party system, where the best way to vote against one candidate will always be to vote for the most credible alternative. But when a majority of voters choose a candidate primarily because of who that candidate is not, then we get some major shifts in the way our government works.

One result of negative partisanship is that those who win elections become much less accountable to the people who voted for them. If a majority of the people who vote for President Smith do so because he is not Candidate Jones—and not because they find Smith trustworthy or competent or because they agree with any of his policy positions—then President Smith will not lose the support of his voters by demonstrating untrustworthiness or incompetence or by taking unpopular policy positions. He just has to keep not being Jones, which is about as low as the bar for success can ever get.

Negative partisanship also leads to much more extreme candidates than its positive counterpart. This happens because of the way that party nominations work. When the main object of a general election is to get more people to vote for your candidate than the other candidate, then the best way to win is to nominate someone who will attract voters from the other party and appeal to independents. When the primary purpose of an election is to rouse your own voters to hate and fear the other candidate, the incentive for moderation disappears.

But negative partisanship is perhaps most dangerous because it eventually weakens the important political norm of mutual tolerance. Wanting to defeat the other party is not the same as wanting to vanquish it. Confusing the two throws us back to the mind-set of the Federalists and the Republicans in 1800: we refuse to acknowledge the legitimacy of our opponents, and we imagine that if we could just get rid of them once and for all, the country could get back to the normal business of democracy. This is a fantasy. The other side is not going away. The people we disagree with aren't going to simply vanish. And figuring out how to share the country with people we profoundly disagree with is precisely the normal business of democracy.

The fatal shift in our understanding occurs not when we want our own side to win or even when we just want the other side to lose. It occurs when we conceive of the other side as threatening to our well-being by its mere existence. When this happens, the guiding logic of our political culture shifts from the logic of the marketplace (where every transaction has the potential to enrich both the buyer and the seller) to the logic of the *Hunger Games* (where everybody is ultimately the enemy and every interaction is a zero-sum game).

This is how democracy dies. The great Athenian historian Thucydides showed us twenty-five hundred years ago what democracy looks like in its death throes. It is not pretty. The following passage, from Book III of *The History of the Peloponnesian War*, discusses the civil war in Corcyra, Athens's key democratic ally, whose conflict with Corinth was one of the main events that propelled the Hellenistic world into war:

> Words had to change their ordinary meaning and to take that which was now given them. Reckless audacity came to be considered the courage of a loyal ally; prudent hesitation, specious cowardice; moderation was held to be a cloak for unmanliness; ability to see all sides of a question, inaptness to act on any. . . . The advocate of extreme measures was always trustworthy; his opponent a man to be suspected. . . . To forestall an intending criminal, or to suggest the idea of a crime where it was wanting, was equally commended until even blood became a weaker tie than party, from the superior readiness of those united by the latter to dare everything without reserve. . . . Meanwhile the moderate part of the citizens perished between the two, either for not joining in the quarrel, or because envy would not suffer them to escape.[19]

Thucydides shows us that no form of government on earth can match the chaos and incompetence of a dysfunctional democracy. In later sections, he describes how, as the Athenian democracy started to fracture, the *polis* lost its ability to debate and decide anything. Disastrous strategic decisions were made by people who had no understanding of military strategy. Truces were made and violated according to the temporary whims of an electorate. Incompetent men were made generals because they roused the assembly with passionate speeches, and capable leaders (such as Thucydides himself) were cashiered when they failed to meet the unreasonable expectations of an angry mob.

One constant in Thucydides's analysis is that democracy stops working when its people divide into tribes and treat each other as enemies. When this happens, the structural mechanisms of democracy itself amplify the enmity by giving any majority, no matter how slight, the power to inflict whatever torments its members can dream up on the minority—which they invariably do because this is how one treats one's enemies. Furthermore, intractable divisions within a society can be exploited by external forces to hasten that society's demise. People who consider their fellow citizens their enemies tend to be less than discriminating about whose citizens they consider their friends.

BACK FROM THE BRINK:
THE JEFFERSON-ADAMS RECONCILIATION

The election of 1800 had personal consequences for its two principal candidates, Thomas Jefferson and John Adams, whose early friendship had profound ramifications for American history. The two founding fathers had first met in June 1775 at the First Continental Congress in Philadelphia, where they took an immediate liking to each other. They worked together on the Declaration of Independence before becoming ambassadors to, respectively, France and England. When they returned to their new nation, they served in the first presidential administration under George Washington, Adams as vice president and Jefferson as secretary of state.

They wrote each other frequently while abroad, interacted cordially when they were at home, and worked passionately together to create a new country. But when the nation divided into factions during George Washington's first term, Jefferson and Adams found themselves on opposite sides of the divide. Jefferson became a leader of the Republican movement, while Adams came to power as a Federalist, though a very moderate one who disagreed with his fellow Federalists as often as he did with Jefferson's Republicans.

When they ran against each other for president in 1796, the two factions had yet to coalesce into concrete parties. Adams became president and Jefferson vice president without a sense that they bore the standards of different political institutions. By 1800, however, things had changed considerably. As we have already seen, the rematch was contentious, bloody, and decisive.

Even though candidates did not campaign directly at the time, the rancor of the race invaded the two men's personal relationship. Jefferson was furious that just weeks before leaving office, Adams had appointed arch-Federalist John Marshall to the Supreme Court; Marshall spent the next eight years thwarting Jefferson's plans whenever he could. Adams, in turn, was devastated when Jefferson pardoned James Callander, a journalist who had slandered Adams viciously during the election and been convicted under the Sedition Act. And he was inconsolable when he learned that Jefferson had paid Callander to write the slanders in the first place.[20] After the election ended, Jefferson and Adams had no contact with each other for eleven years.

But then something remarkable happened. Through the persistent intervention of a mutual friend, Dr. Benjamin Rush, who believed that the divided republic needed its two greatest living heroes to be friends, Adams and Jefferson renewed their friendship. On January 1, 1812, John Adams sent Thomas Jefferson a brief note in advance of what he called "two pieces of homespun" that he was giving Jefferson as a gift. Adams did not explain what the homespun would be (it was two volumes of a new book by his son, John Quincy). He didn't try to catch Jefferson up on his life. Still reeling from the election, he gave Jefferson just the tiniest opening to renew their correspondence if he chose to do so.

Jefferson responded splendidly with a lengthy note expressing his desire to resume their former friendship. "A letter from you calls up recollections very dear to my mind. it carries me back to the times when, beset with difficulties & dangers, we were fellow laborers in the same cause," he wrote. And then he lamented, "Of the signers of the Declaration of Independance I see now living not more than half a dozen on your side of the Patomak, and, on this side, myself alone." He closed with a strong invitation for further correspondence:

> I have heard with pleasure that you also retain good health, and a greater power of exercise in walking than I do. but I would rather have heard this from yourself, & that, writing a letter, like mine, full of egotisms, & of details of your health, your habits, occupations & enjoiments, I should have the pleasure of knowing that, in the race of life, you do not keep, in it's physical decline, the same distance ahead of me which you have done in political honors & atchievements. no circumstances have lessened the interest I feel in these particulars respecting yourself; none have suspended for one moment my sincere esteem for you; and I now salute you with unchanged affections and respect.[21]

Adams wrote an equally enthusiastic letter in return, and, for the next thirteen years, the two ex-presidents carried on a remarkable correspondence in which they discussed everything that came into their minds: Greek philosophy, poetry, religion, education, the origins of the American Indians, and the physical complaints of old age.

And they argued with each other. A lot. About past events as well as current policy. But once separated from the political world that had turned them both into symbols of each other's awfulness, they argued as friends. Understanding how their perspectives differed became part of the essential activity of friendship: understanding other people the way that they understand themselves.

In the early years of their renewed correspondence, the two men spent time discussing the ground rules. "You and I ought not to die, before We have explained ourselves to each other," wrote Adams in 1813.[22] And in one of his first letters, Jefferson told Adams, "If any opinions you may express should be different from mine, I shall receive them with the liberality and indulgence which I ask for my own, and still cherish with warmth the sentiments of affectionate respect of which I can with so much truth tender you the assurance."[23]

In this same letter, Jefferson raised the specter of the partisanship in 1800 by referring to the Alien and Sedition Acts as "terrorism" and claiming that it was "felt by one party only."[24] Adams took this as a challenge and stormed back with a stinging critique of the entire party system:

> The real terrors of both Parties have allways been, and now are, The fear that they shall loose the Elections and consequently the Loaves and Fishes; and that their Antagonists will obtain them. Both parties have excited artificial Terrors and if I were summoned as a Witness to Say upon Oath, which Party had excited, Machiavillialy, the most terror, and which had really felt the most, I could not give a more sincere Answer, than in the vulgar Style "Put Them in a bagg and Shake them, and then See which comes out first."[25]

Jefferson declined to escalate the conflict and instead responded with the observation that, at their age and station in life, they could have no other reason for arguing than to try to understand each other. "I have thus stated my opinion on a point on which we differ, not with a view to controversy," he wrote, "for we are both too old to change opinions which are the result of a long life of enquiry and reflection; but on the suggestion of a former letter of yours that we ought not to die before we have explained ourselves to each other."[26]

In the course of their letters, Jefferson and Adams worked through nearly all the issues that had separated them in 1800: Adams's judicial appointments, Jefferson's pardons, their differing views of a standing military, and their very different perceptions of the French Revolution. These were not minor disagreements, but neither were they battles between absolute good and unalloyed evil. Reasonable people acting in good faith can disagree about things like taxation rates, military spending, and judicial decisions without ceasing to be friends. These are, in fact, precisely the sorts of things that people in a democracy are supposed to disagree about.

Their friendship even survived a new scandal when, early in their renewed correspondence, somebody sent Adams some letters that Jefferson
had written years earlier to the British scientist Joseph Priestly, which had
recently been published in an obscure British memoir. In these letters, Jefferson portrayed Adams as a bigot and an enemy of science. And he did so with
the contempt and ridicule that Adams always feared that Jefferson felt toward
him.[27] In the letter that Adams wrote after reading the memoir, he allowed
outrage to creep into the correspondence for the first time: "The Sentiment,
that you have attributed to me in your letter to Dr Priestley I totally disclaim
and demand in the French Sense of the Word demand of you the proof. It is
totally incongruous to every principle of my mind and every Sentiment of my
heart for Threescore Years at least."[28]

Adams's letter put Jefferson in a difficult position. His private correspondence had been reproduced without his knowledge or permission. In
the letter that Adams did not quote from, Jefferson had expressed religious
sentiments that he was not anxious to have made public. His response had to
be measured and reassuring so as not to jeopardize the reconciliation but also
to make sure that Adams did not feel compelled to publish the embarrassing
letters more widely:

> The last is on the subject of religion, and by it's publication will gratify the
> priesthood with new occasion of repeating their Comminations against
> me. . . . The first letter is political. It recalls to our recollection the gloomy
> transactions of the times, the doctrines they witnessed, and the sensibilities
> they excited. It was a confidential communication of reflections on these
> from one friend to another, deposited in his bosom, and never meant to
> trouble the public mind. Whether the character of the times is justly por-
> trayed or not, posterity will decide.[29]

Jefferson's letter managed to restore Adams's confidence in at least Jefferson's current good intentions toward him.[30] The relationship survived this
difficult disclosure and thrived until the day that both men died because (1)
they had already established an environment in which such an issue could
be discussed frankly, and (2) they valued the current friendship enough to
forgive past slights.

Between 1813 and 1826, Adams and Jefferson wrote more than 150
long and affectionate letters to each other. Their relationship then passed
from history into poetry when they died within hours of each other on July
4, 1826—fifty years to the day after the birth of the nation they founded together. In 1959, the University of North Carolina Press published a complete
edition of John and Abigail Adams's letters to and from Thomas Jefferson,

both before and after the election of 1800. Taken together, this remarkable correspondence is a monument to the power of civic friendship to win out, in the end, over political outrage.

Perhaps the most notable thing about the Jefferson-Adams letters is that, while the two men argued with each other about almost everything, they argued *for* things and not just against things. In 1800, each had played the role of chief bugaboo in campaigns designed to encourage millions of people to vote against something they feared. The race involved very little discussion of what either man stood for.

But letters between old friends can't take the form of political attack ads. To continue their correspondence, they had to try to understand each other's vision on its own terms and then agree or disagree with it on rational grounds that did not bring about the end of the friendship they were trying very hard to preserve. As a consequence, we get a clear vision of what each man thought America should look like—something that rarely comes through in political campaigns, then or now.

Historians do not study the Jefferson-Adams correspondence to gain political insights into the United States at the time. Neither of them had much of an idea of what was going on in the country when they wrote their letters. Both men had left the spotlight and retired far away from the centers of power. The letters are still studied, as Merrill Peterson argues in his book *Adams and Jefferson*, because they "evoked qualities of mind and heart that may have been more significant, because they were shared, than all the continuing clashes of opinion and temperament between the aged patriots."[31]

The Jefferson-Adams correspondence, in other words, remains important today because of what it says about friendship—and especially what it says about friendship between people who disagree with each other politically. This was exactly the message that Benjamin Rush wanted to send to his country, and it is why he spent years trying to persuade his two friends to resume their friendship. Rush saw Jefferson and Adams as "the personification of the American Republic, of its principles and ideas," and he felt that "the prolonged estrangement of the two former presidents was . . . both a personal and a national misfortune."[32]

In 1800, Jefferson and Adams were on opposite sides of a contest that was as nasty and as polarized as anything we have seen in our lifetimes. They endured a culture of echo chambers and media outrage very much like ours, with two factions that sincerely believed their members were the only true Americans and that the other side had no right to exist. Both men participated in this culture and allowed it to destroy their friendship. But they found their way back from the brink.

The reconciliation between Jefferson and Adams occurred because both men consciously decided to make their friendship a priority. Our second and third presidents were separated by enormous political differences and sharply defined political identities. Each had a large enough store of offenses, slights, and resentments toward the other to last the rest of his life. The initial reaction of any human being would be to nurse the resentments and bow to the force of the differences—to follow the easy and crowded path lit by our worst angels. What Adams and Jefferson did when they reconciled required more effort and sustained attention. But it ended up producing much more satisfying results. That's how our better angels work.

· 5 ·

The Great American Outrage Machine

*Outrage is a way to perform for our friends,
not engage our opponents.*

> Resentment and indignation are feelings dangerous to the pos-
> sessor and to be sparingly used. They give comfort too cheaply;
> they rot judgment, and by encouraging passivity, they come to
> require that evil continue for the sake of the grievance to be
> enjoyed.
>
> —Jacques Barzun, *Science: The Glorious Entertainment*

The level of incivility in American political discourse has ebbed and flowed over the years, but it probably reached its high-water mark in 1856—the year that South Carolina congressman Preston Brooks walked into the main chamber of the US Senate and beat Massachusetts senator Charles Sumner senseless with a cane.

The triggering event for Brooks was a speech titled "The Crime against Kansas" that Sumner, a fiery abolitionist, had given three days earlier in the same chamber. At the time, Kansas was the focal point of the national debate over slavery. Under the highly controversial Kansas-Nebraska Act of 1854, Kansas could choose for itself whether to enter the Union as a slave or a free state. Two different state legislatures eventually convened and produced two different constitutions—one that supported and one that opposed slavery. To nobody's surprise, pro-slavery president James Buchanan insisted on accepting the pro-slavery constitution.

As the leading abolitionist in the Senate, Sumner felt morally obligated to denounce the events in Kansas in the strongest terms possible. Even by the

61

standards of antebellum political rhetoric, his speech was harsh and inflammatory. For five hours over two days, he inveighed against slavery, southern
slave power, the Kansas-Nebraska Act, and the act's two sponsors in the Senate: Stephen Douglas from Illinois and Andrew Butler from South Carolina.

As a senator from the most rabidly pro-slavery state in the Union, Butler
came in for special opprobrium. "The Senator from South Carolina has read
many books of chivalry and imagines himself a chivalrous knight," Sumner
thundered, comparing Butler to Don Quixote: "He has chosen a mistress . . .
who, though ugly to others is always lovely to him; though polluted in the sight
of the world is chaste in his sight—I mean the harlot, Slavery."[1] And on the
second day, Sumner broadened his condemnation to the whole state of South
Carolina, which he portrayed as backward, uneducated, bigoted, and tyrannical.

Brooks, who was Butler's second cousin and a lifelong South Carolinian,
heard the first part of the speech in the gallery and read the second part in
the newspaper the next day. Predictably outraged, he felt that he had a special, personal responsibility to punish Sumner for attacking his state and his
kinsman. On May 22, 1856, Brooks walked into the Senate chamber and beat
Sumner with a wooden cane until he was unconscious.

Several important things happened next. First, Sumner recovered and
became a hero throughout the North. He portrayed himself as a martyr to
conscience and the principles of freedom and equality. Moderate northern
politicians who had originally condemned the speech for its incivility had
no choice but to rally behind Sumner when he became the victim of a brutal
beating. The caning incident helped to galvanize northerners and westerners
around the fledgling Republican Party, which held its first nominating convention less than a month later.[2]

Second, Preston Brooks also became a hero. Grateful southerners
cheered him wherever he went, celebrated his actions in public forums, and
sent him hundreds of canes to replace the one that he ruined by almost killing
the senator from Massachusetts.[3] After censure by the House of Representatives and barely surviving an expulsion vote by his colleagues, Brooks resigned
his seat in Congress and was overwhelmingly elected three weeks later to fill
the position he had vacated. When he stood for the seat again later in 1856,
he ran unopposed and attracted not a single write-in vote of opposition.[4]

Third, the United States moved substantially closer to the Civil War,
with the two regions of the country even more entrenched in their positions
than ever before. Both Brooks and Sumner became celebrities because the
story fit so well into each region's existing narratives about the other. To
southerners, it seemed to confirm that violence was the best way to deal with
hostility to their "peculiar institution." And to northerners, it seemed to prove
that southerners could not be reasoned with, so there was no point in trying.

From beginning to end, the caning of Charles Sumner illustrates the way that outrage functions in public discourse. Both Sumner and Brooks trafficked in the politics of outrage—Sumner expressed his outrage in a five-hour speech full of personal attacks and sexual innuendo that energized his friends, incensed his enemies, and persuaded nobody to adopt an opinion not already held. Brooks responded with an act of violence that made him a hero to his friends and an outcast among his enemies—but also didn't change anybody's mind about anything.

Outrage blurs the lines between political disagreement and personal attack. It causes us to see every challenge as a personal affront that we must respond to forcefully and publicly if we don't want to lose our status in the community. We perceive the objects of our outrage as something not quite fully human, and we no longer feel bound to treat them as we think human beings should be treated. These are not people who must be understood or protected but enemies who must be destroyed—or, at the very least, unfriended.

THE PSYCHOLOGY OF OUTRAGE

Feelings of outrage—and the actions they precipitate—have long been associated with a phenomenon that psychologists call "third-party punishment." According to this concept, members of a group internalize its norms and values and take it upon themselves to enforce those values against each other. The threat of social penalties—which are often more certain and more effective deterrents than the threat of legal punishments that may or may not occur—keeps rule breakers and cheaters in line.

For example, anybody who has ever read a Jane Austen novel (or seen one of the many movies derived from these novels) knows the horrors that ensue when a young woman from a good family is "ruined" by sexual contact with a man she is not properly married to. The stigma is absolute and devastating. In *Pride and Prejudice*, Lydia Bennet's family sees her seduction by the rakish George Wickham as worse for them than utter financial ruin. Unless Wickham can be persuaded to marry Lydia, all four of her sisters will be ineligible for marriage within their class, and the family will no longer be welcome at social engagements—such were the heavy penalties of a society's outrage in Jane Austen's world.

In this way society enforced the norm of female chastity, thereby helping to ensure that wealth and titles got passed to the right people. This is how outrage works: people see certain behaviors as violations of important group norms that they have a responsibility to condemn or punish. But even though expressing outrage may involve communicating with others (or beating them senseless), outrage has always been a mechanism for communicating with an in-group. By displaying outrage, we send a series of signals designed to increase our status with people who share our views: I am on your team. I am reliable. I am strong. I am willing to invest time and resources into punishing our common enemies.[5]

Preston Brooks sincerely believed that his standing among his peers would suffer if he failed to address Sumner's transgressions. In his letter resigning from Congress after the attack, Brooks wrote, "I should have forfeited my own self-respect, and perhaps the good opinion of my countrymen, if I had failed to resent such an injury by calling the offender in question to a personal account."[6] And Butler later reported that, before the caning, Brooks "could not go into a parlor, or drawing-room, or to a dinner party, where he did not find an implied reproach that there was an unmanly submission to an insult to his State and his countrymen."[7]

Though Brooks directed his blows at Sumner, he was actually sending a message to his own social group in the South. And though Sumner's "Crime against Kansas" speech directly addressed South Carolina, the actual intended audience was abolitionists in the North. Each man wanted his primary peer group to understand that he was willing to jeopardize his own safety and reputation in order to enforce the group's moral norms on the national stage. Behind the blustering, posturing, and violence lay each man's fundamental desire to be thought well of by his peers.

Outrage can be a useful emotion. It has adaptive advantages for groups, who get the increased cohesion that comes with shared values, and for individuals, who get the social and material benefits that come with increased status. And like most things that convey adaptive advantages, outrage feels good. Feeling righteous indignation gives us pleasure. It makes us feel morally superior, important, engaged, and connected to a greater cause. And we especially enjoy the positive feedback that we get from our friends when we represent their opinions to others in adversarial ways.

In our modern society, almost everything that provides modest pleasure in a natural setting can be stimulated by what Steven Pinker calls "pleasure technologies," or technological innovations "designed to defeat the locks that safeguard our pleasure buttons and to press the buttons in various combinations." Pleasure technologies have no adaptive function and can be remarkably maladaptive, but they are wildly attractive because they provide pleasure in much more concentrated doses than their counterparts in nature. Among the things that Pinker categorizes as "pleasure technologies" are recreational drugs, art, music, literature, cheesecake, and pornography.[8]

Modern media outrage, I would argue, is also a pleasure technology—one with similarities to Pinker's final example: pornography. In 2009, cartoonist Tim Kreider coined the term "outrage porn" to describe the news and commentary that we read, click on, or forward specifically because we enjoy the self-righteous anger that it allows us to feel. Outrage, he writes, "is like a lot of other things that feel good but over time devour us from the inside out. And it's even more insidious than most vices because we don't even consciously acknowledge that it's a pleasure. We prefer to think of it as a disagreeable but fundamentally healthy involuntary reaction to negative stimuli thrust upon us by the world we live in, like pain or nausea, rather than admit that it's a shameful kick we eagerly indulge again and again."[9]

Kreider's equation is apt. Outrage functions in some ways, though not in others, like sexually explicit media. It is intense and addictive, and it gives us the illusion of a human relationship without any of the hard work that real relationships require. And while the Internet didn't invent either pornography or outrage, it has certainly made them both easier to consume. Perhaps the most important thing that outrage and pornography have in common, though, is that "vast and lucrative industries are ready to supply the necessary material."[10] Like pornography, outrage is a multi-billion-dollar industry whose purveyors feel very little concern for the effects of their product and will fight tooth and nail to preserve their profits.

In their 2014 book *The Outrage Industry*, Tufts University professors Jeffrey M. Berry and Sarah Sobieraj try to quantify the prevalence and effect of "outrage journalism," which they define as "efforts to provoke emotional responses (e.g., anger, fear, moral indignation) from the audience through the use of overgeneralizations, sensationalism, misleading or patently inaccurate information, ad hominem attacks, and belittling ridicule of opponents."[11] In 2009, they used a research team to identify thirteen forms of outrage in television shows, blogs, radio programs, and newspaper columns coming from both ends of the political spectrum. Their thirteen categories, in order of frequency, were as follows:

- Mockery
- Misrepresentation/exaggeration
- Insulting language
- Name calling
- Ideologically extremizing language
- Belittling
- Emotional display
- Emotional language
- Obscene language

- Character assassination
- Slippery slope argumentation
- Verbal fighting/sparring
- Conflagration (attempts to escalate nonscandals into scandals)[12]

Berry and Sobieraj found two things that should surprise none of us and concern all of us. First, America's political media stokes a whole lot of outrage. Nearly 90 percent of all content analyzed, including 100 percent of television programs, 99 percent of radio programs, and 83 percent of blog posts, contained at least one example of outrage discourse. Television shows averaged one outrage incident every ninety to one hundred seconds; on radio they occurred even more frequently. And, Berry and Sobieraj found, "the aggregate audience for outrage media is immense." They estimate that outrage-based talk radio attracts a daily audience of close to thirty-five million people, with television programming coming in a distant second at ten million.[13]

Even more disturbing, though, is the way that outrage journalism affects public discourse. Put simply, it makes talking to people who disagree with us harder. Conversations among opponents are hard enough under the best circumstances. Other people are hard. Years of research into political discourse has found that people's anxieties about unfiltered political conversation include "social rejection/isolation, looking uneducated/uninformed, being unable to defend their positions, and social conflict." When we find ourselves in a discussion that becomes political, we are "less likely to voice an opinion on issues when we sense we are in the minority because we believe (consciously or unconsciously) that sharing unpopular opinions will lead to negative consequences."[14]

As a result, most of us try to "avoid political conversations with others whose views are known to be different from our own or whose views are unknown (and hence may differ from our own)."[15] We are scared little mammals with millions of years of evolution telling us to scurry away from anything or anyone who threatens our well-being, but outrage culture gives us a script that we can follow: simply adopt a sneering, angry tone and repeat all of the talking points from our favorite blog or radio show while insisting that anyone who disagrees is crazy, stupid, or evil.

This strategy works especially well in online forums where we can be relatively anonymous and disengage whenever we choose. And the explosion of social media has created entirely new avenues of awfulness for the purveyors of outrage to exploit. Nearly every other media format can be digitized, uploaded, linked to, and shared on social media networks, producing a media environment where people rush to share the most outrageous information they can find. Acclaimed British psychologist Terri Apter describes this environment in her most recent book, *Passing Judgment*:

> The realm of social media thrives on quick, strong but shallow judgments—particularly negative ones. . . . Outrage becomes a kind of entertainment wherein users compete for the stage. This competition—alongside the tendency for angry and negative views to be contagious—reinforces and escalates abuse. Furthermore, on social media, there is no immediate comeback of disapproval, so the bad behavior—and the dopamine jolt that accompanies it—get a free ride. The greater the personal insult, the more abusive the language, the more likely it is that others on the site will join the fray.[16]

The endpoint of this kind of discourse is a nation of silos and echo chambers. Modern social media platforms give us tremendous filtering capabilities. We can decide what kind of information we see, whose messages get through to us, and who will be able to read our posts. And we can change the filters every time we send or receive a message. This gives us a high degree of control over what we see and whom we interact with—which very often leads to an environment in which we spend much of our lives surrounded by virtual voices that amplify our resentment and isolate us from opinions, and even facts, that challenge our existing beliefs.

NORWEGIANS AT THE GATE

Along with degrading the quality of our political discourse and eroding our democracy from within, a culture of perpetual outrage leaves us open to serious threats from without. Foreign invaders rarely just show up at the gates of a strong country and start attacking. They exploit internal divisions to their advantage and find allies willing to help them make it past the gates. When the members of a society consider each other their greatest enemies, external adversaries can destroy them with surprisingly little effort. This is one of the most important lessons we can learn from William Shakespeare's greatest play, *Hamlet*.

Hamlet begins with a conversation among palace guards about the threat of an invasion from Norway, which has recently lost its king and its lands in a war with Denmark. Young Fortinbras, son of the defeated king, is rumored to be marching to Denmark with an army bent on conquest. Denmark's King Hamlet has also died recently—supposedly of a snake bite but really due to poison poured into his ear—and was succeeded by his brother, Claudius, who did the pouring.

The threat of a Norwegian invasion casts a shadow over all the action in *Hamlet*, but it is easy to forget about it, since nobody talks much about it. The characters are too busy with their own palace intrigues and civil wars. Claudius's ascension to the throne is tainted by his arguably incestuous marriage to his brother's wife and by the fact that (as everybody in Shakespeare's audience knew very well) brothers aren't supposed to succeed a king with a living son. But Claudius wins the support of courtiers like Polonius and just skips over the fact that he has no right to the throne.

Upon discovering that Claudius killed his father, Hamlet is properly outraged. But instead of killing Claudius, Hamlet kills Polonius (albeit accidentally), whose son Laertes, also properly outraged, rushes back to Denmark and raises an army of common people to attack the palace. Just as Laertes is about to kill the usurping king, Claudius talks him out of it and convinces him to challenge Hamlet to a friendly sword fight with a blade that just happens to be tipped with poison. In the dramatic final scene, Hamlet and Laertes kill each other with poisoned swords, but Hamlet lives long enough to make several noble statements and run Claudius through as well. Pretty much everybody else dies too.

But here's the thing that people often miss about *Hamlet*: During the entire time that the Danes are plotting and counterplotting against each other, Fortinbras is marching against them. While Hamlet and Laertes are fencing and poisoning each other, a Norwegian army is breaking through the castle's defenses and preparing to seize the seat of government. When Fortinbras finally does arrive on the scene, ready to avenge his father's death and reclaim the lands that Norway lost to Denmark, there is nobody left to kill. He walks into a room full of fresh corpses, picks up the crown from the floor, plops it on his head, and becomes the new king. Hamlet and company have already done the hard work of destroying the government for him.

To understand what Shakespeare is doing in *Hamlet*, we need to look closely at what was going on in England at the end of the sixteenth century (*Hamlet* was written sometime between 1599 and 1602). Elizabeth I was coming to the end of her long and stable reign. Before Elizabeth, Catholics and Protestants had fought each other viciously and produced multiple social upheavals as the monarchy lurched back and forth between rulers of different religions. The Protestant Elizabeth had brought four decades of stability but had no heir, and many people feared that her death would lead to renewed hostilities—during which France or Spain might forge alliances with English Catholics to make a play for the throne.

However else one reads *Hamlet*—as a Freudian tale of Oedipal obsession, perhaps, or as an exploration of the boundaries of madness—it is also a parable about the consequences of internal division and perpetual outrage.

It tells us that if we spend our time and energy fighting battles with each other, then it doesn't really matter who wins because somebody else will always be ready to take control when we have injured ourselves too badly to resist.

Americans found out in 2016 that, much like Fortinbras, our enemies love it when we indulge in recreational outrage instead of focusing on what they are doing. This is how Russian agents were able to conduct extensive cyberattacks against the United States in an attempt to influence the outcome of the 2016 presidential election. They created elaborate phony news sites with inflammatory articles and then used millions of fake Facebook and Twitter accounts to promote them and push them into people's news feeds. And it worked. Articles from Russian news sites dominated American social media during the weeks leading up to the election, with, according to some estimates, up to 20 percent of all political conversations on Twitter driven by Russian bots. And Facebook has now acknowledged that "as many as sixty *million* accounts were fake."[17]

The attack worked for two reasons, both of which have profound implications for our democracy. First, our social media feeds were so segregated into partisan echo chambers and so segmented into demographic categories that foreign spies could penetrate deeply into social networks without triggering alarms. All advertisers on Facebook have the ability to target users by dozens of characteristics, including political preferences, religion, education level, age, income, and zip code.

As Timothy Snyder relates in *The Road to Unfreedom*, this high degree of market segmentation allowed Russian agents to send made-up news items to people "in accordance with their own susceptibilities, as revealed by their practices on the internet."[18] These stories were circulated among like-minded people and confirmed by similar stories from other fake sites so that, when they crossed into more mainstream news feeds, they did so as a kind of common knowledge that "everybody" knew was true. By the time serious journalists and fact checkers could refute the claims in the fake news stories, the election was over.

Russia's plan to subvert American democracy by advertising in our echo chambers could not have succeeded, however, if we had not already done most of the hard work of tearing ourselves apart. Foreign enemies did not convince us to start hating each other; we did that ourselves. We wanted to believe that candidates from the other side were murderers and child abusers and that their supporters despised their own country so much that they didn't care. For the cyberattack to succeed—and by all accounts it succeeded beyond anybody's expectations—we had to be prepared to believe the worst things about each other that a hostile foreign spy could invent.

The recent Russian attack on the integrity of our elections will not be the last. Cyberwarfare is still in its infancy. "Each year, more states employ squads of opinion-shapers to flood on-line sites," warns former secretary of state Madeline Albright. And most of them "can generate products that show people—including democratic politicians—doing things they didn't do and saying things they never said. . . . Imagine a foreign agent creeping into your bedroom every night to whisper lies in your ear, then multiply the number of agents and lies by a billion or more."[19] These attacks exploit the weaknesses of societies that protect key freedoms, such as speech, commerce, and the press—all of which would have to be severely restricted to ensure that foreign interests could not meddle in elections.

As long as we remain an open society, no piece of software or network regulation can prevent a foreign power from using social media platforms against us. But we don't have to do their jobs for them. If somebody wants to set us against each other—to convince us that what splits us apart is more important than what binds us together—then let's at least make them work for it. There is no good reason that Vladimir Putin or anybody else should be able to stroll in like Fortinbras to discover a room full of corpses and the crown of a once proud nation lying on the floor, free for the taking.

OK, FINE, BUT WHAT ABOUT NAZIS?

Anybody who spends any time at all talking about things like civility, civic friendship, and the quality of our political discourse had better be prepared to talk about Nazis. Call it the *argumentum ad nazium*, or the *dicto simplicihitler*, but people seem compelled to let it be known that they have no intention of trying to make friends with Nazis. This is often asserted as a decisive blow: "Don't talk to me about civility. I don't talk nicely to Nazis; I punch them in the face."

I suspect that most of us overestimate the likelihood that we will ever be in a position to punch a Nazi in the face. Like most Americans, I have never met a real-life Nazi, though I have occasionally been called one and have (regrettably) used the word to describe other people. Questions like "Should I try to make friends with a Nazi?" just don't come up that often. The question is really a form of proposition testing. It creates an extreme example to determine whether a principle is truly universal. As long as I can find a three-legged dog somewhere in the world, then "all dogs have four legs" is not a valid premise. This is how one must think when writing formal logic proofs.

It is not, however, how one should think when deciding how to treat other people. Most people who want to carve out a "Nazi exemption" to the requirements of basic human decency—or any exemption based on a proposition-testing outlier instead of lived experience—are not really trying to decide what to do in the unlikely event that they run into someone doing *seig heil* salutes in the checkout line. They want to create an exempt category and populate it with anybody they can force into the definition. This phenomenon happens across the political spectrum. People on the left equate immigration restrictions with *Kristallnacht*, while people on the right post pictures of shoes from Holocaust victims in response to arguments for gun control.

"These repeated references to Nazis showcase the substantial difference between conventional political 'incivility' . . . and outrage," Berry and Sobieraj argue after examining the ways that the Left and the Right both invoke Hitler in their arguments about each other. "Not only is Obama, or Cheney, or Limbaugh described as a terrible leader or broadcaster, they are described as capable of genocide."[20] Contemporary Americans waste a huge amount of imaginative energy thinking up reasons why the other side is like Hitler, not because these comparisons have any value as political analogies but because they paint our opponents with the blackest shades in our culture's palate. As Berry and Sobieraj conclude, "No one looks good in a Hitler Moustache."[21]

Nazis aren't the only people whom good, upstanding citizens refuse to be friends with, of course. I frequently hear people say things like "I believe in being civil and respectful to people who disagree with me, and I can be friends with almost anyone. But there is one issue that I refuse to compromise on. I just can't imagine ever being friends with somebody who thinks that _____." The blank usually gets filled in with a current hot-button issue and a caricature of a position that somewhere around half the people in the country hold.

These deal-breaker issues—the ones that people say they just can't have a civil discussion about—are precisely the ones that we need to have more civil discussions about. These are the issues currently dividing our political body. If we can't talk about them rationally, or at least nonviolently, then we won't have a functioning democracy—just the occasional shouting match followed by a straw poll.

As we have seen, outrage is almost always directed at people who already agree with us—and for reasons that are ultimately quite selfish. Even when we make other people the target of our outrage, we are often just using them as a convenient proxy to signal our virtue and political reliability to our friends. And we too often imagine that we are somehow fulfilling our ethical responsibility to "speak up for our values" when we engage in confrontational discourse that will almost certainly not produce the political changes we want and will very possibly make everything worse.

One good way to deal with actual Nazis—or with anybody else who says and does outrageous things in order to provoke a response from us—is to withhold from them the main thing they want, which is our outrage in return. We can simply drive by people who say reprehensible things. Or we can refute them calmly and rationally in ways likely to persuade other people that they are wrong. When we argue that people should listen to us and not to those who are shouting obscenities, advocating violence, and parading around the public square like unhinged psychopaths in tacky costumes, we would do well to make sure that everyone can tell the difference.

OUTRAGE AND THE SPIRIT OF COMPROMISE

One of the most tragic things about democracy is that campaigning and governing require completely different skill sets. Campaigning requires the ability to create passion. Campaigners must articulate a clear vision and explain why only they can make it a reality. And they need to assure voters that they will get things done without compromising their principles. Governing mainly requires compromising with other people to move agendas forward and accomplish some, but almost never all, of one's goals. As Amy Gutmann and Dennis Thompson write in *The Spirit of Compromise*, "Democracy calls on politicians to resist compromise and to accept it. They may resist it more when they campaign, but they need to accept it more when they govern."[22]

Nobody likes to compromise—especially on things that they feel strongly about. We don't compromise because we want to be nice and avoid hurting people's feelings. It has nothing to do with sharing our toys. We have a system in which power is diffused through multiple branches and levels of government. Stopping things from happening is much easier than making them happen, so meaningful forward movement requires working with opponents, finding common ground, and giving up some things in order to get other things. In a democracy, governing is compromise; everything else is theater.

Forging compromises with political opponents is always hard, but outrage culture makes it virtually impossible. Outraged voters don't want their representatives to compromise with the forces of darkness. They want unconditional victory, and the outrage machine tells them that they can have it—that the other side is an anomaly and that "someday the American public will come to its senses and move decisively to the correct ideological pole."[23] Outrage journalists denounce politicians who compromise with the other side on anything and target them for primary challenges. Even though most voters say they want their representatives to work together to find compromises, most politicians are mortally afraid of what will happen to them if they do.

The outrage industry and the outrage culture that it supports try to sell us a sweet-sounding but completely unrealistic fantasy about how government works. In a column written during the 2012 election, David Brooks called it "the No. 1 political fantasy in America today . . . the fantasy that the other party will not exist."[24] This is the fantasy that your side will so totally devastate the other side in the next election that its values and perceptions will become irrelevant to the governing process. "It's almost entirely make-believe," Brooks concludes. "In the real world, there are almost never ultimate victories, and it is almost never the case (even if you control the White House and Congress) that you get to do what you want."[25]

As fantastic as this idea may seem, it has become the core assumption of modern political rhetoric. Very few political campaigns, talk radio shows, websites, or blogs give even a cursory nod to the reality that, in Brooks's words, "we live in a highly polarized, evenly divided nation" and that to make any progress toward a better society we will have to accept that reality. We know, intellectually, that the other side isn't going away—and most of us would even have qualms about exiling those who disagree with us or stripping them of the right to vote. But we struggle to find ways to talk about governing without pretending that our side can govern without the other side having any say in the matter.

Calls for compromise should not be confused with calls for moderation. A moderate position on an issue is no more inherently logical than a position from any other point on the spectrum. Proposed compromises that just split the difference between two positions are likely to be worse than either of the other options, because the benefits of a proposal don't usually scale as easily as our thinking about them does. If I want a 1 percent sales tax increase to build a new school, and you don't want any increase at all, we can't just split the difference and build half a school. Half a loaf is better than none, but—*pace* Solomon—half a baby is not.

Meaningful compromise does not require political moderation. Few American senators in 1964 were as extreme in their respective ideologies as Democratic whip Hubert Humphrey and Republican minority leader Everett Dirksen. But Humphrey and Dirksen managed to work together to craft the 1964 Civil Rights Act, one of the most significant laws in American history, and to break the southern filibuster that threatened to prevent its passage. Before even sending the bill to the Senate floor, Lyndon Johnson sat Humphrey down and told him, "This bill can't pass unless you get Ev Dirksen. . . . You get in there to see Dirksen! You drink with Dirksen! You talk to Dirksen! You listen to Dirksen."[26]

If Johnson had decided to go it alone with his 65–35 Senate majority, or if Dirksen had decided to deny the president a major victory just four months before he ran for reelection, then there would have been no Civil Rights Act. And if Humphrey and Dirksen had been working with a Senate full of people who knew they would have to face well-funded primary challenges simply because they chose to work with the other party, then the attempt to ensure full civil rights for African Americans a century after the end of the Civil War would have gone down in a well-organized filibuster.

By a 3–1 margin, Americans say that it is more important for political leaders to compromise to get things done than to stick to their political beliefs.[27] But we rarely reward politicians who do exactly so, and we frequently punish them in primary elections, so the standard response of blaming the politicians won't work here. Our houses of Congress are no more dysfunctional than most people's dining rooms on Thanksgiving. We elect politicians who reflect the culture we have created. They reflect our own addiction to outrage and our own skewed perceptions about the other side.

We all need to get off the outrage train; our democracy may well depend on it. But pleasure technologies are notoriously hard to quit. Outrage may not be physically addictive, but it is a pleasurable experience that also tricks us into thinking that we are engaging politically. The first thing people usually do when they decide to reduce the outrage in their lives is stop talking about politics altogether—or at least stop arguing with people who disagree with them. This is exactly the wrong response. We are supposed to argue about politics; we're just supposed to figure out how to do it without shouting at the top of our lungs and calling each other stupid or evil.

Democracy calls us to have uncomfortable conversations. It asks us to listen to each other even when we would rather be listening to ourselves—or to people enough like us that we might as well be listening to ourselves. It is easier and more comfortable for us to live in perpetual high dudgeon inside our echo chambers than it is to have a meaningful conversation with people who disagree with us. The entire outrage industry has been designed to keep us in our bubbles, never challenged by disagreement and never required to think that we might be wrong.

· 6 ·

The Other Opposite of Friendship

Agreeing with people uncritically is flattery, not friendship.

Where there is much desire to learn, there of necessity will be much arguing, much writing, many opinions; for opinion in good men is but knowledge in the making.

—John Milton, "Aeropagetica"

I do not wish to treat friendships daintily, but with the roughest courage. When they are real, they are not glass threads or frost-work, but the solidest thing we know.

—Ralph Waldo Emerson, "Politics"

The quotation "Truth springs from argument among friends" is often attributed to Scottish philosopher David Hume. Hume never said it, or, if he did, he never wrote it down anywhere that anyone can find today. But if Hume had said it, he would have been right. Arguing with our friends is good for democracy. It makes us better friends and better arguers, and it serves as a check on the tendency of fact claims to run amok in friendship networks where nobody ever pushes back against them.[1]

Classical philosophy holds that perpetual agreement with another person is incompatible with friendship. Because no two people can possibly agree on everything, someone who never expresses disagreement with you is acting insincerely—and true friendship requires sincerity above almost everything else. "A genuine friend does not imitate everything or praise everything enthusiastically," wrote the great historian Plutarch. When someone praises

75

our every action and agrees with our every opinion, he concludes, we should say, "I have no need of a friend who changes places when I do and nods in agreement when I do; my shadow is better at that. I need a friend who helps me by telling the truth and having discrimination."[2]

The Greeks and the Romans saw universal agreement as a form of flattery, one of the two opposites of friendship. Most virtues in these ancient cultures had two opposites. They saw desirable traits as occupying a "golden mean" between a deficiency and an excess—the dynamic that shapes the famous story of Icarus, who ignores his father's instructions not to fly too close to the sun or too close to the sea. The virtue of courage, for example, rested at the midpoint between cowardice (a deficiency) and recklessness (an excess). Generosity sat between the extremes of miserliness and prodigality. And friendship represented the golden mean between enmity and flattery.

For the citizens of the world's first democracy, flattery posed a serious threat to public discourse. "The idea was that a free man speaking before his fellow citizens was to speak frankly, truthfully, sincerely," explains Richard Stengel in *You're Too Kind: A Brief History of Flattery*. "The Greeks believed that democracy survived only if men were truthful and frank."[3] In the view of the ancient Greeks, no knave was more knavish than the flatterer, and no fool was more foolish than the person who believed flattery. Together, the flattering knave and the credulous fool could destroy the state.

Warnings against flattery appear throughout the literary traditions of the world. Dante places flatterers in the eighth circle of hell, where they are submerged in excrement for all eternity. In *The Pilgrim's Progress* John Bunyan introduces a character named Flatterer, who leads several pilgrims off the path before he is recognized as "a false apostle, that hath transformed himself into an angel of light"—a formulation that compares him directly to Satan. Unrepentant flatterers and their victims appear regularly in literature as a caution to readers—think of Iago, King Lear's daughters, Tartuffe, Milton's Satan, Uriah Heep in *David Copperfield*, Eddie Haskell in *Leave It to Beaver*, and Wormtongue in *The Lord of the Rings*.

We need these warnings because flattery is so easy to fall for. We tend to see ourselves in the most positive light possible, and we almost always think that our opinions are correct (since, if we thought they were wrong, we would already have changed them). Research suggests that even when we know for certain that flattery is insincere, we still believe it in one part of our brain while discounting it in another—and we still feel more positively toward the flatterer than we would have if that person had not said anything at all.[4]

Flattery is a pleasing but poor substitute for relationships based on mutual affection and trust. It gives us the pleasure of intimacy without the hard work of love. Ralph Waldo Emerson knew very well that, when we try to meet our need for human interaction and validation with shallow affirmations, "we have aimed at a swift and petty benefit, to suck a sudden sweetness." Such relations cannot satisfy us for long, he concluded, because "we have made them a texture of wine and dreams, instead of the tough fibre of the human heart."[5]

FLATTERY VERSUS FRIENDSHIP

Emerson published his first series of essays in 1841, well before "snowflake" became a derisive term for a person who is emotionally fragile and easily offended. But Emerson got very close to our modern phrase and definition with the term "frost-work." While contemporary Americans use the term to ridicule their political enemies, Emerson used it, albeit negatively, to describe friendship. Friends, he insisted, should not treat each other like snowflakes.

Emerson believed that any friendship worthy of the name consisted of two essential elements: tenderness, or honest affection not tied to any material interest, and truth, or a willingness to speak sincerely without fear that frankness will destroy the relationship. Simply agreeing with everything someone says is a sign not of friendship but of insincerity. "Better be a nettle in the side of your friend than his echo," he writes. Friendship should be "an alliance of two large, formidable natures, mutually feared, before yet they recognize the deep identity which, beneath these disparities, unites them."[6]

Three years after publishing "Friendship" in his first series of essays, Emerson incorporated more of his thoughts on the topic into the essay "Politics" in the second series. Here, Emerson contrasts the inherently corrupt nature of both states and political parties with the much more noble nature of individuals. The genius of democracy, he believed, is that it allows individuals to bypass the state and form political bonds directly with each other. The state, then, ultimately consists of nothing more than millions of human relationships based on the principles of friendship. Emerson closes the essay with the dream of a nation in which "thousands of human beings might exercise towards each other the grandest and simplest sentiments as well as a knot of friends, or a pair of lovers."[7]

American political scientist Jason Scorza has argued that Emerson's essays on both friendship and politics provide a better model for civic relationships than the standard notion of "civility," which too often becomes a code word for suppressing tensions and disagreements in order to get along. Civic friendship, Scorza suggests, will not always be civil because sincerity is more important to any friendship than civility. "Friends who cannot be frank with one another, or are afraid that frankness will jeopardize their relationship, cannot be friends in the richest possible sense," he explains. "Such relationships are fragile and unsure. To endure, friendship must develop, and to develop a friendship occasionally must be tested by an element of incivility."[8]

Friends, in other words, argue with each other. They hurt each other's feelings sometimes, apologize and promise to do better, and then do it all over again because they trust that their friendship can handle both disagreement and occasional incivility. Disagreement is not exactly an element of friendship; it is an inevitable consequence of human beings interacting with each other honestly.

This does not mean that we will disagree with every other human being equally. We naturally choose to associate with people who have values and beliefs similar to our own. But there is another kind of relationship that looks like friendship but really isn't. In this second kind of relationship, we choose to associate with a person, and they with us, entirely on the strength of shared beliefs and mutual validation. When the mutual validation ceases, so does the relationship. When a person with whom we have this kind of relationship expresses disagreement with us, we feel hurt and betrayed. This makes us feel insecure about ourselves and our own positions, so we avoid further interaction with the person. The rise of social media has given us an ugly new word to use in such situations: we *unfriend* them.

But what about our real friends? Most of us sometimes worry that disagreeing with a good friend about an important political issue could harm the friendship. Will it? Do we really have to walk on political egg shells with people we love? Even if we take Emerson's advice and treat our friendships "with the roughest courage," will our friends reciprocate? The answer to all these questions is "It depends."

According to a 2005 British research study, the most important variable that determines whether a disagreement harms a relationship is the extent to which people think that disagreements harm relationships. In this study, participants were asked to imagine having a disagreement with their best friend while, at the same time, vocalizing one of several statements about the nature of disagreement. When people vocalized statements like "Disagreeing means that our relationship is not good," they tended to report in post-tests that a disagreement would harm their relationship. The subjects who vocalized statements like "Disagreeing does not mean that our relationship is not good but shows we can say what we think" reported much higher degrees of satisfaction with their friendship after an imagined dispute.[9]

These results suggest something that most people would find intuitive: people who see disagreement as a bad thing will think that disagreeing with a friend will ruin their relationship. Such a person would be more likely to suppress honest disagreements for the sake of friendship. People who see disagreement as either positive or neutral are more likely to consider disagreement among friends a sign of sincerity and, therefore, something that will not jeopardize a friendship and might even make it stronger.

Most of us don't really fear political disagreements with our close friends. We fear not being liked and respected by people we like and respect. Challenging someone's political beliefs can signal (correctly or not) a lack of respect or affection. One way to prevent this from happening is to say something like "I think you are a great person, and I value our friendship, so when I disagree with you it's because I value your opinion and want to learn more about how you see things." If someone manages to communicate this idea to me, then I'm probably not going to hesitate to express my real opinions about controversial issues. It also helps if we don't call each other "stupid," "evil," or "crazy" when "I don't quite see it that way; help me understand what you mean" will do just fine.

Once we get over the fear of damaging our relationships, arguing with friends can be quite pleasant. It helps us get to know each other better and to find the weak spots in our own arguments so that we can make them better in the future. It may result in one of us persuading the other, but it doesn't have to. Honest disagreements help us understand each other's perspectives. And really understanding one person who disagrees with us about something usually helps us understand other people who think the same way.

Arguing with people we *do* want to preserve a relationship with also teaches us how to argue with people we *should* want to preserve a relationship with. When we disagree with our friends, we show respect and deference. We constantly signal that our disagreement is not a reflection of the way we feel about them. We take steps to ensure that arguments don't become personal attacks—that they are intellectual disputes about things that reasonable people of goodwill can view in different ways. We do, in other words, all the things that we should always do when talking to other human beings about things that they consider important.

CIVIC FLATTERY IN THE TWENTY-FIRST-CENTURY ECHO CHAMBER

Arguing with friends is much easier than arguing with political allies—people we don't know very well but whose support we need to advance the issues and causes we believe in. We can talk through our political disagreements with our close friends because we have enough other things in common to support us through occasional disputes. But political alliances are relationships built entirely on political agreement. Expressing disagreement about anything could mess everything up. Common sense seems to dictate that we suppress our disagreements and flatter each other by focusing on what we have in common.

This is precisely how we get partisan echo chambers. When enough people want to have their opinions reinforced and their ideas agreed with, news and media outlets will emerge to accommodate this desire. Affinity networks develop that people can use to flatter and agree with each other and to share media content that will reinforce everything they believe. People who like and agree with each other all the time usually end up spurring each other on to greater and greater levels of nonsense.

Media echo chambers have been with us always. At the time of the founding, newspapers were explicitly partisan and as confrontational as the worst of today's talk radio shows and political blogs. And for most of the nineteenth century, American newspapers were semiofficial organs of the major political parties, with names like the *Ohio Democrat* and the *National Daily Whig*.[10] Only toward the end of that century did anybody see "fair and balanced" as desirable traits for the media to have.

Modern echo chambers differ from their nineteenth-century ancestors mainly in the phenomenal efficiency with which they operate. Instead of two or three partisan newspapers, we have hundreds of satellites TV and radio stations and thousands of websites that can subdivide major political categories into narrow ideological slices. And because the Internet makes all media national, each ideological slice has access to three hundred million potential adherents. So instead of two general echo chambers, we get thousands of groups like "Mormon Democrats Who Don't Like Bernie Sanders" or "Conservative Nuclear Physicists Who Read Thomas Paine."

The proliferation of news sources from various ideological perspectives has occurred alongside the explosive growth of social media sites like Facebook, Twitter, and Instagram. These sites allow us to create carefully curated groups of friends with whom to engage in political commentary and share news stories. The sites give us the ability to filter both news and people according to our personal tastes, and they also use complicated algorithms that filter content to our preferences without even asking. If something we don't like pops up, we just have to unfriend, block, or filter some more, and pretty soon we can make sure that we never have to endure a single idea or assertion that does not agree with everything we already believe.

In an environment where two-thirds of American adults get at least some of their news from social media feeds, our ability to filter out ideas that we disagree with becomes truly frightening.[11] When nineteenth-century partisans bought a copy of the *National Daily Whig*, they knew exactly what kind of news they were getting. But when we interact on social media exclusively with people who think like we do and get most of our news from the links they provide, we can end up living in completely self-reinforcing echo chambers without even knowing it. When this happens, we end up in an environment where political opponents don't even know enough about each other's beliefs and perceptions to disagree rationally.

Highly efficient echo chambers dramatically increase political polarization by segregating like-minded people into groups whose social dynamics force them to be even more like-minded. This can have serious consequences, as Cass Sunstein explains in his 2017 book *#republic*:

> In the United States, political polarization . . . is aggravated by voters' self-segregation into groups of like-minded people, which can make it far more difficult to produce sensible solutions. Even if the self-segregation involves only a small part of the electorate, they can be highly influential, not least because of the intensity of their beliefs. Public officials are accountable to the electorate, and even if they would much like to reach some sort of agreement, they might find that if they do so, they will put their electoral future on the line.[12]

Our primary election system makes this dynamic especially difficult. When most incumbents have more to fear from a primary challenge than a general election opponent, small "groups of like-minded people" at the ideological extremes often have more political influence than the vast majority of voters in the political center.

The most frightening result of our echo-chamber media culture is the phenomenon known by the formidable name "epistemic closure." The term itself comes from the subfield of philosophy called epistemology, or the study of what constitutes knowledge as opposed to simply belief. In 2010, a conservative blogger named Julian Sanchez repurposed the term to describe the tendency of some of his fellow conservatives to reject any challenge to their prevailing narrative as the work of a biased media, thus producing an environment in which all the evidence used to support the movement has to come from sources generated by the movement itself, resulting in a closed circle that no external fact can penetrate.

An epistemically closed system cannot tolerate any internal criticism, Sanchez argues, because dissent "threatens the hermetic seal." As he further explains, "Anything that breaks down the tacit equivalence between 'critic of conservatives' and 'wicked liberal smear artist' undermines the effectiveness of the entire information filter. If disagreement is not in itself evidence of malign intent or moral degeneracy, people start feeling an obligation to engage it sincerely—maybe even when it comes from the *New York Times*. And there is nothing more potentially fatal to the momentum of an insurgency fueled by anger than a conversation."[13]

Sanchez was describing what he saw as the current state of the conservative movement, of which he considered himself a part. But his notion of epistemic closure works equally well for any ideological echo chamber that filters out information that contradicts its ideology. In a 2018 article examining the current state of epistemic closure, Craig Gibson and Trudi Jacobson argued that Sanchez's use of the term "distills in a crucial way our societal—and educational—challenge. The closing off of alternative perspectives, information sources, data, and voices from one's own personal information landscape results in an attenuated and impoverished capacity to reflect and to learn."[14]

Civic flattery—or a political culture that allows people to appear to engage in civic discourse without ever having their opinions, or even their claims of fact, seriously challenged—is ultimately more damaging to democracy than civic enmity. When we incorporate civic flattery into our personal relationships, we get shallow, insincere friendships. When we use it as the basis for political alliances, we get echo chambers. And when a skilled political manipulator flatters a large portion of the population in an attempt to acquire and consolidate power, we get perhaps the most dangerous test that a democratic society can ever face: the emergence of a demagogue.

FLATTERING THE DEMOS: THE DANGER OF THE DEMAGOGUE

Flattery of kings and emperors has long been seen as a grave threat to a nation's security. By playing on the insecurities and vanities of the sovereign, an unscrupulous courtier can sway the ship of state in calamitous directions. But what happens when the people are the sovereign, as they are in a democracy? Can an unscrupulous sycophant come to power by flattering "the people" in the same way that a courtier flatters a king? Unfortunately, the answer is yes, the people can be seduced by an unscrupulous flatterer who will use their approval to secure power and destroy the machinery of democracy. We call such people "demagogues," and they represent a structural weakness in the fabric of democracy.

Demagogues like Creon and Alcibiades nearly destroyed the Athenian democracy by plunging it deeper and deeper into the Peloponnesian War. The demagogue Julius Caesar destroyed the Roman Republic and replaced it with an empire. In the twentieth century, demagogues such as Benito Mussolini and Adolf Hitler were elected democratically before destroying the democracies that gave them power. And contemporary demagogues have been responsible for much of the democratic backsliding that has occurred in the twenty-first century, including Vladimir Putin in Russia, Hugo Chávez in Venezuela, Recep Erdoğan in Turkey, and Viktor Orbán in Hungary.

So, what is a demagogue? In the wake of destruction left by one of America's most famous demagogues, Senator Joe McCarthy, Columbia University scholar Reinhard Luthin wrote an influential book on demagogues in America. In the preface, he gives a definition of "demagogue" that we can use as a starting point for discussion:

> What is a demagogue? He is a politician skilled in oratory, flattery, and invective; evasive in discussing vital issues; promising everything to everybody; appealing to the passions rather than the reason of the public; and arousing racial, religious, and class prejudices—a man whose lust for power without recourse to principle leads him to seek to become a master of the masses. He has for centuries practiced his profession of "man of the people." He is a product of a political tradition nearly as old as western civilization itself.[15]

Demagoguery is the special problem of democracy. Both words come from the same root: *dēmos* ("the people"). Democracy, or *dēmokratía*, means "rule of the people." Demagogue, or *dēmagōgos*, means "leader of the people." And therein lies the problem: in a democracy, where the people have the ultimate sovereign power, they are supposed to be their own leader. But having power also means having the ability to give that power away. This is the design flaw: if people have the power to do anything they want, then they can give that power away to someone who flatters them.

The greatest philosophers in ancient Athens—Plato and Aristotle—both paid scrupulous attention to the demagogue problem in their political works. Plato, whose mentor, Socrates, was condemned to death by vote of the Athenian assembly, tried to imagine a political order in his *Republic* that could not be manipulated to unjust ends. Any attempt to give meaningful political power to the people, Plato knew, would be subject to demagoguery—so he constructed a political system that did not give power to the people. As Michael Signer notes in his book *Demagogue*, "The savage, wolf-like demagogue who haunted Plato's imagination helped spawn a political philosophy based on control, crushing the passions of a demagogue, and eliminating the possibility of a demagogue ever becoming a tyrant."[16]

America's founders also understood the demagogue problem very well and took great pains to address it in the Constitution. In Federalist #1, Alexander Hamilton observes that "of those men who have overturned the liberties of republics, the greatest number have begun their career by paying an obsequious court to the people; commencing Demagogues, and ending Tyrants."[17] Hamilton was not just mentioning demagoguery in passing. A primary purpose of the Federalist Papers was to show how the Constitution would prevent the emergence of a democratically elected dictator.

Demagoguery was a constant concern of Americans in the nineteenth century, when the United States stood virtually alone as the world's only democracy. One of the clearest and most insightful descriptions of demagoguery ever produced in the United States comes from a brief essay by American frontier writer James Fenimore Cooper, author of *The Leatherstocking Tales* (*The Deerslayer*, *The Last of the Mohicans*, etc.), who in 1838 wrote a collection of political essays called *The American Democrat*. One of these essays, titled simply "On Demagogues," lays out a set of clear characteristics by which Americans, should they ever need to, could recognize a demagogue:

1. "The peculiar office of a demagogue is to advance his own interests, by affecting a deep devotion to the interests of the people."[18] Demagogues invariably present themselves as the voice of the people, maintaining the fiction that "the people" speak in a united voice and are universally opposed to the voices of "the elites." In American usage, "the people" usually becomes either "the American people" or "We, the People," while the enemy becomes (depending on the demagogue's political base) something like "the media elite," "the Wall Street elite," "the Hollywood elite," "liberal academics," "wealthy industrialists," or "the one percent." In the rhetoric of the demagogue, these elites don't count as "the people." They are "not the people," a group that frustrates the legitimate desires of the actual people. And if these elites could just be made to disappear, the real people could govern themselves. (And most demagogues eventually get around to trying to make them disappear.)

2. "The man who is constantly telling the people that they are unerring in judgment . . . is a demagogue."[19] The essence of flattery is telling people that they are right. The essence of civic flattery is telling the people that they are right, that whatever challenges they face are somebody else's fault, and that they do not have to change the way they think or act in order to have successful lives and good government. This sounds like a natural thing for politicians to do, and indeed it is. But it can have severe consequences, since it leads populations to scapegoat the people whom the demagogue identifies as the ones who are "really" to blame for a nation's problems.

3. "The demagogue always puts the people before the constitution and the laws."[20] As we have already seen, the difference between a democracy and a majoritarian tyranny is that a democracy has a system of laws, checks, balances, and safeguards collectively called "the

rule of law." A major purpose of the rule of law in a democracy is to set up guardrails that prevent the emergence of demagogues. When checked by these mechanisms—court decisions, legislative vetoes, constitutional requirements—would-be demagogues invariably call them "undemocratic." They argue that, because they were elected by "the people," their decisions should have precedence over "unelected judges" or "old-fashioned legislative rules." These actions weaken the rule of law and pave the way for autocracy.

4. Demagogues "defer to prejudices, and ignorance, and even to popular jealousies and popular injustice, that a safe direction may be given to the publick [*sic*] mind."[21] The demagogue claims to want to apply the principles of democracy to every question—not just matters of public policy but also questions of fact and moral value. Everything is subject to a vote, and every proposed fact must be ratified by the voice of the people. To flatter the people completely, the demagogue must pretend to accept their judgment on everything, and those who disagree with the public judgment (perhaps because they are experts in the field under discussion) must be castigated as both wrong and undemocratic. In this way, demagogues vanquish not only individual experts but also the entire concept of expertise: science, history, language, comparative politics, and all the rest of the things that people can spend their lives learning about vanish with a wave of the hand.

5. "This is a test that most often betrays the demagogue, for while loudest in proclaiming his devotion to the majority, he is, in truth, opposing the will of the entire people, in order to effect his purposes with a part."[22] For all they may talk about the people as a coherent group, demagogues are actually devoted to pitting the people against each other. Demagogues rarely create new prejudices; they amplify those that already exist, giving people permission to say things that had previously been unpopular or taboo. Much as demagogues work to weaken the rule of law, they try to weaken the social norms that enforce civic friendship, opening old wounds and encouraging the eruption of anger and hatred that have been kept below the surface by a thin but crucially important layer of civility and civic decency.

The final point is especially important. Demagogues don't simply flatter the populace. They flatter a portion of the people by attacking and demonizing everyone else. Those who stand with the demagogue become "the people." Everybody else becomes effectively subhuman: "animals," "vermin," "criminals," "enemies of the state." In this way, demagogues ensure that a portion of the people will always side with them against their common enemy. At the same time, they create the perception of emergency to justify their destruction of the constitutional safeguards that would otherwise check their power. A demagogue needs division the way that a fire needs oxygen. They succeed only because they are able to fan the flames.

The only way to defeat a demagogue is to overcome the polarization that feeds his or her power. This is the advice of Venezuelan economist and journalist Andrés Miguel Rondón, who was part of the opposition to the populist demagogue Hugo Chávez during his ten years in power. "Don't feed polarization, disarm it," Rondón wrote in the *Washington Post*, reflecting on the mistakes made by Chávez's opponents:

> It took opposition leaders 10 years to figure out that they needed to actually go to the slums and the countryside. Not for a speech or a rally, but for a game of dominoes or to dance salsa—to show they were Venezuelans, too, that they weren't just dour scolds and could hit a baseball, could tell a joke that landed. That they could break the tribal divide, come down off the billboards and show that they were real. This is not populism by other means. It is the only way of establishing your standing. It's deciding not to live in an echo chamber. To press pause on the siren song of polarization.[23]

The demagogue is the ticking time bomb buried deep in democracy's basement; given enough time, one will always emerge and find a path to power. But demagogues need certain conditions to thrive, and they come with warning signs that we ignore at our peril. They require polarization, and they exploit it to their advantage, but they don't create it; it must already be in place and already have weakened the norms and guardrails they intend to destroy. They tell us that people who don't look or think like we do are our enemies and that only they can protect us. They tell us that we are right and nobody really understands us the way that they do. And they promise to hate who we hate and punish those who hate us. And if we believe them, they steal our democracy.

WE HAVE MET THE ENEMY, AND HE IS US

In 1936, Sinclair Lewis, America's first Nobel laureate in literature, published *It Can't Happen Here*, a speculative novel about the emergence of a demagogue in America. Lewis was writing for a very specific historical audience: Adolf Hitler was chancellor of Germany, but war had not yet broken out, so Americans could admire him openly without appearing treasonous. Benito Mussolini was still well thought of in some quarters as a man of action who had made trains run on time. At the same time, Louisiana senator Huey

Long, whose political career had been a case study in modern demagoguery, was planning to challenge Franklin Roosevelt in the Democratic primary election.[24]

Doremus Jessup, the protagonist of *It Can't Happen Here*, is a journalist in the fictional town of Fort Beulah, Vermont. In the first part of the novel, Jessup comments from the sidelines as a senator named Berzelius "Buzz" Windrip announces his bid for the presidency. Windrip, a populist modeled after Huey Long, directs his campaign to the "Forgotten Men"—white, male Americans who have been hit hard by the Great Depression and are looking to the government to restore what they see as their rightful place in American society. Windrip is openly racist and anti-Semitic. He promises to take the right to vote away from African Americans and the right to work away from women.

Every time Jessup tries to sound the alarm about Windrip's fascist tendencies, he is met with the phrase in the title of the book: "It can't happen here." This is perhaps the most important point of the novel. Americans have always had a high degree of confidence that our democratic institutions will protect us from dictatorship. This confidence makes us vulnerable when we assume that these institutions will work automatically—or when we neglect them or allow them to be weakened when it suits our interests to do so. When a dictator emerges in a place where people do not believe that dictatorship can happen, everybody will assume that he is something other than a dictator until it is too late to do anything about it.

This is exactly what happens in *It Can't Happen Here*. Windrip defeats Roosevelt in the Democratic primary and goes on to win the election. When the new president strips Congress of its powers and organizes his own private army, Jessup joins the resistance and begins to publish an opposition newspaper—a crime in the new regime for which he is arrested and sentenced to life in a concentration camp. While sitting in jail the night after his arrest, Jessup soberly assigns the blame for what has happened to his country and to himself:

> The tyranny of this dictatorship isn't primarily the fault of Big Business, nor of the demagogues who do their dirty work. It's the fault of Doremus Jessup! Of all the conscientious, respectable, lazy-minded Doremus Jessups who have let the demagogues wriggle in, without fierce enough protest.
>
> . . .
>
> It's my sort, the Responsible Citizens who've felt ourselves superior because we've been well-to-do and what we thought was "educated," who brought on the Civil War, the French Revolution, and now the Fascist Dictatorship. It's I who murdered Rabbi de Verez. It's I who persecuted

the Jews and the Negroes. I can blame . . . only my own timid soul and drowsy mind. Forgive, O Lord!

This is the crucial passage of *It Can't Happen Here*. It is Sinclair Lewis's message to his country, and it is something that every citizen has to understand: In a democracy, we bear responsibility for the type of government we end up with. We create the culture in which our politicians operate. We get what we encourage or permit—or don't sufficiently oppose. When Jessup finally acknowledges his own responsibility for the problem, he empowers himself to start working to solve it.

Jessup also recognizes that demagogues succeed because people let them succeed. And we rarely recognize them in time because they look so much like other politicians. Flattering voters is not the special province of ambitious and corrupt office seekers. All politicians do it because voters demand to be flattered. As much as we claim to value sincerity in our politicians, most of us won't vote for anyone who doesn't flatter us relentlessly. This is why politicians rarely even hint that we should take responsibility for any of our own problems. If we are unhappy, they tell us, somebody else must be to blame.

Imagine what would happen if a candidate for public office walked into a crowded auditorium and told the audience that they were idiots for believing every negative ad that they heard on the radio. Or that our country's finances were a mess because they kept demanding that elected officials give them more stuff and cut their taxes at the same time. Nobody wants to hear politicians talk like this. We want to hear that we are good, wise, and perpetually misunderstood—and that other people are causing all the problems that make us unhappy. This is usually wrong, and it is always flattery—and it comes with a potentially very serious price.

When we demand that anyone running for elected office flatter us, we create precisely the environment that demagogues need to thrive. Actual self-government is hard and messy, and it often means negotiating and compromising with our political opponents and sacrificing some things in order to get other things. Demagogues tell us that democracy is easy, that we can have everything we want, and that other people have caused all our problems. They will say whatever they think we want to hear and promise us whatever we say we want—and they will make sure that somebody else pays for it. If the history of democracy has shown us anything at all, it has shown us that when people give the reins of government to those who flatter them and pit them against each other, they end up with something that no longer looks much like a democracy.

· 7 ·

The Majesty of Persuasion

We persuade people by who we are, not what we say.

If you have any reverence for Persuasion
the majesty of Persuasion,
the spell of my voice that would appease your fury—
Oh please stay.

—Athena in Aeschylus's *The Eumenides*

It is hardly possible to overrate the value, in the present low
state of human improvement, of placing human beings in contact with persons dissimilar to themselves, and with modes of
thought and action unlike those with which they are familiar. . . .
Such communication has always been, and is peculiarly in the
present age, one of the primary sources of progress.

—John Stuart Mill, *The Principles of Political Economy*

*W*hen John Adams sent Thomas Jefferson a note indicating that he would soon be receiving "two pieces of homespun," Jefferson responded with a long paragraph praising American textiles. Jefferson had to write a second letter two days later when he realized that Adams had been joking. The "home-spun" in question was actually a two-volume book written by Adams's son, John Quincy, who had recently become the US ambassador to Russia. Before this appointment, he had divided his time between Washington, DC, where he served as a US senator from Massachusetts, and Boston, where he held the newly endowed Boylston Professorship of Rhetoric and Oratory at Harvard University.

The two-volume book that the elder Adams sent to Jefferson in 1812 was *Lectures on Rhetoric and Oratory*, a compilation of the lectures that his son had given at Harvard in 1806 and 1807. The lectures traced the history and current state of rhetoric, or the study of persuasion. Since the Middle Ages, rhetoric (along with grammar and logic) had been considered part of the *trivium*—the foundation of the liberal arts (and the source of our word "trivia"). Formal instruction in rhetoric traced back to ancient times and included the work of such luminaries as Aristotle in Greece and Cicero in Rome.

John Quincy Adams used his lectures to make a series of bold and controversial statements about rhetoric, the most important being that the study of rhetoric could best be advanced in a democracy like the United States. This idea was a direct challenge to the prevailing understanding of rhetoric in the English-speaking world, which had been shaped by the writers of the Scottish Enlightenment, such as Hugh Blair, George Campbell, and Adam Smith. These writers emphasized the role of rhetoric in producing aesthetic pleasure, which turned the study of rhetoric into a form of literary criticism, or a way to organize ideas, words, and sounds to enhance the experience of readers.

John Quincy Adams tried to recover the original political function of rhetoric—and to argue that America was the best place in the world for that tradition to continue. The study of persuasive speaking, he argued, could only have evolved in self-governing societies like democratic Athens and republican Rome. In these societies, making speeches had real consequences and high stakes. This made them worth people's time and attention, so they became part of the civic education of young citizens. "The art of speaking must be most eagerly sought, where it is found to be most useful," he argued, "and that can be in no other state of things, than where the power of persuasion operates upon the will, and prompts the actions of free men. The only birthplace of eloquence therefore must be a free state."[1]

John Quincy Adams wasted no time in drawing the conclusion that his own nation was "at this time precisely under the same circumstances, which were so propitious to the advancement of rhetoric and oratory among the Greeks."[2] He was not just bragging about American liberty but also arguing that Americans should receive formal instruction in persuasive speaking as part of their basic education. As both a senator and a professor of rhetoric, Adams understood the profound connections between rhetoric and democracy. In his own eloquent words, the art of persuasion is "grappled, as with hooks of steel, to the soul of liberty."[3]

For democracy to function, its citizens must be able to make arguments capable of persuading other people to their point of view. This doesn't mean persuading everybody, or even persuading anybody, to see things 100 percent the same way that we do. But to have an effective self-governing society, some people must be able to persuade a majority of their fellow citizens to vote for them or for their proposals or their ideas. When people's worldviews are so far apart that they cannot find enough common ground to have a conversation, democracy has a hard time surviving. When persuasion becomes impossible, force becomes inevitable.

THE FIRST POET OF DEMOCRACY

Democracy in Athens emerged gradually, as the citizens' assembly wrested more and more power away from the wealthy aristocratic families who had run the city-state for centuries. Usually this was done with the help of canny leaders like Cleisthenes and Pericles, themselves members of the aristocracy, who understood the value of having the common people as allies in their power struggles with other aristocrats.

But this is not how Athenians explained the history of their democracy to themselves. Their founding myth was much more dramatic than their actual history, and it still tells us a lot about what the world's first democracy thought was important. According to the myth, Athens was founded by its namesake, Athena, the goddess of wisdom, shortly after the end of the Trojan War. Athena wanted her city to be different from the rest of the Greek world. Specifically, she wanted justice administered by law courts and not by aggrieved relatives, as was the Greek custom—which had recently pitched the Hellenic world into a disastrous war fought to avenge the honor of one man, Menelaus, whose wife was seduced by a Trojan prince.

The most important text we have for Athens's mythic origin story is *The Oresteia*, a three-play cycle by the tragic playwright Aeschylus, first performed at the Dionysia festival in 458 BCE. Aeschylus was the first "poet of democracy," thousands of years before Walt Whitman claimed the title. The cycle's three plays—*Agamemnon*, *The Libation Bearers*, and *The Eumenides*—trace the consequences of a brutal act that occurred before the Trojan War. According to legend, the supreme commander of Greek forces, Agamemnon, sacrificed his daughter Iphigenia in order to secure favorable winds for the voyage of his massive fleet of more than one thousand ships. Predictably, this decision did not endear him to his wife, Clytemnestra, who took a lover named Aegisthus while her husband was off leading the siege of Troy. The first play of the *Oresteia* takes place ten years later, on the day that Agamemnon returns to Argos.

The first two plays deal with retributive murders. When Agamemnon returns after his great victory, Clytemnestra arranges for her lover to kill him at his moment of great triumph. This situation causes a huge problem for Clytemnestra and Agamemnon's son, Orestes. In the absence of any kind of judicial system, Orestes is responsible for avenging his father's murder. To do so, however, he must kill his mother—a horrendous act proscribed by the same moral code that requires him to avenge his father.

To make matters worse, the god Apollo himself commands Orestes to kill Clytemnestra. He is in a no-win situation: If he leaves his father unavenged, he will anger a god. But if he kills his mother, he will incur the wrath of the Furies—the embodiments of justice who tormented those who committed matricide and other horrible acts. *The Libation Bearers* ends with Orestes killing Clytemnestra and bringing the wrath of the Furies upon himself.

The first two plays of the *Oresteia* dramatize the main problem that Athena's democracy was supposed to solve. In the absence of the rule of law, kinship networks must administer justice: you kill my father, I will kill you, then your son will have to kill me, and so on. Even when the person who kills your father is not your mother, this kind of justice poses real problems. It rarely stops at one killing, resulting in cycles of retributive violence that can easily spin out of control and engulf entire communities. The element of democracy that most impresses Aeschylus is not that people vote for their rulers but that juries vote to determine the guilt or innocence of people accused of crimes. This arrangement removes justice from the private sphere and creates a rule of law.

The final play, *The Eumenides*, depicts the founding of both Athens and the rule of law. To protect Orestes from the Furies, Apollo spirits him to the Areopagus, where Athena is in the process of setting up her city. Apollo's support for Orestes does not guarantee his safety, however. The Furies are divine beings too, belonging to the older generation of gods who were succeeded, but not entirely supplanted, by the Olympians. Apollo decides to address the problem through the classic tools of outrage: he calls them "grotesque" and "loathsome" and threatens them with his superior power.[4]

Athena does not have the comfortable luxury of outrage. She can't compel the Furies to cooperate. She is more powerful than they are, but only marginally; they have enough power to ensure that her new city will never enjoy a profitable harvest or a moment of peace. If Athena wants Athens to succeed, then she has to solve the crisis with Orestes in a way that incorporates the Furies into the endgame as willing players. She can't do this by calling them stupid or ugly. She can't do it by shouting obscenities. She can't even do it by forming an "Anti-Fury Party" and beating them in a landslide. She has to persuade them to be on her side, or her city won't get built.

Fortunately, her new city has a process for settling disputes. The first thing Athena does is propose that the case of Orestes be submitted to a jury and that everybody agree to be bound by the decision. Athena takes a grave risk in doing this, as she gives up control over the final verdict. The jury could decide against Orestes, which would be tremendously embarrassing for her brother, Apollo, and would cast doubt on her own power. But she also knows that she has to give up the absolute power of an autocrat to access the power of persuasion. She cannot win the Furies over unless she creates a fair process that they agree, in advance, to be bound by. When the ten-person jury deadlocks 5–5, Athena casts the tie-breaking vote for Orestes. This action sends the Furies into, well, a fury, and they charge her with manipulating the results:

> You, you younger gods!—you have ridden down
> The ancient laws, wrenched them from my grasp—
> And I, robbed of my birthright, suffering, great with wrath,
> I loose my poison over the soil, aieee!—
> Poison to match my grief comes pouring out my heart,—
> Cursing the land to burn it sterile and now
> Rising up from its roots a cancer blasting leaf and child,
> Now for Justice, Justice![5]

Athena realizes that she must do much more than convince the Furies to accept her decision about Orestes. They have much deeper concerns. They feel that they have been tossed aside by a new generation. They take great pride in the role that they play in the social order: they ensure justice by tormenting those who commit the most grievous of crimes. Athena's innovations—trial by jury and the rule of law—pose a legitimate threat to their position. The Furies are not just fighting for the right to torment Orestes; they are also trying to prevent Athena from taking away their role in society and making them irrelevant.

The real debate between Athena and the Furies concerns deep insecurities in the face of change and the latter's anger at being dismissed by somebody who does not understand their importance. They fear losing power and prestige, and they want to be respected and admired for the good things they do. As it turns out, political arguments are almost always about just these things. People want to feel respected and valued, and they are desperately afraid that there won't be a place for them in the new world that others want to create. Until we resolve these real concerns, we will never make any headway at all with the stuff we are pretending to discuss.

Athena can't get what she needs to build Athens by telling the Furies that they are stupid idiots who only care about themselves or by saying, "For heaven's sake, it's the fifth century now, so get your heads out of the Bronze

Age." Nor can she persuade them of anything by calmly and rationally explaining why they are wrong and she is right. Such discussions can only occur after the real persuasion has already happened. Athena's initial argument to the Furies contains three main points: (1) I respect you; (2) you can trust me; and (3) I am not going to destroy you. These remain three of the best arguments to make when an audience wants to scratch your eyes out with their scaly talons.

Athena's arguments illustrate the importance of what rhetoricians call the speaker's ethos. Aristotle recognized three general modes of persuasion: *pathos*, or appeals to emotions; *logos*, or appeals to logic; and *ethos*, or "the personal character of the speaker."[6] According to Aristotle, the speaker's ethos should consist of "good sense, good moral character, and goodwill." These characteristics in a speaker can convince us "to believe a thing apart from any proof of it."[7] Like everything else that humans do, Aristotle believed, persuasion occurs within the context of relationships that can be based on all sorts of things: coercion, reciprocity, antagonism, flattery, or friendship, just to name a few. The nature of this relationship is, by a wide margin, the most important aspect of any persuasive appeal.

This is why our initial response to being disagreed with is almost always wrong. Our scared-mammal brain immediately classifies challengers as "not us"—enemies to attack or threats to avoid. This happens before we can even process what is going on, and it causes us to respond in the least persuasive ways imaginable. We try to establish dominance and superiority. We bare our teeth, insult, delegitimize, and offend. Our only thought is that we must do whatever it takes to win. In the old days, we challenged people to duels. In the really old days, when we were still chimpanzees, we threw poop at them. Now the poop is metaphorical, but it is no more compelling.

The "I'm-going-to-destroy-you" ethos is not even slightly persuasive, nor are the "I'm-smarter-than-you-will-ever-be" ethos, the "Hitler-said-the-same-thing" ethos, or the "you-are-a-vile-disgusting-reptile-who-should-be-kept-in-a-cage" ethos. These sorts of postures feel good. They often win atta-boys from our friends, and if we are good at them, we may even make our opponents feel bad. But we will not persuade anybody of anything. To be persuasive, you have to be the sort of person your audience wants to believe. And people want to believe people who like them, treat them with respect, and share their most important values.

I am frequently surprised by how much resistance I encounter when I say that we should try to be friends with people we disagree with. Some people see it as a betrayal of their ideals. More than one of my good friends has told me something like "You are just wrong about this. We need to call out evil when we see it, even when it hurts someone's feelings. One should always try to be civil, but there is no way that I could ever be friends with someone who thinks *x*. There are moral principles at stake."

It is precisely because of the moral principles at stake that I believe we must try to be better friends with people who disagree with us. Those who have strong opinions about what should happen in a society have a moral obligation to advocate effectively for their beliefs. If I sincerely believe that something is immoral, then this belief should compel me to find the most effective way possible to keep that thing from happening. Unfortunately for the future of public discourse, our brains tend to confuse antagonizing our opponents with doing something worthwhile. We imagine that the things we see wrong with society come about because people don't know that they are stupid and evil—and if we just let them in on the secret, everything will get better.

A foundational assumption of this book is that human beings can change their minds and their behavior in response to other human beings. Persuasion is possible. In democratic societies, persuading other people is often the only way to translate our values into policies. We do not act in accordance with our own values when we sacrifice meaningful engagement with other people, which might actually win them to our cause, for the emotionally satisfying but ultimately unproductive rewards of cheap outrage. When we really believe that something is important, we have a moral obligation to be persuasive.

IS PERSUASION REALLY POSSIBLE?

Not everybody believes in the possibility of political persuasion. Many people see political positions as expressions of innate personality traits—hard-wired into us either by our genes or by an irreversible process of socialization. Why should we waste time trying to be persuasive when people never really change their minds? This is a reasonable concern.

The idea that persuasion doesn't work comes from a bad application of good science. A substantial body of research suggests that our political beliefs are shaped by more or less fixed psychological characteristics. Jonathan Haidt outlines much of this research in his best-selling 2012 book *The Righteous Mind*. According to Haidt, liberals and conservatives have different built-in matrices for moral reasoning. Both liberals and conservatives use values such as caring, liberty, and fairness in their matrices, but the conservative matrix also includes loyalty, respect for authority, and sanctity. These different foundations for making value judgments shape the way we see the world, leading to different positions on most controversial issues.[8]

Research like this, however, tells us about the difficulty of conversion, not persuasion. These are not the same things. We too often misrepresent the task of political persuasion by thinking of the most strident partisan we have ever encountered and imagining what it would take to turn that person into an equally strident partisan for the other side. This sort of Paul-on-the-Road-to-Damascus conversion rarely happens in politics. Most people don't change their fundamental values, and if we expect them to, we are going to be very disappointed.

But we usually don't need people to change their fundamental values in order to convince them to adopt a particular position. The fact that people have fundamental values makes it possible to persuade them by appealing to those values. But we have to find values that we really share. No meaningful argument can occur between people who don't share at least some core assumptions about how the world should work—since "meaningful argument" largely entails convincing people that certain actions and beliefs are consistent with those core assumptions.

Thus we can frame the task of political persuasion as involving the attempt to convince people to update their current beliefs with new information. Research shows that we do this all the time. When people encounter new evidence and new arguments that contradict their positions, they almost always change their views in ways that are consistent, predictable, and measurable. They just don't change them very much. But, as it turns out, we don't really need them to.

For his 2016 dissertation at Columbia University, Yale political scientist Alexander Coppock conducted a series of experiments designed to measure incremental changes in political opinion when people are presented with new information about a topic. In one study, he used a seven-point scale to determine subjects' support for capital punishment (1 = strongly against / 7 = strongly for) and for the proposition that capital punishment deters crime (1 = certain that it does not deter crime / 7 = certain that it does). Subjects who identified as either strongly for or strongly against capital punishment were invited to continue the study and asked to read two of six articles about the deterrent effect of capital punishment. Two articles supported the argument that capital punishment deters crime, two articles opposed it, and two articles were inconclusive, and equal numbers of participants received each of the six possible combinations.

Coppock then gave subjects a post-test to see where they fell on the same two seven-point scales. His most interesting finding was that, among those who read two articles with the same conclusion, both opponents and proponents of capital punishment moved one full point on a seven-point scale in the direction of the evidence. This doesn't mean that death-penalty supporters were suddenly willing to put on armbands and light candles. But it does mean that people at every level of belief intensity changed—slightly but perceptibly—in the direction of evidence designed to persuade them. Though nobody in the study was converted, everybody was, to some extent, persuaded.[9]

Coppock repeated this experiment on twenty different issues, and while the intensity of the results differed from issue to issue, he was able to draw four consistent conclusions about the way that our brains react to new political information:

1. Effects are nearly uniformly positive: individuals are persuaded in the direction of evidence.
2. Effects are small: changes in opinion are incremental.
3. Effects are relatively homogeneous: regardless of background, individuals respond to information by similar degrees.
4. Effects are durable: at a minimum, effects endure for weeks, albeit somewhat diminished.[10]

For Coppock, these conclusions point to the brain as a Bayesian processor—one that constantly updates its opinions by combining new information with old information and shifting incrementally in the direction of the new information. This means that people do not change their opinions dramatically in a short amount of time. But it also means that partisans don't reject good arguments and good evidence when they encounter it just because it does not conform to their worldview. This can be hard to see. People who move from a 7.0 to a 6.5 on a seven-point scale of certainty will still argue passionately for what they are only slightly less certain about. But this doesn't mean that they have not been persuaded—only that they have not been converted.

Small acts of persuasion matter, because there is much less distance between people's beliefs than we often suppose. We easily confuse the distance between people's political positions with the intensity of their convictions about them. It is entirely possible for people to become sharply divided, and even hostile, over relatively minor disagreements. Americans have fought epic political battles over things like baking wedding cakes and kneeling during the national anthem. And we once fought a shooting war over a whiskey tax of ten cents per gallon. The ferocity of these battles has nothing to do with the actual distance between different positions, which, when compared to the entire range of opinions possible in the world, is almost negligible.

None of this means that we can persuade our opponents easily. Persuading people to change their minds is excruciatingly difficult. It doesn't always work, and it rarely works the way we think it will. But it does work, and the fact that it works makes it possible for us to have a democracy.

THE ECOSYSTEM OF POLITICAL PERSUASION

Persuasion is messy because it takes place among human beings, and human beings are messy. For many years, I taught students all about inductive and deductive reasoning and logical fallacies as though people spent most of their time thinking about things logically and making decisions based on reason. We do have the ability to think rationally, but we exercise reason in a context that includes a lot of other things, such as emotions, relationships, moral beliefs, insecurities, and biases. These things all influence what we see as "reasonable" and "unreasonable." When persuasion occurs, it rarely looks like we think it should.

Real persuasion happens around the edges of public discourse, and it has a lot more to do with our feelings about people than with our thoughts about issues. When we engage in civic discourse, we are usually addressing multiple audiences at the same time and making several arguments at once. Often we don't even realize whom we are talking to and what we are telling them. We become so intensely focused on winning a particular argument with a specific person that we stop focusing on all the other conversations we are having at the same time.

Persuasive communication occurs within a dynamic ecosystem. Like any ecosystem, it has multiple elements that all interact with and influence each other. A fundamental law of ecology is that you can never do just one thing. You can isolate a single interaction for the sake of analysis, but you can't ignore the fact that everything else in the ecosystem is affected when two elements interact with each other. Below are some guidelines to keep in mind when trying to navigate the intricacies of a persuasive communication ecosystem.

The Person You Are Addressing Is Not Your Only Audience

The Lincoln-Douglas debates of 1858 were among the most consequential acts of persuasion in America's history, but neither Abraham Lincoln nor Stephen Douglas was trying to change the other's mind. They knew their minds; they wanted to change the minds of the people in the audience. And though each debate dealt entirely with the single topic of slavery, the purpose was not primarily to convince people to take a certain position on that issue. Nor was it even to convince people to elect Lincoln or Douglas to the Senate—since, before the ratification of the Seventeenth Amendment in 1914, state legislatures elected US senators. The most immediate objective of the Lincoln-Douglas debates was to convince voters in legislative elections to support either the Republican or the Democratic candidate.

Debates like this were not the norm in Senate races. They required enormous effort and expense and had no track record of influencing legislative elections. But both Lincoln and Douglas had presidential ambitions. Douglas was already the leading contender for the Democratic nomination in 1860, and Lincoln was trying to position himself within the newly formed Republican Party for an eventual presidential run. Douglas's reputation ensured that every word of the debates would be recorded by trained stenographers and reprinted in newspapers throughout the country, which meant that, even though all the debates occurred in Illinois, Lincoln and Douglas were both playing to a national audience and trying to present themselves as presidential material.

Politicians aren't the only ones who must appeal to multiple audiences when they debate. Most of our political discussions occur within view of an audience. This is especially true of online discussions on social media, blog posts, and so forth. These forums often have huge potential audiences, only a fraction of whose members ever announce themselves or participate in discussions. Most face-to-face discussions have onlookers too: children, neighbors, friends, and classmates. And these onlookers are often more persuadable than the people we argue with directly. People constantly watch us to learn what people like us believe—and how we act when we talk to people like them. As Stephen Sondheim wrote in *Into the Woods*, "Children will listen." Everyone else will too.

The Things You Are Saying Aren't Your Only Arguments

Most of the time, we aren't really talking about the things that we think we are talking about—because most people care much more about the things beneath the surface of a conversation. This is especially true when someone disagrees with us and we feel attacked. If someone calls my view of, say, capital punishment "stupid," then the only argument that I really want to make in return is "I'm not stupid." Whatever I say next will appear to be about capital punishment but will really make the argument that I am a smart, moral person whose opinions deserve respect.

Even when we really are arguing about the things we think we are arguing about, we are arguing about other things too. People who are participating in or even observing a debate about a political issue are usually thinking about a lot of other things. The questions on their minds might include the following:

- Is this issue important enough for me to worry about?
- What do people like the person I consider myself to be think about this issue?
- If I change my mind about this issue, do I have to think differently about myself?
- How will other people judge me on my opinion about this issue?
- Will my having an opinion, or a different opinion, about this issue have any effect at all on the problem?

Even when we don't want them to, our arguments about other things also make arguments about these things. Realizing this fact can help us create arguments that address all the questions at issue in a discussion rather than simply the most obvious topic of the debate.

Persuading Is Not the Same Thing as Winning

"Can people be persuaded?" is a very different question from "Can arguments be won?" People change their minds about things all the time, but I'm not sure that anybody ever wins an argument. Persuasion is not a zero-sum game. It occurs when somebody moves, even slightly, away from one position and toward another. It is entirely possible for two (or more) people to move closer to each other's positions during an argument without either one being able to claim victory over the other.

But we like to win, and we hate to lose, so the fact that people don't usually win arguments doesn't stop most of us from trying. And we all think we know what winning means: It means crushing opponents and making them cry. It means humiliating them in front of their friends while our friends cheer us from the sidelines. It means forcing them to acknowledge our magnificence and their own nothingness in front of a crowd. And it means displaying our power and our rightness for all the world to see and acknowledge. And this means that we often end up trying to win by employing rhetorical strategies that are fundamentally incapable of persuading anybody of anything. And that looks a lot like losing.

Opinions Come First; Reasons Come Later

You have probably had the experience of trying to convince somebody of something that seemed completely self-evident to you only to find that he or she didn't see it the same way. You probably assumed that you just weren't explaining it well enough, and if you could just find the right words, the other person would immediately see the logic of your position. So you restated the case in different words and thought of examples that, you were certain, would remove any doubt. But it didn't, so you concluded that the person must be intellectually or morally incapable of understanding the truth or too cognitively impaired to recognize it. Stupid, crazy, or evil. And he or she probably thought the same about you.

The first principle of moral reasoning that Jonathan Haidt identifies in *The Righteous Mind* is "intuitions come first; strategic reasoning second." We must understand this concept if we want to engage in productive political discussions. People aren't irrational, but rational argument is a higher-order skill that we bring to our opinions after we form them. Strategic reasoning helps us explain and defend our beliefs to others and even to ourselves. But we arrive at our beliefs through a much more intuitive process that involves the foundational principles of our moral reasoning, our relationships with other people, and our answer to the question "What should a person like me think?"

A fair amount of our public discourse boils down to trying to reason people out of beliefs that they were not reasoned into. This happens across the political spectrum. We believe things that seem consistent with the beliefs of people we like and trust. Mountains of facts and logical arguments don't always persuade us because we process such arguments differently when they confirm our intuitions than we do when they contradict them. "Reasoning can take us to almost any conclusion we want to reach," Haidt explains, "because we ask, 'Can I believe it?' when we want to believe something, but 'Must I believe it?' when we don't want to believe. The answer is almost always yes to the first question and no to the second."[11]

To persuade somebody with logical arguments, we need to first persuade them that they want to believe us—that we are like them, share their values, love our country, and are arguing in good faith about how to improve it. If we can convince them that they should want to believe us, then they will evaluate the evidence we present with a different set of assumptions than they will if we do not. As it has since the days of Aeschylus, our ability to persuade comes down to our ethos.

Everything You Say Is an Argument about Who You Are

When I teach composition courses, I tell my students that every paper consists of at least two arguments. The first argument is contained in the thesis statement. It can be about almost anything, but it should be clear, focused, arguable, and interesting. The second argument always has the same thesis statement: "You should give me a good grade on this paper because I am an intelligent, careful, conscientious student who took this assignment seriously and produced a thoughtful response." Your position on the first argument doesn't matter to me at all. But you had better get the second argument right. If you want a good grade, your paper has to convince me that you are the sort of student who ought to get an A.

For a composition student, a good ethos requires following instructions, turning papers in on time, proofreading carefully to avoid errors, revising sentences for clarity, creating transitions between major ideas—all of which generally shows that someone has paid attention in class and made a real effort to produce good work. A student who turns in a badly handwritten essay with lots of grammatical errors several days after the deadline will not get a good grade, even if it is the most brilliant essay in the history of freshman comp. Ethos matters.

When we carry on political discussions with other people, especially people who disagree with us, we are making two arguments as well. We are trying to convince them to change their minds about immigration or taxes or health care. But we are also trying to convince them that we are intelligent, moral people that other people look up to and admire, so they should too. There are many ways to do this effectively. Calling people stupid is not one of them.

CHESTER ARTHUR'S ROAD TO DAMASCUS

For most people, the name Chester A. Arthur will conjure up . . . nothing. Our twenty-first president is mainly remembered for not being remembered for anything. A 2014 study published in *Science* asked five hundred American adults to write down as many presidents as they could remember in five minutes. Arthur came in dead last, with only 6.7 percent of respondents able to remember his name.[12] In a follow-up study in which participants were given names and asked which belonged to former presidents, Arthur again came in last, with only 46 percent of respondents identifying him correctly. The average participant in the study would have done better flipping a coin than trying to remember whether Chester A. Arthur had ever been president.[13]

The eminent forgettableness of Chester Arthur obscures the fact that he did one of the most memorable things of the nineteenth century: he reformed the civil service and ended the practice of political patronage. When Arthur became president in 1881, the US government employed nearly one hundred thousand of the nation's fifty million people. Since the time of Andrew

Jackson, the vast majority of these positions had been subject to the "spoils system," through which the winner of each presidential election distributed patronage appointments to loyal supporters. By the time of the Civil War, members of Congress controlled most patronage appointments in their states, and this became the basis of their political power. All federal employees were assessed mandatory contributions to the party bosses who controlled their jobs.

The spoils system enshrined corruption. People needed to make contributions back to their patrons, and as long as they did, nobody looked too hard at where the money came from. Sometimes this involved illegal activities—Indian agents were notorious for selling items meant for Native tribes and keeping the profits. But there were also completely legal ways to augment civil service salaries. Customs inspectors, for example, could keep and sell a portion of any goods they found being smuggled into a US port. In this way, the head collector for the New York Customs House in the 1870s managed to earn $50,000 a year (more than $1 million in 2018). His name? Chester A. Arthur.

For years, Arthur was the poster child for an out-of-control patronage system. He lived lavishly on what should have been a modest salary. He rarely showed up for work before noon and spent every night socializing with wealthy New Yorkers and political donors. His patron and mentor, the powerful New York senator Roscoe Conkling, controlled the largest political machine in the country. During Ulysses S. Grant's presidency, Conkling gained complete control over New York's vast patronage network and used it to become the most powerful man in the nation's most powerful state. Conkling was the king of patronage, and Chester Arthur was his loyal knight.

But the patronage system was not universally popular. By the time Grant took office, a movement had taken root within the Republican Party to move to a nonpartisan, merit-based civil service system. Grant initially embraced civil service reform and created the Civil Service Commission to come up with and implement suggestions. But the powerful senators and representatives who relied on patronage fought back hard. After two years, Congress refused to fund Grant's commission, and Grant's struggles with corruption in his own administration soon overshadowed his desire to reform government employment.

In 1876, Grant was succeeded by Rutherford B. Hayes, a committed reformer who was determined to end the spoils system. Hayes clashed with his own party for most of his term, and he was not able to convince Congress to pass any civil service reform legislation. Hayes did, however, issue an executive order in 1877 forbidding political assessments.[14] And the main target of his attack was Arthur's New York Customs House. When Arthur refused to implement the president's order, Hayes fired him, making Arthur the most important casualty in the fight to reform the civil service—and a martyr to the cause of those who opposed reform.[15]

Hayes's actions angered members of his own party so greatly that he was not nominated for reelection in 1882. Republicans replaced him with James Garfield, a congressman from Ohio who also identified with the reformers but was perceived as more moderate and cautious on the issue. But because Republicans could not lose New York and win the election, they had to placate Roscoe Conkling, who had backed Grant for a third term at the convention. To do this, they placed Conkling's chief lieutenant—a man whose entire professional life was defined by and associated with the spoils system—on the ticket. And thus Chester A. Arthur, who had never held an elected office in his life, became the vice president of the United States. Four months into his term of office, James Garfield was shot, and Arthur was as astonished as everyone else in the country to find himself president two and a half months later when Garfield died.

The circumstances of Garfield's assassination changed the conversation about the civil service. The assassin, a frustrated office seeker named Charles Guiteau, believed that his service to the Republican Party during the election merited a high-level appointment. After months of trying unsuccessfully to see Garfield (who had no idea who he was), Guiteau determined that Garfield was destroying the patronage system and the only way to save it was to make Chester Arthur president. A voluminous writer, Guiteau spelled all this out in great detail in letters published after the assassination, leading to a huge groundswell of support for civil service reform.

Nobody thought it would happen with Chester Arthur as president. Most people believed that Arthur, who had no real government experience, would appoint Conkling to his cabinet and let his patron run the show. Conkling, in fact, showed up in Washington before the inauguration and demanded to be made secretary of state. Arthur refused and showed him the door. To the horror of his allies and the shock of the entire nation, Arthur embraced civil service reform.

So, what changed Chester Arthur's mind? Several things. First, he could sense that Garfield's assassination had reshaped the debate and created a movement with huge momentum, and he didn't want to stand in the way of history. He may have concluded that civil service reform was going to pass no matter what he did and that he would be forever cast as a villain if he tried to block it. And there is some evidence that he resented Roscoe Conkling's assumption that he could walk into the Oval Office and start calling the shots. Arthur knew that everybody expected him to back Conkling and oppose reform because no one believed he had the character or integrity to do otherwise. And he did not want to be known forever as someone who came into office and fulfilled everybody's low expectations.

But none of this quite explains Arthur's conversion. Even if he concluded that some kind of civil service reform needed to pass, he could have watered it down, given his allies control over the process, and enforced it half-heartedly. But he did none of these things. In his first message to Congress after becoming president, he asked that body to outlaw political assessments and reauthorize the Civil Service Commission. It did nothing. When Republicans sustained major losses in the 1882 midterm election, Arthur reached across party lines and supported a bill written by Democratic senator George Pendleton. In 1883, Arthur signed the Pendleton Civil Service Reform Act, which, over time, eliminated the spoils system and created the merit-based civil service that is still in place today.

Arthur's actions were extremely unpopular with his own party, which depended on the patronage system for its political dominance. At the 1884 convention, Arthur was passed over for the nomination in favor of James Blaine, who had been his secretary of state. Arthur died a year later at fifty-seven years old and began his slide into presidential anonymity.

Arthur is one of our history's greatest examples of a person who changed his mind. But let's be clear about exactly what part of his mind got changed. He didn't go from thinking that patronage was a good idea to thinking it was a bad one. Nobody in 1880 actually believed that political patronage produced better civil servants than a merit-based system would. It persisted because sitting politicians found it useful and refused to get rid of it. This was especially true of Arthur's Republican Party, which controlled the richest patronage sites in the country and used them to maintain its dominant position in the post–Civil War era. To end patronage, Arthur had to be persuaded to place the interests of the nation ahead of the short-term interests of his political party.

This tension between party and country has always been part of American politics, and it has colored some of the most controversial issues of our history: immigration, public works spending, the direct election of senators, women's suffrage, civil rights, congressional redistricting, campaign finance—and all sorts of other issues that produce tangible winners and losers. It becomes very difficult with such issues to think of the long-term health of democracy instead of the short-term wins and losses of a particular faction. Much of our progress as a nation, however, has come because people like Chester A. Arthur have been persuaded that the interests of the tribe must give way to the long-term health of American democracy.

Agreeing to Disagree

Arguments don't have to be zero-sum games.

We shall render our hearers willing to receive information, if we explain the sum total of the cause with plainness and brevity, that is to say, the point on which the dispute hinges.

—Cicero, *De Inventione*

The futility of most debates as a means of modifying outlooks can be traced to the unwillingness or the inability of the opponents to listen to one another.

—Anatol Rapoport, *Fights, Games, and Debates*

The phrase "agreeing to disagree" can mean two very different things. In standard usage, it means something like "We've each had our say, and clearly neither of us is going to convince the other, so let's talk about something more pleasant that we can agree on, even if it is just the weather." This usage is ultimately ironic: agreeing to disagree means agreeing to stop disagreeing.

When we agree to disagree in this way, we are acting on two assumptions that, unfortunately, shape a lot of our political conversations. First, we assume that disagreement between two people is an unnatural condition—like a toothache or a high fever—that requires immediate resolution so that everything can return to normal. The second assumption is that the only possible reason to express a disagreement with somebody else is to "win" by convincing that person to change his or her mind and agree with us. The first assumption makes argument an unpleasant chore, and the second makes it a zero-sum game.

But "agreeing to disagree" doesn't have to be a conversation ender. It can also be a way to begin arguing with a friend. Agreeing to disagree can describe a process in which people determine exactly what kind of disagreement they are going to have. This sort of agreeing to disagree, when it occurs, can turn an angry shouting match into a productive debate.

Most people intuitively conceive of arguing as a zero-sum game: an activity like arm wrestling or blackjack that conveys rewards to a "winner" in exact proportion to the costs incurred by a "loser." When we understand an argument in these terms, we naturally want to win. Evolution leaves us little choice in the matter, as we are all descended from millions of organisms who, when faced with a zero-sum competition for survival, chose the winning moves. When we encounter a situation that must have a winner and a loser, we are hard-wired to want to be the winner.

But arguments are not zero-sum games—or, at least, they don't have to be. For one thing, they rarely have a clear definition of victory, like checkmating the king or making the most baskets. We tend to think that we win an argument when we produce an argument that we find more compelling than the arguments of the other person. As long as somebody doesn't change our minds, we claim victory. Most arguments, therefore, end with all sides thinking that they won.

However, the actual rewards that come from arguing with other people have nothing to do with winning and losing. A good argument helps us refine our own ideas and discover where our reasoning is the weakest. Other people's opposition can help us turn our own half-formed ideas into clear assertions backed by solid reasoning. And setting our ideas and opinions against someone else's helps us know each other better, which makes us better friends. We get these benefits from arguments when we collaborate with a partner. We do not get them when we try to destroy an enemy. That is how non-zero-sum games work.

In a non-zero-sum situation, winning and losing are not mutually exclusive. Take, for example, buying a car. When I was a poor graduate student, I bought a used car from a friend for $500. It was a ten-year-old Honda Civic with two hundred thousand miles on it, but I needed a car badly, and this was all I could afford. I drove it for two years before it finally died. I needed the car much more than I needed $500. At the same time, my friend was about to move across the country, and he needed to sell the car immediately. Not many people wanted to pay anything at all for a car with two hundred thousand miles on it, and my friend needed the money to help him move. He needed the $500 much more than he needed the car. Our transaction was not the least bit oppositional. We both did everything possible to facilitate the transaction, and both of us came away winners.

We see this same dynamic over and over again in our human relationships. Most of the contests we engage in for entertainment or sport are zero-sum games, but most of our meaningful interactions with other people are non-zero-sum games. And most of our problems in life arise because we don't know how to tell the difference. When we see a political argument as a non-zero-sum game, our objective is not to win but to help each other have the best and most productive argument that we can have.

RAPOPORT'S RULES

The terms "zero-sum game" and "non-zero-sum game" come from the branch of mathematics known as game theory. In the latter half of the twentieth century, game-theory models became important to the study of conflict resolution. By breaking some of the causes of conflict down into gamelike scenarios, researchers could study people's responses to conflict in laboratory conditions and even create computer simulations to determine how various assumptions interacted with each other to produce group behaviors.

One of the most important scholars to study conflict in these ways was Anatol Rapoport, a Russian-born mathematician and professor of peace studies at the University of Toronto. Rapoport spent years studying a game-theory scenario called "the prisoner's dilemma." This simple two-person game requires players to cooperate with or defect from each other (usually by playing a card with either a *C* or a *D* on it).[1] Point values change in different versions of the game, but in a true prisoner's dilemma, players must receive a modest reward if both choose to cooperate and a mild punishment if both choose to defect. If one chooses to cooperate and the other chooses to defect, the defector receives a large reward and the cooperator an equally large penalty.

Theorists have long known that, in a single iteration of the prisoner's dilemma, rational players will always defect, as the potential reward is huge and the potential penalty is much less severe than the penalty for cooperating when the other player defects. But when the same players play multiple times against each other, cooperation can evolve. In 1980, Rapoport wrote the winning program for a computer-based prisoner's dilemma tournament hosted by Robert Axelrod, a political scientist at the University of Michigan. Axelrod solicited programs from fifteen game-theory specialists who each created a series of decision rules dictating when the program would cooperate and when it would defect. The programs were then matched against each other in five games of two hundred moves each.

Rapoport's program, called TIT FOR TAT, had the simplest instructions of all the programs submitted: always cooperate on the first turn and then do whatever the other player does. Rapoport won the tournament handily with this simple strategy, and then, in a follow-up tournament with sixty-three entrants—all of whom had read Axelrod's account of the first tournament—Rapoport's TIT FOR TAT won again. These results have been discussed in dozens of books and thousands of articles as proof of a kind that altruism and cooperation can emerge in an environment that rewards only self-interested actions.

In his now classic book *The Evolution of Cooperation*, Axelrod uses the results of the tournaments to draw some conclusions about the qualities that lead to successful human interactions. Axelrod concludes that TIT FOR TAT won the tournament because of several important characteristics that are comparable to (but not exactly the same as) qualities we find in some human beings.

> *Niceness:* "Surprisingly," Axelrod explains, "there is a single property which distinguishes the relatively high-scoring entries from the relatively low-scoring entries. This is the property of being *nice*."[2] A nice strategy is one that never defects first but only does so in response to a defection by another player. The eight highest-scoring strategies in the tournament were nice. The other seven strategies were "nasty"— strategies that, under some circumstances, would defect without another player defecting in order to try to capture the larger payoff. All eight of the nice strategies in the tournament outperformed all seven of the nasty strategies.
>
> *Forgiveness:* A "forgiving" strategy is one that cooperates after another strategy has defected. TIT FOR TAT is a forgiving strategy because it only defects once in response to another player's defection and then offers to cooperate again. One strategy in the tournament called GRUDGER was nice but not forgiving. It cooperated until another player defected, and then it never cooperated again. This strategy did worse than all but one of the other nice strategies in the tournament.[3] The value of forgiveness does have limits. Programs that always cooperate end up being taken advantage of by nasty programs, so it is important that even the nicest programs build in some form of retaliation. But Axelrod was able to determine after the tournament that a program called TIT FOR TWO TATS—a program that cooperates until the other player defects twice—would have won the tournament if it had been part of the mix.[4]

Generosity: TIT FOR TAT was not the only strategy in the tournament that was both nice and forgiving. Axelrod determined that a third quality made Rapoport's strategy the winner: it was not envious. It never tried to win a single game—and, in fact, could never win a game. The best it could do in any single matchup was tie. It won the tournament "not by beating the other player, but by eliciting behavior from the other player which allowed both to do well. TIT FOR TAT was so consistent at eliciting mutually rewarding outcomes that it attained a higher overall score than any other strategy."[5]

Clarity: A final characteristic of TIT FOR TAT was the absolute predictability of its actions. It always did the same things in the same situations. Other programs tried to be clever. They waited until late in the game and then defected once in an attempt to capture a few more points by being unpredictable. Others had an element of randomness built in—they would change strategies for a single turn in an attempt to confuse other players. None of this worked. The clarity of TIT FOR TAT created predictability and (to the extent possible with computer programs) trust. This, in turn, encouraged cooperation.[6]

The terms that Axelrod uses to describe these strategies—nice, forgiving, nonenvious—are drawn from what humans would call a moral vocabulary. But the computer programs were not trying to be moral. They were not designed to try to avoid hurting other programs' feelings or to respect the dignity of every line of code. They were developed to try to win a tournament by getting as many points as possible. The genius of TIT FOR TAT was that it recognized and exploited the non-zero-sum nature of the game.

Under the rules of the tournament, if one player cooperated every round and the other player defected every turn, the defector would receive one thousand points and the cooperator zero points. But if both players cooperated every turn, each would receive six hundred points, or a total of twelve hundred points—so there were more total points available to cooperators than to defectors. Rapoport, who wrote a book on the prisoner's dilemma in 1965, understood this dynamic better than anybody else and created a program designed to maximize the total points per round, not the total points per player. TIT FOR TAT won because it never treated the opposite player as an opponent but always as a team member in a game whose purpose was to get as many total points as possible. This is the best way to win a non-zero-sum game.

What does all of this have to do with arguing? Quite a bit, actually. In his 1960 book *Fights, Games, and Debates*, Rapoport makes the connection himself by describing an argument as a non-zero-sum activity that can benefit all participants.[7] A Russian American writing during the chilliest days of the Cold War, Rapoport spent much of his professional life trying to frame international relations as non-zero-sum games. The alternative, he knew, was a prisoner's dilemma situation in which a mutual defection meant blowing up the world.

Debate, for Rapoport, is essential to making peace. It is normally not possible to resolve a conflict without honest argument, but most people feel so threatened by the prospect of losing arguments that they rarely engage in them honestly. The key to a successful debate, Rapoport argues, is to remove the threat and allow people to see it as something positive rather than hostile. This changes the argument into a non-zero-sum activity instead of a contest that must have a winner and a loser. Rapoport offers three rules, which he calls the "rules of ethical debate," to accomplish this shift.

Rule #1: Convey to Opponents That They Have Been Heard and Understood

Understanding what somebody else is arguing, and then demonstrating that understanding, removes the threat of manipulation and focuses the argument on the issues of honest disagreement. Philosopher Daniel Dennett summarizes Rapoport's first rule in this way: "You should attempt to re-express your target's position so clearly, vividly, and fairly that your target says, 'Thanks, I wish I'd thought of putting it that way.'"[8]

When we proceed this way, two things happen that fundamentally change the nature of the debate. First, the other person feels heard and respected and no longer fears being misrepresented and humiliated because we have signaled our willingness to listen carefully and understand his or her argument on its own terms. This turns the argument into a positive connection between human beings and invites our interlocutor to reciprocate.

Second, when somebody summarizes an argument thoughtfully before offering a counterargument, the resulting debate tends to be more meaningful and productive. Much of what passes for argument in our society consists of people badly misrepresenting each other's arguments and responding to points that another person is not making. This inevitably leads to frustration and anger and a feeling of being rhetorically manipulated instead of honestly challenged. Correctly paraphrasing somebody's position makes it much harder to misrepresent that position while trying to argue against it.

Rule #2: Delineate the Region of Validity in the Opponent's Stand

Rapoport's second rule of debate is to identify any areas of agreement that you have with an opponent's position. Such areas will always exist, Rapoport believes, because "it is hard to find a statement in ordinary language without *any* region of validity. There are, roughly speaking, no absolutely false assertions."[9] To put this more concisely, you will never disagree with someone completely. There will always be areas of overlap between your position and theirs; thus you can always find something to speak positively about. Read charitably, even an Orwellian statement like "War is peace," Rapoport insists, could well be interpreted as "emphasizing the well-known unifying effect of war on a nation waging it."

The idea of agreeing with an opponent about anything, however, works against our initial reflexes. When we feel challenged, we immediately move to rhetorical absolutes: things are "totally wrong" and "absolutely unjustified." And the people who say them have to be "pure evil" or "completely insane." Even when we do agree with some of the things an opponent says, we don't want to admit it. When we see debate as a zero-sum game, then anything we concede to the enemy adds to his or her point total and detracts from ours, so we must minimize areas of actual agreement to avoid giving aid and comfort to the enemy.

Partially agreeing with somebody is a way to move an argument from zero-sum to non-zero-sum assumptions. It frames the debate as a collaborative search for truth rather than a game to be won or lost. "The idea," Rapoport explains, "is to steer the debate away from polarities and towards the examination of contexts. If both parties do this . . . progress may be made toward the resolution of the issue."[10]

Rule #3: Induce the Assumption of Similarity

Rapoport's third rule is simply an inversion of his second rule. "Having shown the opponent that we *can* see his image and that we recognize the contexts in which this image is valid . . . we must invite him to perform the same exercise with respect to us."[11] We need, in other words, to convince our opponent to see us as a cooperator and not a defector. For this to happen, Rapoport insists, "the debate must be a genuine debate, not a fight and not a game. And . . . the debate must be a debate between equals."[12]

Once again, this flies in the face of the standard debate stance. When I argue with somebody, I want to feel that I am arguing from a position of strength—that I am smarter than my opponent or much more knowledgeable about the things we are discussing. And I want to press this advantage by foregrounding the books I have read, the people I know, or the experiences I have had. At the same time, I must minimize or belittle any experiences my opponent might have had. If I cannot appeal to my own authority in an argument, then I give up an important advantage, which might cause me to lose. In a zero-sum argument, one never wants to acknowledge an opponent as an equal. And my opponent feels exactly the same way.

A non-zero-sum argument requires two people who perceive each other as similar. Any attempt to create asymmetries—be they in power, knowledge, experience, or morality—forces zero-sum assumptions back onto the discussion. Dennett suggests that one good way to avoid such asymmetries is "to mention anything you have learned from your target."[13] This emphasizes the intellectual value of the other position and the nature of debate as a mutual learning experience—and encourages our opponent to adopt the same perspective.

All three of Rapoport's rules of debate work on the assumption that, if we offer to argue with someone in a cooperative way, we encourage them to reciprocate and turn the debate into a productive and mutually beneficial experience. This is precisely the same assumption that TIT FOR TAT makes in the prisoner's dilemma game. Clear and trustworthy offers to cooperate are usually reciprocated because they create an environment that makes cooperation more profitable than defection. Players who always start out willing to cooperate usually win the long game—not by beating their opponents in every contest but by encouraging everybody involved to realize and profit from the non-zero-sum nature of the game.

THE POWER OF STASIS

In 2018, a Pew Research Center study tested the effects of political bias by showing more than five thousand adults ten politically charged statements and measuring their responses. Five of these were claims of fact that could be disputed but must, by their very nature, be either true or false—such as "President Barack Obama was born in the United States." The other five claims were statements that clearly expressed either values or policy positions, like "Democracy is the greatest form of government" and "Abortion should be legal in most cases."[14]

Predictably, people's political affiliation influenced their views of whether the claims of fact were true or whether the opinions were valid. But the Pew study found that political bias extended to people's evaluation of the category of claim being made. Participants were instructed to disregard their view of the truth of each assertion and label it a factual statement "if they thought that the statement could be proved or disproved based on objective evidence" or an opinion statement "if they thought that it was based on the values and beliefs of the journalist or the source making the statement."[15]

Only 26 percent of respondents could label all five factual statements correctly, and a bare majority could correctly label three of the five statements in each set—about the same percentage that we would expect with random guesses.[16] Participants tended to identify factual statements that they disagreed with as opinions and opinion statements that they did agree with as facts. For example, 36 percent of Republican respondents classified the place where Barack Obama was born as an "opinion" rather than verifiable or falsifiable claim of fact. Not to be outdone, 45 percent of Democrats classified the statement "Spending on Social Security, Medicare, and Medicaid makes up the largest portion of the U.S. federal budget" as an opinion that could not be verified by examining a factual source such as, say, the federal budget.

The underlying problem that this study illuminates goes much deeper than people not being able to distinguish between truth and falsehood. Somebody who accepts a falsehood as true or rejects a true statement as false is at least getting the general category right: "true" and "false" are evaluations that we can assign to things that claim to be facts. When we disagree with someone about the truth of a factual statement, we have reached an agreement about what we are disagreeing about—and we know how to proceed. But when one party to an argument is defending a fact that another party considers an opinion, we have not even reached the minimum level of agreement necessary to have a disagreement. We are simply talking past each other.

This is yet another possible aspect of "agreeing to disagree" that we need to consider: for any kind of productive disagreement to occur, participants need to agree about what they are disagreeing about. The ancient Greeks had a word for an agreement about the subject of a disagreement: they called it *stasis*, or "stand." The point of stasis in an argument is the place where both sides take their stand. When an argument is in stasis, the arguers are offering arguments for and against the same proposition. It is usually impossible to resolve an argument that is not in stasis because, without a point of stasis, there is no conflict to resolve. People may be arguing *against* each other, but without stasis they are almost never arguing *with* each other.

Let's look at an example of an argument that is not in stasis. For years, abortion has been one of the most divisive issues in American politics. Commenters have referred it as "a clash of absolutes"—a political issue that pits people's fundamental and nonnegotiable worldviews against each other.[17] Perhaps it does, but I would suggest that the arguments people make about abortion rarely produce a clash of absolutes, or a clash of anything else, because they never really connect with each other. They do not produce a point of stasis in which people are arguing against what others are saying. Such a conflict can never be resolved because it is not, properly speaking, a conflict.

Let me explain what I mean by this: One side of the argument claims that life begins at conception and from there concludes that abortion is a type of murder. If this is true (the argument continues), then it simply doesn't matter whether a woman has the right to control her body. Nobody has a right to commit murder. The other side argues that the government should not have the authority to compel a woman to carry a child to term. They perceive laws against abortion as laws that co-opt a person's bodily integrity—much as a law requiring organ donation or blood donation would. If this is true (the argument continues), then the personhood status of a fetus simply doesn't matter. Nobody has a right to use somebody else's body, even if they need it to live.

Here is the problem: The assertions "life begins at conception" and "women have a right to choose what happens to their bodies" are not inherently in conflict with each other. It is entirely possible to accept both statements without producing a conflict—to believe either (1) that the right to bodily integrity does not supersede the right to life or (2) that an embryo is a fully legitimate human being that does not have a claim on another human being's body, even if it needs that body to continue living.

So, when each side picks up one of these assertions and wields it as a rhetorical rapier, the swords never cross. There is no clash, no actual argument—just a lot of yelling. To actually have a debate about abortion, people have to engage with the things that, from their perspective, "simply don't matter." This means that those on the pro-choice side should acknowledge that the decision to permit abortion has profound implications for something close enough to a human life to command our moral attention. And people on the pro-life side should similarly acknowledge that criminalizing abortion requires an enormous and wholly intrusive exercise of state power against an individual.

Framed this way, the debate is about balancing different rights, determining partial goods and lesser evils, and finding workable solutions to extremely difficult problems. This is not nearly as much fun as being 100 percent right and attacking an opponent for being 100 percent wrong. But it does have the advantage of actually being an argument—and of allowing people to find enough common ground with each other to stand on while disagreeing about the things that they really disagree about. This is the nutshell version of what ancient rhetoricians meant by *stasis*.

CICERO AND STASIS THEORY

Almost everything the ancients understood about stasis theory comes to us through the writings of Marcus Tullius Cicero (106–43 BCE), perhaps the best-known politician of the ancient Roman Republic. Cicero came from a rural family of equestrian rank—a background that technically qualified him for government service, though only barely and through extraordinary merit and effort. But Cicero was the most gifted orator that Rome had ever produced, and he soon won fame as a lawyer and entered politics, where he rose through the ranks quickly to become consul—the highest elected office in the Roman Republic—in 63 BCE.

In his political roles, Cicero frequently found himself at odds with the three most powerful men of his day: the immensely rich Crassus, the great general Pompey, and the brilliant young senator Julius Caesar. As the power struggles between and among these three men threatened to destroy the republic, Cicero stood firm as a defender of the Senate and republican rule. And when Caesar proclaimed himself dictator and was assassinated on the Senate floor, Cicero led the opposition to Mark Antony, who eventually had him killed.

What made Cicero remarkable in Rome was not just his power of persuasive speech but also the fact that the power of persuasive speech was all he had going for him. Unlike his rivals, he did not have great wealth or strong family connections to help him acquire political power or an army of loyal soldiers to help him take it by force. He owed everything that he accomplished to his ability to construct and deliver powerful arguments. In his various periods of exile, Cicero spent his time writing down everything he knew about persuasion and creating books that, because of his fame as a politician and orator, survived the Middle Ages and became the basis of the modern science of rhetoric. And none of his work has been more influential than his writings on stasis theory.

According to Cicero, the first step in getting to a point of stasis is understanding what kind of assertions are being made. He argued that any claim a person makes will fall into one of four categories: it will be an assertion that something is true (*a claim of fact*), that something is good or bad (*a claim of value*), that somebody should do something (*a claim of policy*), or that something has a certain meaning (*a claim of definition*). These are, of course, very broad categories, and each has a number of subcategories and special cases. But for more than two thousand years, rhetoricians have found these categories useful for describing the kinds of arguments people make.

Each kind of claim produces a different kind of disagreement. We argue about facts differently than we argue about values, definitions, and policies—and most arguments in the wild contain elements of all four types of assertions. Consider how you might go about disagreeing with the following statement:

> We need to require that all backyard swimming pools be covered at night because fifteen thousand children die every year in preventable swimming pool accidents.

Let's break down the four possible areas where we might find a point of stasis to disagree with this argument.

- *Fact:* There is only one important fact claim in the assertion: that fifteen thousand children die in swimming pool accidents every year. As it turns out, I just made this number up, and when I did, I had no idea how many children die each year in swimming pool accidents. But fifteen thousand seemed like it would get everyone's attention, so I used it. The actual number, of course, is going to depend on how the key terms are defined, but it is probably somewhere between three hundred and twelve hundred. So, there is a clear point of stasis here in arguing about the correct statistic, but that also means agreeing on a source for finding statistics about things like this.
- *Definition:* Clarifying definitions is a huge part of having meaningful arguments. In this case, the correct number of accidental deaths depends on who we decide to classify as a "child." If we set the bar at four years old and under, then the number is about three hundred. If we set it at fourteen and under, it goes up to about seven hundred. But the definition also matters because the precautions necessary to prevent a toddler from drowning in a swimming pool are not the same as those necessary to prevent a teenager from drowning. So, once everybody agrees on a source for statistical information, then the question at issue becomes how we define "children" for the sake of the argument. This is a second legitimate point of stasis.
- *Value:* The most important implied value in the original assertion is that children dying is a bad thing. Most people will (and all people should) concede the point, so this is not a good place to make the stand. But the argument implies another value through the word "preventable." Technically, any accident is preventable, but not all accidents can be prevented at a cost to society that most people would consider reasonable. In their most high-minded moments, most people will say that we must spare no expense to save any human life. But nobody actually believes this. For example, we could probably eliminate a large portion of highway deaths with a rigorously enforced national speed limit of fifteen miles per hour, but this would also negate the purpose of the highway system, which is to get places quickly. Similarly, we could eliminate all swimming pool deaths by outlawing swimming pools altogether and requiring that they be filled with concrete—and we would probably do exactly this if swimming pool deaths reached, say, fifteen million a year. But just how many deaths justify just how much expense and inconvenience? This is the

crucial value judgment buried in the original assertion, and because it is a value judgment, reasonable people can disagree by several orders of magnitude—providing a crucial point of stasis for a debate.

- *Policy:* The original assertion—*we need to require that all backyard swimming pools be covered at night*—is a claim of policy, and it must stand or fall as an argument that a specific thing (covering swimming pools) should be done in order to solve a specific problem (children drowning). At other points of stasis, we might question whether the problem is really a problem, or whether it can be solved with a reasonable investment of resources and attention. But the ultimate question at issue in any policy assertion is "Will it work?" Since we cannot know for sure what will happen in the future, the question at issue becomes "Is it reasonable to believe that the proposed solution will actually solve the problem?" In this specific case, the assertion requires its proponent to demonstrate that covering swimming pools at night will decrease swimming pool deaths. One could do this by pointing to other countries or local jurisdictions that have reduced deaths by covering swimming pools at night, by showing how many of the deaths take place at night, by demonstrating the effectiveness of swimming pool covers at preventing drownings, and so on.

Each of the categories of assertion gives us at least one point of stasis that generates a debatable question. For there to be a meaningful debate, both (or all) parties must disagree about the same question. It would not do, for example, for one party to assert that swimming pool covers will not prevent children from drowning and the other party to assert that thousands of children die each year in uncovered swimming pools. These swords don't cross, as someone can agree that something is a problem that needs to be solved and, at the same time, disagree that a specific proposal will solve the problem. Only arguments that reach a point of stasis—the place where people are actually speaking to each other's points—have any chance of persuading people to change their minds.

Determining which questions are at issue in a debate takes time and attention. And we accomplish this most successfully when we talk about it with each other in advance. Once we create the stasis point, we still have to agree on some things in order to have a debate about others. We have to agree about facts and definitions before we can talk meaningfully about anything else. And in order to argue about value claims, we have to appeal to values that we share. Until we spend the time necessary to foreground these areas of agreement, we cannot have meaningful disagreements. All we can do is yell a lot. Meaningful debate, unlike meaningless yelling, is a collaborative enterprise.

THE LINCOLN-DOUGLAS DEBATES AND
THE POWER OF CLARIFYING THE ARGUMENT

The Lincoln-Douglas debates would not be possible today. They were nothing like the sanitized joint appearances that we call debates, where candidates give brief answers to generic questions and try as hard as they can not to say anything that anyone could ever hold against them. The format that Abraham Lincoln and Stephen Douglas used for their debates was very different. There were no moderators, no questions, just the two candidates who each spoke for a full hour and a half, with one candidate giving a thirty-minute opening speech, the second a ninety-minute rebuttal, and the first a sixty-minute rejoinder. These debates are rightly considered the high-water mark of political argument in America.

The Lincoln-Douglas debates covered the single topic of slavery. No other issues mattered in 1858. We were a one-issue country, and the entire federal system would be paralyzed until that one issue was solved. But even though only one issue mattered, that one issue could not be neatly packaged into two "sides," one pro-slavery and one anti-slavery. There were multiple values and policy positions at issue in the debate, as table 8.1 attempts to demonstrate.

Neither Lincoln nor Douglas was an abolitionist in 1858. Though quite a few people in the country were abolitionists, immediate, universal emancipation was not even at issue in the elections that year. Very much at issue, however, was the question of how to handle slavery in the new territories. Douglas had hitched his wagon to the star of "popular sovereignty," or the position that each territory should decide for itself whether to allow slavery. Lincoln, by contrast, argued that while slavery should not be allowed to expand further than it already had, the federal government did not have the constitutional authority to interfere with slavery where it already existed.

The Lincoln-Douglas debates give us an excellent laboratory for understanding how debate sharpens, and even helps to create, good arguments. During the early debates, Lincoln spent much of his time defending himself against Douglas's charges: that he was an abolitionist, that he believed in full racial equality, that he supported interracial marriage. These charges not only kept Lincoln on the defensive for much of the first four debates but also prevented him from staking out a coherent anti-slavery argument that did not conflict with one of these denials. Douglas, however, was free to press his signature issue: "popular sovereignty," or the assertion that the people of every state had the right to decide for themselves what to do about slavery.

Table 8.1. Pre–Civil War Positions on Slavery

Moral Value	*Possible Policy Positions*
Slavery is morally evil • because members of all races are fully equal and deserve the same rights and freedoms; • because all human beings deserve compassion, even if they are not fully equal; • because slave labor drives down the price of free labor and negatively affects white laborers.	Slavery should be abolished immediately and full citizenship rights granted to all races. Gradual emancipation should be accomplished by preventing the expansion of slavery into new territories and allowing it to fade out gradually (Lincoln's position). The government should pursue compensated emancipation (i.e., buying the slaves from the owners) and the resettlement of slaves. Slaves should be deported to Liberia or another African or a Caribbean nation.
Slavery is morally neutral • therefore, decisions about slavery are economic decisions that should be made by states; • therefore, decisions about slavery are personal decisions that should be made by individuals; • therefore, we should acknowledge that it is part of the heritage of some states and protect the rights of the people in those states to own slaves and to transport them anywhere in the country.	There should be an equal number of free and slave states admitted into the Union so that the interests of both types of state will always be protected. Popular sovereignty: each existing state and each incoming state should be allowed to decide for itself whether it wants to be a free or a slave state (Douglas's position).
Slavery is morally good • because the white race is the only race that matters; • because Africans are natural slaves and are happiest and most fulfilled when they have masters.	Universal allowance of slavery: all states should permit slavery, and all Africans should be required to live as slaves. The United States should aggressively seek to annex new slave states in Cuba, Haiti, Dominica, and other plantation economies.

All of this changed during the fifth debate, at Knox College in Galesburg, Illinois. Galesburg was a Republican stronghold and a center of abolitionist sentiment, so Lincoln had one of the friendliest audiences he would encounter during the debates. Douglas had the opening speech, and he tried a new tactic. He came prepared with a quotation from a speech that Lincoln had given several months earlier in Chicago in which he argued that the phrase "all men are created equal" in the Declaration of Independence was intended to apply to both white and black men.

Douglas then read other remarks that Lincoln had made during the other debates arguing that the races were not equal—which, Douglas argued, proved that Lincoln was a secret abolitionist who hid his intentions when speaking to people who did not believe in racial equality. Believing that the Declaration of Independence applied to slaves was the same as believing that slaves should be freed and granted the rights of citizenship. Douglas agreed that states that wanted to could grant such rights but asserted that no federal entity could decide the question for the people of any state—and he insisted that only agreement on this point could hold the Union together.

Douglas's speech was effective, but he made a logical error that Lincoln exploited masterfully. To use the vocabulary of the current chapter, Douglas did not counter the arguments that he quoted from a point of stasis. He cited several apparently contradictory value statements that Lincoln had made and then argued against the policy that he believed those values implied. His final argument for popular sovereignty, therefore, was a claim of policy offered as a counterargument to a claim of value. This had been a common theme of Douglas's arguments, and up until this point, Lincoln did his best to explain his policy of containing slavery where it existed and prohibiting it in new states and territories.

In Galesburg, however, he came up with a much more powerful response by simply finding a way to put the argument in stasis:

> I suppose that the real difference between Judge Douglas and his friends, and the Republicans on the contrary, is, that the Judge is not in favor of making any difference between slavery and liberty—that he is in favor of eradicating, of pressing out of view, the questions of preference in this country for free or slave institutions; and consequently every sentiment he utters discards the idea that there is any wrong in slavery. . . . If you will take the Judge's speeches, and select the short and pointed sentences expressed by him—as his declaration that he "don't care whether slavery is voted up or down"—you will see at once that this is perfectly logical, if you do not admit that slavery is wrong. If you do admit that it is wrong, Judge Douglas cannot logically say he don't care whether a wrong is voted up or voted down. Judge Douglas declares that if any community want[s] slavery they have a right to have it. He can say that logically, if he says that there is no wrong in slavery; but if you admit that there is a wrong in it, he cannot logically say that any body has a right to do wrong. He insists that, upon the score of equality, the owners of slaves and owners of property—of horses and every other sort of property—should be alike and hold them alike in a new Territory. That is perfectly logical, if the two species of property are alike and are equally founded in right. But if you

admit that one of them is wrong, you cannot institute any equality between right and wrong.[18]

By putting the argument in stasis—and demanding that his opponent speak to the morality of slavery rather than to his specific policy proposals—Lincoln placed Douglas on the horns of a dilemma. Douglas could not answer the question on its own terms. If he said that slavery was morally evil, he would lose any chance of receiving the Democratic nomination for president. If he said that it was morally good, he would open himself up to demands that it be allowed in all states. All he could do was repeat the argument that states had to decide for themselves what to do about slavery, which gave Lincoln the opportunity to counter, convincingly, that moral values cannot be decided by popular vote.

This immediately became Lincoln's strongest anti-slavery argument: not that it should be abolished, or even that it should be curtailed, but that it should be considered "a moral, social, and political evil" that might have to be tolerated but could never be embraced.[19] He made this argument effectively in his Cooper Union speech and in his First Inaugural Address. For the next two years, he insisted in all his speeches that he was making a moral argument against slavery, not a policy argument, and this allowed him to win plaudits from abolitionists by denouncing slavery without running up against the politically dangerous policy issue of abolition.

But consistently labeling slavery a moral evil did have policy implications. Before the war, Lincoln did not believe that abolition was possible or constitutionally permissible, so he focused on condemning slavery rather than promising to abolish it. However, the Civil War made impossible things possible. Lincoln was able to issue the Emancipation Proclamation as a war measure, freeing all slaves in states that were part of the rebellion. And he was able to secure passage of the Thirteenth Amendment, which changed the Constitution to prohibit slavery everywhere. But he could only do these things because he had already created the argument that slavery was a moral evil that should be eradicated whenever possible.

We cannot overstate how much these debates helped Lincoln's political career. Though Douglas eventually won reelection to the Senate, the debates instantly established Lincoln as a heavyweight—somebody who could go toe-to-toe with the highest-profile politicians in the country and make the positions of the new Republican Party sound good. Lincoln's performance in the debates led directly to an invitation to address the Republican faithful in New York City's Cooper Union. And that speech led directly to his nomination for the presidency.

Does this mean that Lincoln won the debates even though he lost the election that followed them? If you have read this chapter carefully, you know that this is the wrong question to ask. Both Lincoln and Douglas profited from them. Both got the national exposure they needed to launch their presidential campaigns, both were strengthened in their own political parties, and both improved their arguments about slavery by testing them against an intelligent and articulate opponent.

The Lincoln-Douglas debates did not have a winner and a loser because they were not part of a zero-sum game. And they provide all the proof we need that political arguments can work to the benefit of all participants and to the overall good of a self-governing nation.

· 9 ·

"Think It Possible You May Be Mistaken"

*Arguing in good faith means acknowledging
that you might be wrong.*

Human understanding is like a false mirror, which, receiving
rays irregularly, distorts and discolours the nature of things by
mingling its own nature with it.

—Francis Bacon, *Novum Organum*

I beseech you, in the bowels of Christ, think it possible you may
be mistaken.

—Oliver Cromwell

*Y*ou are wrong. You are profoundly and disturbingly wrong about a spectacularly large number of things. You accept facts that are not facts, values
that are incompatible with each other, and a fair number of truly dumb ideas
about how to change the world. If you ever really understood the extent of
your wrongness, you would never trust another word you said.

You need not feel ashamed about this. I am wrong too; everybody is
wrong about a lot of things. Given the number of things that all of us believe (or do not believe) to be facts, the number of things that we consider
(or do not consider) valuable, and the number of policies that we think (or
do not think) will work, there is no possible way that anybody is going to be
right about everything—or even most things. You already accept this about
99.9999 percent of the human population. You know perfectly well that everybody else is wrong about a lot of things. And if you really think about it,

125

you will realize that you are probably not the only person in the world who is always right.

We all understand this in the abstract. We even understand it retroactively and can remember any number of things that we got wrong in the past. I am willing to bet, however, that you can't think of a single thing that you are wrong about right now. None of us can. The minute we realize that we think something wrong, we immediately revise our beliefs to be right again. This is just how human cognition works; we can't imagine ourselves being wrong.

Blame it on evolution. An absolute sense of our own rightness is nature's way of protecting us from indecision. When escaping from bears and such, just about any decision we can make (run left, run right, climb a tree) is better than just sitting there and being eaten. Not trusting our own judgment can be dangerous, especially since we are all right about a lot of things too. And whether we are right or wrong about something, pursuing our choice vigorously will almost always be better than wallowing in indecision and self-doubt. According to the rigorous logic of natural selection, organisms who *think* they are right all the time have an advantage over those who *are* right all the time.

We can also blame evolution for the fact that we spend so much time being wrong about things. It's not that there is an evolutionary advantage to making bad decisions; there is an evolutionary advantage to making quick decisions and not wasting time and resources getting things righter than they need to be. Thinking about things for a long time wastes effort and incurs a heavy opportunity cost because it prevents us from thinking about other things—and it usually gives us better answers than we need. If I am pressed for time and need to know how long it will take to get to the hardware store, "about ten minutes away" will do just fine. I can probably calculate a better estimate if I spend more time doing so, but that would defeat the purpose of trying to make it a quick trip.

So, our brains are wired to take shortcuts, work from preexisting templates, make educated guesses, reduce complexity, and generally try to find good-enough answers to complicated questions with the smallest possible investment of resources. To do this, our logical brain outsources as much work as it can to our intuitions and our emotions—and then they all come back and try to convince us that everything has been analyzed in elaborate detail. We can now form an opinion that will be exactly the right opinion, and we can defend it to the death. We might suspect that our emotions and intuitions are lying to us, but we go with it anyway because this way of doing things usually works well enough.

Except when it doesn't. And here are some of the most important ways that our brains can lead us astray.

PATTERN RECOGNITION BIASES

Human beings love finding patterns and relationships, and we are very good at it. We are so good at it, in fact, that we often find patterns that aren't there. Patterns allow us to predict the future and control our environments, and we find the knowledge that patterns exist comforting because it makes the universe seem predictable and controllable. Random events—things that we can neither predict nor control—frighten us and create anxiety. To manage this anxiety, we often impose patterns on random collections of facts.

By far, the most important pattern in our cognitive toolbox is cause and effect. We need to understand why and how things happen if we want to change anything about our environment, which means that we have to know how to trace effects back to their causes. This understanding has been crucial to human progress. To develop agriculture, people had to understand that planting seeds in the ground causes things to grow. To enter the Bronze Age, people had to understand what happens when you mix copper and tin together at high temperatures. The ability to create cause-and-effect narratives may be humanity's greatest superpower.

But we are so good at telling ourselves cause-and-effect stories that we frequently invent them when they don't apply.[1] If somebody's cow dies for no apparent reason, we need to find and burn the witch who made it happen. If a volcano looks like it might erupt, we toss in a virgin or two to make the gods happy. Superstitions of all kinds emerge as we use our reasoning ability to match observable effects with controllable causes—so that, at least in our own minds, we can create a world full of things that we can predict and control.

The best-known error of causation goes by the fancy Latin name *post hoc ergo propter hoc* (often shortened to just "post hoc fallacy"), which means "after the thing therefore because of the thing." It occurs when someone points to two things that happened in sequence and argues, without any evidence beyond the sequence of events, that the first thing caused the second thing.

A nontrivial portion of human civilization has been built on top of post hoc fallacies—including many of the assumptions that drive our elections. Most Americans believe (or at least act like they believe) that a president can control everything that happens anywhere in the world. Presidents routinely get blamed for high gas prices, low wages, recessions, and even wars in other countries that happen when they are in office. However, they invariably take the credit for low unemployment rates, economic growth, and every other good thing that happens on their watch. Just about everybody involved perpetuates the illusion that presidents control everything.

Presidents have far less control over the economy than most people suppose, and they have virtually no control at all over the price of a worldwide commodity like crude oil or the behavior of foreign dictators. Yet one rarely hears a presidential candidate answer a question like "What are you going to do to lower gas prices?" with "I'm not going to do anything, because gas prices are set by a worldwide market that no American politician can control." Candidates don't say this because constituents don't want to hear it. We all want to believe that complicated things can be controlled. And most of us will give our votes to the politicians who promise—however implausibly—to control them.

Our overwhelming reliance on post hoc reasoning creates an expectation-management problem for anyone who wins an election. People believe that politicians who really want to make good things happen can control all the chaos and randomness in the world. A president who really cares, then, should be able to eliminate unemployment, keep wages high and prices low, stop school shootings, get drugs off the streets, and bring peace to the Middle East. Dartmouth political scientist Brendan Nyhan calls this the Green Lantern theory, or the idea that a president or other politician "can achieve any political or policy objective if only he tries hard enough."[2]

These expectations pauperize our political discourse by focusing much of our energy on the wrong things—apportioning praise and blame for largely random events in the past and demanding fixes for problems not really under the control of the people tasked with fixing them. They can also lead us to waste our efforts on activities that create the *illusion of control*, an often-studied cognitive phenomenon by which people perform actions and rituals that they know to be irrational but which, on some level, they think will allow them to control something in their environment.[3]

We experience a classic example of the illusion-of-control phenomenon when we repeatedly press an elevator button while waiting in a lobby—even though we know that pressing it more than once accomplishes nothing—because we feel an overwhelming urge to do something, and pushing the button is the only action available. We do the same sorts of things in our political lives too. We circulate petitions, change our Facebook profiles, make poorly considered donations, and express our outrage to anybody around because we need to do *something*, and these things are available and require only a very modest effort. This becomes a serious problem when we see such activities as a substitute for the considerable effort required to influence things that we really do have some control over.

Most people's overwhelming fear of randomness, combined with the infinite human ability to construct plausible-sounding narratives, can create a political culture driven by conspiracy theories, unreasonable expectations, and extreme oversimplifications. When we reduce a complicated and near-infinite set of variables to a handful of simple cause-and-effect stories, we make the world seem much more predictable and controllable. But when we organize our conversations around this imaginary world instead of the actual one, we end up understanding the world badly and trying to structure our government accordingly.

CONFIRMATION BIAS

The *confirmation bias* is exactly what it sounds like: a powerful bias that human beings have toward information that confirms their own position or that of the "team" they perceive themselves to be on. Precisely because we always think we are right, we have a strong tendency to search out, notice, pay attention to, think well of, and be persuaded by information that supports what we already believe.

The confirmation bias factors into just about everything that counts as civic discourse. Once we choose our political "side," we devote our considerable reasoning skills to justifying that choice to ourselves—and to convincing other people that we are right. Like all good energy-conserving organisms, we filter out things that don't relate directly to those objectives. Research shows that we are less likely to engage with information that contradicts our political beliefs—less likely to notice it, less likely to watch or read it when we do notice it, less likely to believe it when we watch or read it, and less likely to tell anybody else about it—than with information that supports our side.[4] Nothing surprising about any of this—it's how filters work. Energy must be conserved.

The confirmation bias also kicks in when we encounter evidence that relates to our beliefs but does not inherently support or contradict them. When this happens, we start building a narrative into which we can embed the new data in a way that confirms our position.

For example, consider the argument that Americans have with each other when there is a mass-shooting incident in a school or public venue. One side of the argument will see the tragedy as proof that there are too many guns in America and that they are too easy to get. They will use this evidence to argue for making guns harder to access. The other side will argue that an armed bystander could have prevented the shooting. For these people, the best way to prevent mass shootings is to arm more citizens to ensure that there is always someone around with the firepower necessary to stop a crazed sociopath with a gun.

The people who participate in this debate rarely come to it as disinterested observers, waiting to evaluate the relevant evidence before deciding what to believe. Most of us already know what we think about guns, gun control, and mass shootings. When something new happens, we work very hard to fit it into our existing narratives. We are better storytellers than we are logicians. So when new evidence comes along, we try very hard to meet the challenge with a story that explains how we were right all along.

All the scientific studies aside, confirmation bias is really just another term for taking your own side in a fight, which is something that we all do instinctively. Because we almost always think we are right, we have a hard time seeing it as a cognitive defect when we do, so the confirmation bias conceals itself from us by convincing us that we actually are right and have no need to correct for any biases. Every time I speak to students or civic audiences about the confirmation bias, people come up to me afterward and thank me for explaining why their neighbors and relatives are always so wrong. Nobody has ever said, "I guess I am wrong sometimes too."

But another side to the confirmation bias often gets missed in popular discussions. In fact, many cognitive scientists use the term "myside bias" to refer to what I have been defining as the confirmation bias because they want to reserve the term "confirmation bias" to refer to a preference for affirmative evidence (evidence that confirms a belief or hypothesis) over negative evidence (evidence that contradicts or falsifies a hypothesis), even when negative arguments prove more than affirmative arguments do.

This usage of "confirmation bias" traces back to the 1960s and the experiments of psychologist Peter Wason, who coined the term. Wason's experiments used cards with printing on both the front and the back, which participants were instructed to turn over to test various hypotheses. For example, consider the four cards below. With the understanding that each card contains a letter on one side and a number on the other, which card or cards would someone need to turn over to test the proposition that a card that has a 3 on one side has an *A* on the other?

| S | A | 3 | 9 |

The correct answers are 3 and *S*. If there is a 3 on the other side of the *S* or anything other than an *A* on the other side of the 3, then the rule is falsified, and we know it is not valid. Turning over the *A* seems like a good choice, since a 3 on the other side would confirm one instance of the rule. But the rule does not say that only 3s are paired with *A*s, so there is no reason to turn it over; any number on the other side will confirm the rule.

Fewer than 10 percent of the respondents chose the correct two cards. The overwhelming majority chose the *A*, which gives the illusion of confirmation, and failed to choose the *S*, which contains the potential for falsification. From this result, Wason theorized that we are biased in favor of trying to prove our beliefs true by confirming them rather than by trying (and failing) to falsify them.[5]

Trained scientists understand that experimental research should try to falsify, rather than confirm, a hypothesis. For the rest of us, though, confirmation seems more compelling, and we imagine that it proves more than it actually does. Falsification is a much more powerful reasoning tool than confirmation because most propositions can be falsified conclusively but only confirmed provisionally. This is the essence of the famous black swan problem in philosophy. We have centuries of accumulated evidence "proving" the proposition that all swans are white, but it took only a single black swan to falsify the proposition and make all the confirmations irrelevant.

Psychologists who have followed Wason have discovered that humans are much better at falsifying propositions than the original experiments suggested. We know how to find the inconsistencies in people's arguments, poke holes in their reasoning, point out assertions made without evidence, explain where a complicated chain of reasoning breaks down, and identify counterexamples that disprove the principles upon which their arguments rest. We regularly perform these operations on arguments that we disagree with. We just can't do it for ourselves, even when we try our best, because we use a different cognitive process to evaluate our own arguments than we do for those that we want to reject.

The nature of the confirmation bias makes it almost impossible for us to correct it by ourselves. Once we identify an opinion or pick a political side, our brains will keep hiding the ball from us. We will find confirmation for our beliefs everywhere and have a hard time seeing anything else, and if we happen to encounter evidence that contradicts our opinion, we will rigorously attempt to falsify it. But, Jonathan Haidt argues, there is a simple way to control for the effects of confirmation bias: we just need to surround ourselves with people who see things differently than we do and invite them to try to falsify our positions:

We should not expect individuals to produce good, open-minded, truth-seeking reasoning, particularly when self-interest or reputational concerns are in play. But if you put individuals together in the right way, such that some individuals can use their reasoning powers to disconfirm the claims of others, and all individuals feel some common bond or shared fate that allows them to interact civilly, you can create a group that ends up producing good reasoning as an emergent property of the social system. This is why it's so important to have intellectual and ideological diversity within any group or institution whose goal is to find truth . . . or to produce good public policy.

If we scale Haidt's advice to our entire society, we get something that looks a lot like civic friendship and public debate. If we can manage not to treat each other as enemies who must be destroyed, spirited political conversation can become a mechanism for countering our own biases. We can, in effect, turn our political opponents into our very own bias checkers by inviting them to try their best to prove us wrong.

THE AVAILABILITY HEURISTIC

When I received tenure at the university where I began my career, I got a very kind and affirming letter from the provost. He listed some of my accomplishments, quoted from some of the letters written on my behalf, mentioned a few of my publications, and, in the end, congratulated "Dr. Jennifer Burke" on reaching this important career landmark. Not being Dr. Jennifer Burke, I was a bit confused.

When I became a provost myself and wrote dozens of these letters every year, I realized exactly what happened. Faced with the task of writing a stack of letters that said many of the same things, he wrote the first letter and then used it as a template for the others. He reused all the official language that had to go in each letter and only changed the specific things that applied to me. This allowed him to partially automate a repetitive task and write many letters in a fraction of the time that it would take to write each one from scratch. He simply forgot to change one of the things that applied specifically to me. I have done the same thing myself, and I have made the same mistake.

This letter-writing process mirrors something that happens in our brains every day. When we encounter a new situation that requires us to process information and make decisions, we look for templates that we have already created—similar situations that have required similar decisions—and just change the things that apply to the new situation. We save a lot of time and energy this way, since we don't have to reconsider every aspect of every situation. But the fact that this strategy saves us so much time often tricks us into overestimating similarities between situations and not considering enough of the differences.

In the 1970s, two Israeli psychologists—Daniel Kahneman and Amos Tversky—conducted a series of groundbreaking experiments on what they called "heuristics," or mental shortcuts that people use to assess probabilities and make decisions under pressure. A heuristic works a lot like a template for writing letters. It gives us a basic structure for thinking about situations to which we can add information as necessary, thus allowing us to make decisions in a fraction of the time that it would take to consider every aspect of a complex situation individually. Heuristics allow us to partially automate repetitive thinking tasks. They usually produce workable responses, but sometimes they fail spectacularly.

One of the most important mental shortcuts that Tversky and Kahneman identified was the tendency to base our decisions on the information that we can retrieve most easily. They called this the *availability heuristic* because it causes us to use availability as the measure of information's importance. This is a pretty good rule of thumb. Even in a world of near-limitless access to information, there is usually a fairly high correlation between the availability of information and its usefulness. If I spend fifteen minutes a day reading a few of the most prominent online news sites, there is a pretty good chance that I will encounter most of the really important things that are happening in the world. And if I just go to Google and type in "best composers of the nineteenth century," there is a very good chance that the first page of results will contain at least a defensible list of ten.[6]

But availability isn't quite the same thing as utility, and confusing the two can lead us astray. A scene in the 1998 movie *Rain Man* illustrates this concept nicely. In this scene, Tom Cruise's character, Charlie Babbitt, has just met his brother Raymond, an autistic savant played by Dustin Hoffman. Charlie needs to get Raymond from Cincinnati to Los Angeles as soon as possible. They go to an airport, but Raymond won't get on a plane. Among the many things he has committed to memory are all the planes—including airline and flight number—that have ever crashed. Every time his brother tries to get him on a flight, Raymond lists an accident that the airline has been involved in. Raymond refuses to budge, so Charlie has to drive him across the country, which is the main action of the movie.

Like many people, Raymond focuses on the available information to construct an incorrect argument about probability. Air travel was then, and is now, significantly safer than driving across the country in a car. But information about airplane deaths is much more *available* because airplane crashes always make the news. This same reasoning tends to cause us to overestimate some potential dangers—terrorist attacks, mass shootings, shoe bombs—while dramatically underestimating far more dangerous things (like, say, untreated diabetes or talking on the phone while driving) that kill and injure far more people every year.

So, what constitutes availability for the purposes of this heuristic? The three most important factors that determine the availability of information are *recency*, *memorability*, and *accessibility*. Information is available if we acquired it recently, if we have stored it in our memory banks in ways that make it easy to recall, or if we can locate it quickly with resources easily available to us. Each of these can create problems in the way that we talk to each other about politics.

Recency

The cognitive bias in favor of recent events has been well documented in a dozen different fields, from finance (where recent market events have a disproportionate effect on investment decisions) to human resource management (where annual performance evaluations consistently overemphasize the last few months of an evaluation period).[7] In most cases, we pay much more attention to things that have happened recently than we do to things that happened a long time ago. This causes politicians to live in fear of an "October surprise"—a huge revelation or major event that hits the papers a week or so before a November election. And it causes many people to cast their votes in a way that reflects their satisfaction with government on the day that they step into the voting booth.

Memorability

When we do remember past events, we do not remember them all in the same way. We use other heuristic strategies to tag and store information for retrieval. For most of us, sensational information is easier to recall than ordinary information, pictures are easier to recall than words, stories are easier to recall than statistics, and people are easier to recall than problems. This means that the information we recall the most—and that will play the largest role in our discussions—will usually be vivid and spectacular and will foreground personal stories over statistics and data.

If we are not careful, the availability heuristic can lead to public policy decisions that divert resources to the most visible problems instead of the most pressing ones. I call this the "baby seal effect." Videos of pelt-hunters clubbing baby seals to death fill us with compassion for the seals and outrage at the hunters. It just seems so wrong, and we simply have to do something before another baby seal is sacrificed to the gods of fashion.

The untimely death of baby seals is not the most pressing environmental problem we face—not even close. However, "climate change and ocean acidification has been responsible for the degradation of 80% of the world's coral reefs" is a boring statistic. "Look at that evil hunter clubbing that cute little baby to death" is a sensational story with a powerful visual component. The fact that the world can't survive without coral reefs seems somehow less important than the fate of something adorable.

Accessibility

Not too long ago, the availability heuristic was constrained by the relatively modest amount of information that most of us had easy access to, which meant that major media coverage had an enormous effect on what people talked about in political conversations. This is no longer the case. Most people can access more information on their phones in twenty minutes than their parents could access with a month in a good-sized library.

But this doesn't mean that all the information on the Internet is accessible to us. *Having* access to a hundred billion pages of information is not quite the same as *being able* to access a hundred billion pages of information. Access to information in the twenty-first century is largely a matter of filtering. "Accessible" information is information that can get through whatever filters stand between us and the enormous resources of the Internet.

We create some of these filters ourselves, and others are created by the corporations that own the information we want to access. But an increasingly large percentage of the algorithms that filter our information are created for us, by our interactions, in ways that we barely understand. Every time we interact with something, we teach an algorithm to show us more things like that and fewer things like anything else. The end result of all this filtering is that, without even trying, we create what journalist Eli Pariser calls a "filter bubble"—a virtual space in which our past choices and interactions constrain our present access to information.[8]

George Orwell, in other words, got it exactly wrong. We do not live in a society where Big Brother is constantly spying on us, invading our privacy, and monitoring our political opinions. We live in a society where we spy on ourselves, willingly sacrifice our privacy for the sake of good entertainment, and ask Big Brother for directions to the resistance meeting.

THE ANCHORING HEURISTIC

In one of their earliest and most famous experiments, Tversky and Kahneman asked high school students to estimate, in five seconds or less, the product of the following two strings of numbers:

$$1 \times 2 \times 3 \times 4 \times 5 \times 6 \times 7 \times 8$$
$$8 \times 7 \times 6 \times 5 \times 4 \times 3 \times 2 \times 1$$

The two calculations, of course, have the same answer: 40,320. But not many high school students (or anybody else) could perform such a calculation mentally in five seconds, so they had to rely on their intuition, which was the point of the experiment. The median estimates were, respectively, 512 and 2,250.[9] The first number in the sequence dramatically affected people's intuitive estimates.

It turns out that the first piece of information we encounter about something has an outsize influence on our perception—it influences not just our intellectual understanding of something but also our feelings about that subject. Intellectually, we all know that the difference between $99.99 and $100 is insignificant. But marketers know that we will never understand this so well that we will stop feeling like $99.99 is closer to $90 than to $100. We feel the emotional pull of the anchor even when we know exactly what it is doing.

In the same way that a ship's anchor restricts movement but does not make the ship completely stationary, a cognitive anchor fixes our ideas within a range but does not entirely determine them. Most people do not know, off the top of their head, the freezing point of sea water in degrees Fahrenheit. But if I asked you to guess, you would have an anchor to use as a reference point because you know that the freezing point of fresh water is 32° Fahrenheit. Sea water will probably be different by a few degrees, but it won't be 75° or −30°. It will be somewhere around 32°—say, +/− 5°. The correct answer, 28.4°, is well within the range established by the anchor.

In political discourse, the anchoring heuristic is closely related to the *framing effect*, through which people influence the way that others perceive an issue by changing the context in which it is presented. The way an issue is framed the first time we encounter it anchors the way we understand it in the future.

As an example of the framing effect, consider the following story from Ron Hansen's novel *Exiles*, which explores the poet Gerard Manley Hopkins's experience in a Jesuit seminary:

He overheard Reverend Jones telling . . . a joke about a Jesuit and a Dominican who smoked cigarettes as they read their breviaries outside together. The Dominican felt scruples about the propriety of that and thought they ought to consult their Superiors. When they next got together, he was surprised that the Jesuit was still smoking. The Jesuit asked how he'd framed the question to his Superior, and the Dominican said, "Am I permitted to smoke while I'm praying?" The Jesuit took another drag and said nothing. "Well, what did *you* say?" the Dominican asked. And the Jesuit answered, "Am I permitted to pray while I'm smoking?"[10]

We must do a lot of cognitive heavy lifting to get this joke. We have to understand that "praying while smoking" and "smoking while praying" mean exactly the same thing as declarative statements but very different things as interrogatives. Though both priests were asking whether they could smoke and pray at the same time, the Dominican framed his question as "Is it OK if I smoke?" and the Jesuit framed his question as "Is it OK if I pray?" The truth upon which all the humor rests is that people can hear the same question in a different way and perceive it as a different question.

Tversky and Kahneman's experiments revealed that framing biases dramatically change the way people understand risk and reward. In one study, they gave faculty members at the Harvard Medical School information about a surgical treatment for lung cancer and then asked them to choose between that treatment and a riskier option of radiation treatment. Half the participants read that the surgical treatment had a 90 percent survival rate in the first month. The other half read that the treatment had a 10 percent mortality rate. Only half the doctors who learned about the mortality rate chose the surgical option, compared to 84 percent of the doctors who learned about the survival rate—even though a 90 percent survival rate and a 10 percent mortality rate mean exactly the same thing.[11]

To see how this framing bias might affect public policy, consider the argument from the last chapter that we need to do something to make swimming pools safer because fifteen thousand children a year die in swimming accidents. Let's imagine that somebody has invented a simple swimming pool cover that would prevent ten thousand fatal accidents at a cost of $10 per pool if one million pool owners installed it. One could frame an argument about swimming pool covers in two ways:

Frame 1: We could save ten thousand lives a year by requiring all swimming pool owners to spend $10 on a simple device.
Frame 2: We could spend $10 million installing some newfangled device, and five thousand children would still die every year in swimming pool accidents.

It should not be difficult to see that the first and second frames will elicit very different responses, even though they are mathematically identical statements. Such is the power of a frame.

We would all do well to understand things like the anchoring and framing heuristics thoroughly, as most of the people trying to manipulate us understand them very well. Advertisers, political strategists, media outlets, and propagandists have spent millions of dollars and thousands of research hours exploring ways to trick our brains into working against our better angels. They have access to talent, expertise, and large piles of money—and they are not that concerned about what is good for us. If we don't understand the tools they deploy against us every day, we might as well just hand our wallets and our keys over to the first person who asks for them and flip a coin every time we go into the voting booth.

THE AFFECT HEURISTIC

For years, logicians have seen emotional appeals—or arguments that people should allow their emotions to override purely rational decisions—as logical fallacies. Take the formidably named *argumentum ad misericordiam*, or "appeal to pity." According to most logic textbooks, it is a formal fallacy to ask someone to make a decision based on feeling sorry for someone else. If you owe me money, that is purely a matter of business; the fact that you were just diagnosed with a fatal disease places no logical burden on me to forgive the debt.

But human beings don't work that way. We empathize with other people. We care about other people's suffering, and we sometimes make decisions based on our feelings—and there is absolutely nothing wrong with that. For this reason, it makes much more sense to consider emotional thinking not as a series of pitfalls and fallacies but as a mental heuristic that usually takes us to the right place but can, on occasion, mislead us.

In *Thinking, Fast and Slow*, Kahneman explains the affect heuristic as "an instance of substitution, in which the answer to an easy question (How do I feel about it?) serves as an answer to a much harder question (What do I think about it?)."[12] As Kahneman explains, this saves a huge amount of time because we process our feelings intuitively with our "fast thinking," but we come to rational conclusions laboriously with our "slow thinking."

Usually this works out fine. We are pretty good at snap judgments about the things that affect us. We are all descended from a long line of people who survived by making important decisions quickly. They often had just seconds to decide which people to trust, which animals to run away from, which mushrooms were OK to eat, and so on. Human beings who made these decisions badly did not survive long enough to become anybody's ancestors.

Like all heuristics, however, emotional thinking can be fooled and manipulated to take us down the wrong path. "The affect heuristic enables us to be rational actors in many important situations," Paul Slovic and his collaborators conclude in their classic paper on the subject. "It works beautifully when our experience enables us to anticipate accurately how we will like the consequences of our decisions. It fails miserably when the consequences turn out to be much different in character than we anticipated."[13]

A main way that the affect heuristic damages civic discourse is by causing us to see proposals as either all good or all bad. Realistic public discussions deal primarily with costs and benefits—and almost any proposal worth talking about has elements of both. But costs and benefits are exactly the things that the affect heuristic causes us to handle badly. When we approve of something, we tend to overestimate its rewards and underestimate its risks. When we disapprove of something, we tend to overestimate its costs and underestimate its potential benefits. We don't want to live in a world of trade-offs. We want to live in a world of clear and obvious choices, and the affect heuristic tells us that we do.

But the real world is not nearly so clear cut. We rarely get to choose between an obvious good and an undeniable evil. Real political progress requires us to slog through a minefield of difficult trade-offs, partial goods, lesser evils, hidden costs, and uncertain rewards. As Kahneman writes, "Reliance on the affect heuristic is common in politically charged arguments. The positions we favor have no cost and those we oppose have no benefits. We should be able to do better."[14]

CAN WE UNBIAS OURSELVES? BACON'S METHOD AND CROMWELL'S LAW

Though most of the scientific research into biases and heuristics has been done in the last fifty years or so, the biases themselves have been known and understood for much, much longer. In 1620, English politician and philosopher Francis Bacon published his most important book, *Novum Organum*, which many people today consider the foundational text of the scientific revolution. In *Novum Organum*, Bacon attempts to isolate what he calls the "idols of the mind" or "false notions which are now in possession of the human understanding, and have taken deep root therein."[15]

A quick glance at the idols that Bacon calls "Idols of the Tribe" (errors that stem from the inherent limitations of human nature) will show us that the basic errors of human cognition identified in this chapter have been well understood for four hundred years:

- "The human understanding is moved by those things most which strike and enter the mind simultaneously and suddenly, and so fill the imagination; and then it feigns and supposes all other things to be somehow . . . similar to those few things by which it is surrounded." (anchoring heuristic)[16]
- "The human understanding is of its own nature prone to suppose the existence of more order and regularity in the world than it finds." (pattern recognition bias)[17]
- "The human understanding when it has once adopted an opinion . . . draws all things else to support and agree with it." (confirmation bias)[18]
- "But by far the greatest hindrance and aberration of the human understanding proceeds from the dullness, incompetency, and deceptions of the senses; in that things which strike the sense outweigh things which do not immediately strike it, though they be more important." (availability heuristic)[19]
- "The human understanding is no dry light, but receives an infusion from the will and affections; whence proceed sciences which may be called 'sciences as one would.' For what a man had rather were true he more readily believes." (affect heuristic)[20]

When Bacon wrote *Novum Organum*, science was considered a branch of philosophy, and "natural philosophers" drew conclusions about human nature by reasoning deductively from known principles—many of which traced back either to the Bible or to the works of Aristotle. Bacon understood that such a system could not generate true scientific principles because it was completely self-referential. It relied too much on human reason and had no way to correct its own errors. Flawed premises produce flawed conclusions, which go on to become premises for new arguments and new conclusions.

Bacon argued that the only way to control for the errors of human reason was to adopt a rigorous scientific process based on observation, experimentation, hypothesis testing, and induction. Such a method encourages us to use reason and sensory perception to check each other's blind spots. And the method is also self-correcting because it operates on the principle of falsifying hypotheses rather than confirming them, thus neutralizing the effects of the confirmation bias.

Bacon's method became the impetus for the standard procedures that working scientists use today. And while contemporary scientists don't always live up to Bacon's ideals, this notion of observation and experimentation has now been hard-wired into our understanding of what science aims to do. As a result, human understanding of the universe and the natural world—which changed very little in the two thousand years between Aristotle and Bacon—has been expanding at an unimaginably rapid rate for more than three hundred years.

Bacon's methodology is not just a way of doing science, however. It also offers us a way to use reason to its full potential while controlling for its blind spots and recognizing the possibility of error. And these skills can be exported to many other areas of human endeavor—including civic discourse in a democracy. The problems that democracy must solve are not that different from the questions that scientists try to answer: How do we ensure that our schools are educating young people for an environment that does not exist yet? What is the best way to provide health care to our large population? How do we keep people safe from potential terrorists? And, ultimately, how do we maximize human potential?

These are all questions that—along with all the ideological baggage they come with—generate testable hypotheses that can be analyzed and falsified. But we have to find ways to talk about them that minimize our own biases. And every possible way to do this requires us to internalize one core assumption of Bacon's scientific method: the very real possibility that we might be wrong.

I call this the "Cromwell rule" after Oliver Cromwell, who led the English parliamentary forces during England's Civil War and governed that country as its "lord protector" from 1653 through 1658. I have taken the title of this chapter from a letter that Cromwell wrote when he invaded Scotland to punish the Scottish Presbyterian Church for declaring loyalty to King Charles II. Cromwell believed that the Scottish Calvinists should see him as their natural ally, but they believed that they had a divine duty to support the king.

Before committing his troops to battle, Cromwell wrote a letter to the Scottish church asking it to reconsider its position. In this letter, he issued his now famous plea: "I beseech you, in the bowels of Christ, think it possible you may be mistaken." This rule remains valuable advice for all sorts of human interactions—especially because it can also be framed as "Think it possible that the other person may be right." This is a nonnegotiable element of civic (or any other) friendship.

Arguing in good faith means being willing to consider the possibility that we are wrong and that the person we are arguing with is right. It means constantly monitoring and trying to control for our own biases. And it means being willing to revise our positions once we realize that we can no longer defend them. This doesn't require self-doubt or indecision. But it does require humility and enough respect for reality to understand that we really will be wrong from time to time. Once we admit this, we should also be able to see that always acknowledging the possibility that we might be wrong is the only way to make sure that we are always at least right about something.

· 10 ·

The Vision and the Dream

*Charity and kindness are the best foundations
for lasting civic peace.*

With malice toward none, with charity for all, with firmness
in the right as God gives us to see the right, let us strive on to
finish the work we are in, to bind up the nation's wounds, to care
for him who shall have borne the battle and for his widow and
his orphan, to do all which may achieve and cherish a just and
lasting peace among ourselves and with all nations.

—Abraham Lincoln, Second Inaugural Address,
March 4, 1865

Through our scientific genius we have made of this world a
neighborhood, and now through our moral and ethical commit-
ment, we must make of it a brotherhood. We must all learn to
live together as brothers or we will all perish together as fools.

—Martin Luther King Jr., address at Lincoln University,
June 6, 1961

*I*f America can be said to have a civic religion, then Abraham Lincoln and
Martin Luther King Jr. should be considered our greatest national prophets.
Like the prophets of the Old Testament, they created visions of frightening
beauty and communicated them to the nation with urgency and resolve. The
visions of both men can be summarized in just one sentence: to thrive, America must become a genuinely democratic society that gives equal opportunity

143

and equal protection to its people regardless of race, gender, religion, life experience, political affiliation, or point of view.

As both Lincoln and King made clear, their vision for America is the same vision that the founders articulated in the Declaration of Independence and the Constitution—with one crucial exception: the original documents excluded people of color from the human family, but Lincoln and King did not. Lincoln made this point subtly in the Gettysburg Address when he equated the cause for which the Union soldiers "gave the last full measure of devotion" with "the proposition that all men are created equal." King was much more direct when he said, "I have a dream that one day this nation will rise up and live out the true meaning of its creed: 'We hold these truths to be self-evident: that all men are created equal.'"

Most Americans now agree with this vision in its broadest sense, but we disagree substantially on how it should be implemented. Different members of our society have dramatically different understandings of terms like "equal opportunity" and "equal protection"—and we are still not united on which people qualify as members of the political body. Furthermore, we have widely different ideas about what to do when various elements of the vision conflict with each other.

But this is how visions work. Prophets don't micromanage the details; they declare God's will, tell us we need to repent, assure us that we will be destroyed if we don't, and articulate the broad outlines of a better world. Prophets communicate a dream; we have to figure out how to solve the thousands of practical problems that prevent us from making the dream come true. Differences in how to best implement the vision arise because human beings differ in their views about almost everything. It is vital, however, that we all work toward the same goal: to create a society that includes different kinds of people and people with different ideas into a political body that guarantees freedom, equality under the law, and equal opportunity for everyone.

Lincoln and King, I suggest, gave us two excellent strategies for managing our disagreements and working together to create a meaningful democracy. Both strategies originated as religious virtues but can be adapted—sometimes in surprising ways—to civic life. The first is *charity*, or the willingness to make the same kinds of assumptions about other people that we make about ourselves. The second is *kindness*, or the ability to see all humans as part of the same category, or kind, of moral beings. In this final chapter, I will attempt to persuade you that charity and kindness are the only foundations upon which we can build meaningful civic relations.

LINCOLN'S VISION: MALICE TOWARD NONE, CHARITY FOR ALL

Exactly four years after delivering his First Inaugural Address in 1861, a very different Abraham Lincoln addressed a very different nation. In 1861, the new president had to prepare the nation for war. Four years later, the war was all but over: Atlanta had fallen, Sherman had burned his way to the Atlantic and was marching up the coast, and Grant had pinned Lee's forces down at Petersburg. The war was coming to an end, and Lincoln had to prepare the nation for peace.

But it would not be an easy peace. Lincoln knew that the nation could not go back to the *status quo ante bellum*. The original compact between the states—which had specifically permitted slavery—had been dissolved forever. The social contract had to be renegotiated, and the new society would have to reintegrate the Confederate states into the Union while, at the same time, incorporating four million freed slaves into the body politic.

Both tasks required monumental effort. To reintegrate the nation, Lincoln would have to prevent northerners from treating the rebellious states as conquered provinces while, at the same time, convincing southerners to recommit to the Union and share their communities with newly freed slaves. Enfranchising former slaves would require a federal military presence and would severely antagonize southerners, making it almost impossible to win back their loyalty. Giving the southern states a free hand in implementing the Thirteenth Amendment, however, would almost certainly (and in fact did) result in riots, massacres, and the reinstitution of slavery under other names.

These were all nearly intractable political problems, but Lincoln did not see his second inauguration as a political moment. He certainly knew how to be political. He had spent most of January and February twisting arms and buying votes in order to pass the Thirteenth Amendment and outlaw slavery once and for all. Had he lived, he no doubt would have done the same for the constitutional revisions that became the Fourteenth and Fifteenth Amendments. Lincoln knew how to make sausage.

But the inaugural address was not the time for sausage; it was the time for bold vision and civic prophecy. His first task was to construct a new theological interpretation of the Civil War. Both sides had already constructed their own interpretations, Lincoln argued, and both had gotten it wrong. "Both read the same Bible and pray to the same God, and each invokes His aid against the other." But neither side could avoid God's wrath because the horrors of the Civil War were punishment for the national sin of slavery:

The prayers of both could not be answered. That of neither has been answered fully. The Almighty has His own purposes. "Woe unto the world because of offenses; for it must needs be that offenses come, but woe to that man by whom the offense cometh." If we shall suppose that American slavery is one of those offenses which, in the providence of God, must needs come, but which, having continued through His appointed time, He now wills to remove, and that He gives to both North and South this terrible war as the woe due to those by whom the offense came, shall we discern therein any departure from those divine attributes which the believers in a living God always ascribe to Him?[1]

Lincoln places the entire nation under God's condemnation for the sin of slavery—not just the southern states or the Confederacy. The great sin lay not in separating the states of the Union, as he had argued four years earlier, but in separating human beings from the political body and workers from the economic benefit of their labor. The entire nation had to pay for these crimes because the entire nation had committed them. Had Lincoln refused to acknowledge this—had he followed most northerners in blaming both slavery and secession entirely on the South—he would have had to concede that the United States was something other than a single nation, which was the one thing that he steadfastly refused to do.

This assertion of shared responsibility was part of Lincoln's overall strategy for the address. As political scientist Matthew Holland explains, "The considerable lengths that he goes to in this brief speech to hammer away early and often at the similarities between the two sides showcases Lincoln's determination to restore national bonds of affection."[2] In reframing the war as God's punishment of the entire nation, Lincoln negated the war's primary effect—the division of the Union into two belligerent factions. Slavery was not a sectional sin. It was not something that the South inflicted on the North or that the North was trying to deny to the South. It was an American sin that had been built into the Constitution as the price of union.

In Lincoln's version of the American story, slavery was the original sin that America had to atone for. Though he hoped that the war would end soon, he warned that God might choose to allow it to continue "until all the wealth piled by the bondsman's two hundred and fifty years of unrequited toil shall be sunk, and until every drop of blood drawn with the lash shall be paid by another drawn with the sword."[3]

But divine punishment was only half of Lincoln's story. He concluded the speech with a prophecy of national redemption—a redemption that could be shared by North and South alike once slavery and its attendant evils had been purged from the political body. The story of redemption comes in the shape of a vision of the kind of nation that the United States might become:

With malice toward none; with charity for all; with firmness in the right, as God gives us to see the right, let us strive on to finish the work we are in; to bind up the nation's wounds; to care for him who shall have borne the battle, and for his widow, and his orphan—to do all which may achieve and cherish a just, and a lasting peace, among ourselves, and with all nations.[4]

Rhetorically, Lincoln's final paragraph takes the form of an admonition and a consequence. The admonition is "Let us strive to have charity and avoid malice," and the consequence is "If we do, we will have a just and lasting peace." We should not allow ourselves to be fooled by the economy of these words. Like the even shorter Gettysburg Address, the Second Inaugural Address managed to reframe our national story in a matter of minutes. In the 272 words of the Gettysburg Address, Lincoln renarrated the standard version of America's past by reading black people back into the words of the Declaration of Independence.[5] In the 703 words of the Second Inaugural Address, he renarrated the standard version of America's future.

In both of these great speeches, Lincoln took the soaring rhetoric of the founding fathers about equality, inalienable rights, and self-determination and spoke as though this rhetoric had always included black people. The "just and lasting peace" that Lincoln pointed to had to include both the North and the South as one nation and both black Americans and white Americans as one people. Otherwise, it would be neither just nor lasting.

The only thing that could get the nation to a just and lasting peace, Lincoln believed, was charity. But what exactly did Lincoln mean by "charity"? This is perhaps the most important question we can ask about the speech. It is a big word with a lot of possible definitions, but Lincoln gave us hints that we could use to construct a civic version of what the New Testament labels as the greatest canonical virtue.[6]

The New Testament virtue of charity—a translation of the Greek *agape*, or selfless love—means something like "loving other people in the same way that God loves them." This is a noble sentiment, and it follows naturally from the sermonic nature of Lincoln's speech. But it is difficult to imagine a large republic based on the sort of absolute, universal love that Paul describes to the Corinthians. The religion in Lincoln's Second Inaugural Address was the American civil religion, not the Kingdom of God, and the charity he called the nation to practice was a civic charity rather than a perfect love.

Lincoln's phrase "with malice towards none; with charity for all" gives us a pretty good starting point for defining a civic version of charity. Having malice toward others means wishing them ill—either wanting to harm them or wanting bad things to happen to them through some other agent. Charity means wishing others well—wanting to help them or wanting good things to happen to them. Civic charity, then, means that we desire the happiness and well-being of those with whom we share our nation.

This is an abstract sort of affection—which is the only kind of affection we can feel for hundreds of millions of people we will never meet. Civic charity does not call us to forgive murderous psychopaths, or even to bless those who curse us and pray for those who spitefully use us. It merely requires us to acknowledge that, all things being equal, we would rather see good things happen to our fellow citizens than bad things—even if some of them believe things that we find reprehensible or that offend us deeply.

This does not, of course, mean that we should accept everybody's beliefs, or agree with them, or stop doing everything we can to oppose them and convince other people to oppose them too. This is all part of our civic duty. But we can do all of this without malice—without actively working to harm them or secretly hoping that they fall down an elevator shaft. At an absolute minimum, charity means not actively wanting the people we disagree with to suffer or going out of our way to cause them pain.

The mere absence of malice is a necessary but not a sufficient element of a genuinely democratic civic discourse. In his book *The Bonds of Affection: Civic Charity and the Making of America*, Holland describes a more mature version of civic charity as "a generous and forgiving affection among citizens."[7] This is an excellent description of what Lincoln meant, and it continues to describe the traits that should govern our political conversations—specifically, generosity and forgiveness.

When we argue with a generous affection, we assume the best about people that can reasonably be assumed. We try our best to believe that our opponents are patriotic, intelligent, well-intentioned people who sincerely believe their positions and want what is best for the nation and their families. When they say things that can be understood in different ways, we assume the most morally and intellectually coherent meaning that their words will bear.

When people say things that we find offensive, civic charity asks that we resist the urge to attribute to immorality or prejudice views that can be equally well explained by other motives. It asks us to give the benefit of doubts, the assumption of goodwill, and the gift of attention. When people say things that we agree with or that respond thoughtfully to our arguments, we acknowledge that they have done so. We compliment where we can do so honestly, and we praise whatever we can legitimately find praiseworthy in their beliefs or their actions.

When we argue with a forgiving affection, we recognize that people are often carried away by passions when discussing things of great importance to them. We overlook slights and insults and decline to respond in kind. We apologize when we get something wrong or when we hurt someone's feelings, and we allow others to apologize to us when they do the same.

When people don't apologize, we still don't hold grudges or hurt them intentionally, even if we feel that they have intentionally hurt us. If somebody is abusive or obnoxious, we may decline to participate in further conversation, but we don't retaliate or attempt to make them suffer. And we try really hard not to give in to the overwhelming feeling that arguments must be won—and opponents destroyed—if we want to protect our own status or sense of worth. We never forget that our opponents are human beings who possess innate dignity and fellow citizens who deserve respect.

Civic charity is easy to talk about but tremendously difficult to practice—mainly because a lot of people don't reciprocate. Some people will be rude and obnoxious and will laugh at us when we try to engage with them charitably. They will see our generosity as a sign of weakness and take advantage of our good nature to abuse us further. We will forgive them the requisite seventy times seven times, and they will keep on offending us. Charity always works this way, both the civic kind and the "love-other-people-like-God-loves-you" kind.

We need not think, however, that we are shirking our duties or abandoning our causes when we decline to angrily denounce those on the other side or to treat them like subhuman imbeciles. Charitable engagement does not always change people's hearts and minds, but the number of times it has done so is not zero—which gives charity a better track record than anger, contempt, and derision. Ultimately, though, mature and thoughtful people do not allow the way other people treat them to determine how they treat other people; when we do this, we surrender an enormous amount of power to people who do not wish us well.

KING'S DREAM: THE WORLD AS A BROTHERHOOD

In nearly all the world's ethical systems we find a moral imperative along the lines of "Treat other people the way that you want to be treated yourself." For Christians, this is sometimes called the Golden Rule (Matthew 7:12). For Confucians, it is the core principle of *shu*, or "benevolence." Nearly identical statements can be found in the sacred texts of Judaism, Islam, Buddhism, Hinduism, Taoism, Zoroastrianism, Wicca, and many other religious traditions. Stripped of its divine provenance, the same basic principle appears in most secular discussions of ethics and morality. It is as close as the world has ever come to a universal moral rule.

But, strictly speaking, the Golden Rule isn't a rule at all. It doesn't tell us how to treat other people. It doesn't allow or disallow certain actions or insist that we do, or refrain from doing, specific things. Rather, it assumes that we already know how to treat people because we know how we want to be treated. We treat others badly not because we don't understand how people should be treated but because we don't really consider them people.

The essence of the Christian Golden Rule and nearly every other ethical system in the world can be aptly summarized as "Be kind." Used this way, "kindness" means something very different from its sometimes synonym "niceness." "Nice" comes from the Latin word for "ignorant" and originally meant "foolish" or "simple." "Kind," by contrast, comes from the same Old English word as "kin" and refers to the way that one treats a relative or clan member.

"Kind," of course, can also mean "category," as in "What kind of soup are we having for dinner?" If we look carefully, we can see that these two senses of the word are closely related. We try to be *kind* to people when we consider them the same *kind* of creature as we are. Treating people with kindness means considering them fully human in the same sense that we are fully human. Treating them with unkindness means rejecting our common humanity and seeing them as something unlike ourselves. Being kind simply means (1) treating people the way that we think people ought to be treated and (2) believing that all people are actually people.

Those who organize human beings into groups—religions, political parties, armies, trade unions—have long known that the best way to encourage kindness is to portray the groups as extensions of family networks. They often encourage people to call each other "brother" and "sister" or to refer to certain leaders as "father" (and, in some less reputable groups, "godfather"). In this way, human beings over the last ten thousand years or so have moved from seeing themselves as tribal groups of 150–200 people to seeing themselves as members of large social bodies that number well into the millions.

This has not happened easily. One of the hardest things to accomplish in the modern world has been the creation of multiethnic, religiously diverse nations. Such things emerged fairly recently in the world's history. Until the twentieth century, most political bodies were either relatively homogenous nations or ethnically diverse empires. America's founders imagined a diverse nation where membership in the political body was not dependent on origin or belief. In practice, their view of diversity did not initially extend much beyond a few varieties of northern European Protestants. In theory, though, the nation they described could accommodate anybody.

We might narrate the entire history of the United States as the logical expansion of our founding principles. We inherited a shockingly radical view of the way that human beings should be treated: every single person should be considered equally valuable to the nation and must be protected equally by the law. Everybody has the right to participate equally in the creation of laws and the selection of representatives. Every person's voice matters. As a nation, we have always believed these things. For the last 230 years, we have been continually engaged in the process of renegotiating who counts as "people."

We have made progress through a process of punctuated equilibrium—relatively slow, incremental changes interrupted by a few quantum leaps that dramatically expanded the political community. The work of Abraham Lincoln produced one of these dramatic leaps, as did the work of the many women's suffrage activists whose efforts led to the Nineteenth Amendment. Unlike the work of women's suffrage, however, Lincoln's work was reversed by the segregationist regime that emerged after Reconstruction ended. The three Civil War amendments guaranteed full civil rights to freed slaves and their descendants in perpetuity. For nearly a hundred years, though, these constitutional rights were ignored and suppressed by state and local governments.

The great victories of emancipation and African American suffrage were overturned by segregated facilities, poll taxes, grandfather clauses, literacy tests, and violent intimidation sponsored—or at least not discouraged—by the states. The powerful vision that Lincoln articulated in his Second Inaugural Address languished until the civil rights movement, which began in the 1950s with the desegregation of schools and culminated (but did not conclude) with the Civil Rights Act of 1964.

Reverend Martin Luther King Jr., the figure most identified with the American civil rights movement, stands as the direct heir to Lincoln's vision of a multiethnic democracy. In August 1963, King delivered his most famous speech, "I Have a Dream," in a way designed to emphasize the connection of his vision to Lincoln's. He delivered the speech in front of the Lincoln Memorial in Washington, DC, and began with both a rhetorical nod to Lincoln and a tribute to his Emancipation Proclamation: "Five score years ago, a great American, in whose symbolic shadow we stand, signed the Emancipation Proclamation." He made it clear that the dream he described was the same dream that Lincoln had articulated a hundred years earlier.

Unlike Lincoln, however, King used the language of kinship to describe his dream. To enact Lincoln's vision, King argued, Americans must treat each other as brothers and sisters. This is a pervasive theme in the speech:

> Now is the time to lift our nation from the quicksands of racial injustice to the solid rock of brotherhood. Now is the time to make justice a reality for all of God's children.

The marvelous new militancy which has engulfed the Negro community must not lead us to distrust of all white people, for many of our white brothers, as evidenced by their presence here today, have come to realize that their destiny is tied up with our destiny.

I have a dream that one day on the red hills of Georgia the sons of former slaves and the sons of former slave-owners will be able to sit down together at a table of brotherhood.

I have a dream that one day, down in Alabama, with its vicious racists, with its governor having his lips dripping with the words of interposition and nullification; one day right there in Alabama little black boys and little black girls will be able to join hands with little white boys and white girls as sisters and brothers.

With this faith we will be able to transform the jangling discords of our nation into a beautiful symphony of brotherhood.[8]

King imported the rhetoric of brotherhood into his civil rights speeches, but his overall argument was more practical than ethical. Just as Lincoln believed that "a house divided against itself cannot stand,"[9] King believed that "we must all learn to live together as brothers or we will all perish together as fools."[10] Both men understood that the people of the nation have to be held together by something.

The homogeneity of the traditional nation-state—a useful fiction composed of people of the same ethnic, linguistic, and religious background—created a natural sense of kinship that could be amplified easily by symbols, myths, and common experiences. The further a nation moves from homogeneity, the more work symbols, myths, and common experiences must do—and the more effort everybody has to devote to creating a sense of kinship. When King said that he believed we can "transform the jangling discords of our nation into a beautiful symphony of brotherhood," he was actually engaging in practical nation building. Jangling discords don't create sustainable nations.

We need not look far to see what happens when the people of a nation fail to develop this sense of kinship. Recent instances of genocide in the former Yugoslavia and in the African nations of Rwanda and Sudan tell a clear and horrific story of what happens when unresolved intragroup tensions come to the surface. People who have been living together for years with a semblance of civic peace, and even friendship, become mortal enemies. Demagogues whip their followers into a frenzy and set them to murder their fellow citizens.

In her astounding memoir *Left to Tell*, Immaculée Ilibagiza—a Tutsi woman who survived the Rwandan genocide by hiding in a small bathroom with seven other women—describes what she experienced when a gang of Hutus who had been her friends and neighbors came to kill her:

I heard the killers call my name. They were on the other side of the wall. Less than an inch of plaster and wood separated us. Their voices were cold, hard, and determined. "She's here. We know she's here somewhere. Find Immaculée," they were saying. There were many voices and many killers. I could see them in my mind: my former friends and neighbors, who had always greeted me with love and kindness, moving through the house carrying spears and machetes. "I've killed 399 cockroaches, and Immaculée will make 400. It's a good number to kill."[11]

Ilibagiza's story resonates eerily with the recollections of an unnamed Muslim schoolteacher who survived the Bosnian genocide, as reported by Croatian theologian Miroslav Volf in his book *Exclusion and Embrace*:

My student, Zoran, the only son of my neighbor, urinated into my mouth. As the bearded hooligans standing around laughed, he told me: "You are good for nothing else, you stinking Muslim woman. . . ." I do not know whether I first heard the cry or felt the blow. My former colleague, a teacher of physics, was yelling like mad . . . [a]nd kept hitting me. Wherever he could. I have become insensitive to pain. But my soul? It hurts. I taught them to love and all the while they were making preparations to destroy everything that is not of the Orthodox faith.[12]

These reflections remind us how fragile ordinary civic peace can be. All nations are fictions created by stories and symbols that endow certain lines on a map with an almost magical significance. But the magic requires that the stories and symbols of the nation surpass the stories and symbols of the tribes that constitute it. The easy stories—the ones about how our tribe is the best and the members of other tribes aren't really people—have disastrous effects when they emerge in a diverse democratic society. Such narratives fundamentally undermine the civic relationships that make democracy work. They transfer our civic allegiance from the messy, chaotic society that is trying to govern itself to the much more controllable subset of people who look, talk, or think like we do—creating nations within nations that work like corrosive acid on the political body.

We modern Americans have no reason to think ourselves immune to the kinds of upheaval we have seen in other parts of the world. We should not tell ourselves that our democratic institutions will save us or that something called "civilization" will pop up and make everything all right. It won't. When the bonds that hold a nation together dissolve, the dissolution is usually accompanied by cataclysmic violence that engulfs everything in its way—including democratic institutions and civilization. The poet W. H. Auden perhaps said it best: "We must love one another or die."

THE RISK OF EMBRACE

A substantial amount of evidence—much of it presented in this book—shows that Americans are becoming less charitable and less kind to those who identify with a different party or political philosophy. This means that political labels are becoming our primary civic identity. We are ceasing to be Americans and becoming members of two competing political tribes defined primarily by whom they hate. We are a nation not so much of liberals and conservatives as of anti-conservatives and liberal-haters whose only fundamental beliefs are that the nation is irreparably broken and that it cannot be fixed until the other side is vanquished forever. But this won't work. The other side isn't going anywhere. If we can't figure out how to be one country, we are going to have to figure out how to be two.

What can we do about it? Quite a lot, actually: We can argue as friends. We can learn to have difficult conversations with charity and kindness. We can change the way we talk to each other. We can do our part to restore the civic tradition that has always defined our nation at its best. But somebody has to go first.

"Who goes first?" is always the most important question when it comes to disarming and de-escalating conflict. Even when everybody agrees in theory that it needs to happen, nobody wants to be the first to put down his or her weapons—the one who takes the greatest risk and experiences the most vulnerability. This is the classic prisoner's dilemma situation: both parties would benefit from mutual cooperation, but both end up defecting because neither wants to risk being the only one to cooperate.

Volf calls this the "risk of embrace." Having lived through the breakup of Yugoslavia and the ethnic cleansing in Bosnia, Volf speaks with more authority than most about the consequences of division and civic enmity: "Finally, there is the *risk of embrace*. . . . I open my arms, make a movement of the self towards the other, the enemy, and do not know whether I will be misunderstood, despised, even violated, or whether my action will be appreciated, understood, and reciprocated. I can become a savior or a victim—possibly both. Embrace is grace, and 'grace is a gamble, always.'"[13]

Somebody has to go first, and it might not work, and we might get laughed at, insulted, made fun of, or mischaracterized. We might try to forgive somebody who doesn't want to be forgiven, and we might end up offering our hand in friendship to somebody who slaps it away in anger or disgust. We might lose control of the situation. We might lose a friend by taking a position, and we might offend our allies by insufficiently hating the common enemy.

But sometimes it will work. Sometimes people will see our embrace as the invitation that it is. Sometimes we will have good conversations that end without anybody changing his or her mind but with all participants understanding a little bit more about a position they disagree with. Sometimes we will persuade people not, perhaps, to change their lives and join our team but maybe to soften their position on an issue or temper their hostility to a group. Sometimes we will be the ones who get softened and tempered and who change just a little bit.

Ultimately, this is how we create the society we want to live in. We vote every two or four years for the people we want to represent us in our government. But we vote every day for the kind of country that we want to live in. We vote by how we choose to participate—or not participate—in the civic life of our democracy. Every time we have a political conversation, we are casting a vote for the kind of political conversations we want to have. We also vote when we decline to have a conversation because we just don't want the conflict.

Civic conversations in a democracy are hard. They are supposed to be hard because we aren't supposed to agree about things. Realizing the shared vision of Abraham Lincoln and Martin Luther King Jr.—a diverse democracy that incorporates all of its people into the political body on fundamentally equal terms—is perhaps the most difficult thing that anybody in the world has ever tried to do. No nation has managed it yet. It stands as a goal that we can move either toward or away from. I believe that we can only succeed as a nation to the extent that we move continually forward.

Appendix A

James Madison, Federalist #10

THE UTILITY OF THE UNION AS A SAFEGUARD AGAINST DOMESTIC FACTION AND INSURRECTION

AMONG the numerous advantages promised by a well-constructed Union, none deserves to be more accurately developed than its tendency to break and control the violence of faction. The friend of popular governments never finds himself so much alarmed for their character and fate, as when he contemplates their propensity to this dangerous vice. He will not fail, therefore, to set a due value on any plan which, without violating the principles to which he is attached, provides a proper cure for it.

The instability, injustice, and confusion introduced into the public councils, have, in truth, been the mortal diseases under which popular governments have everywhere perished; as they continue to be the favorite and fruitful topics from which the adversaries to liberty derive their most specious declamations. The valuable improvements made by the American constitutions on the popular models, both ancient and modern, cannot certainly be too much admired; but it would be an unwarrantable partiality, to contend that they have as effectually obviated the danger on this side, as was wished and expected. Complaints are everywhere heard from our most considerate and virtuous citizens, equally the friends of public and private faith, and of public and personal liberty, that our governments are too unstable, that the public good is disregarded in the conflicts of rival parties, and that measures are too often decided, not according to the rules of justice and the rights of the minor party, but by the superior force of an interested and overbearing majority. However anxiously we may wish that these complaints had no foundation, the evidence of known facts will not permit us to deny that they are in some degree true.

It will be found, indeed, on a candid review of our situation, that some of the distresses under which we labor have been erroneously charged on the operation of our governments; but it will be found, at the same time, that other causes will not alone account for many of our heaviest misfortunes; and, particularly, for that prevailing and increasing distrust of public engagements, and alarm for private rights, which are echoed from one end of the continent to the other. These must be chiefly, if not wholly, effects of the unsteadiness and injustice with which a factious spirit has tainted our public administrations.

By a faction, I understand a number of citizens, whether amounting to a majority or a minority of the whole, who are united and actuated by some common impulse of passion, or of interest, adverse to the rights of other citizens, or to the permanent and aggregate interests of the community.

There are two methods of curing the mischiefs of faction: the one, by removing its causes; the other, by controlling its effects.

There are again two methods of removing the causes of faction: the one, by destroying the liberty which is essential to its existence; the other, by giving to every citizen the same opinions, the same passions, and the same interests.

It could never be more truly said than of the first remedy, that it was worse than the disease. Liberty is to faction what air is to fire, an aliment without which it instantly expires. But it could not be less folly to abolish liberty, which is essential to political life, because it nourishes faction, than it would be to wish the annihilation of air, which is essential to animal life, because it imparts to fire its destructive agency.

The second expedient is as impracticable as the first would be unwise. As long as the reason of man continues fallible, and he is at liberty to exercise it, different opinions will be formed. As long as the connection subsists between his reason and his self-love, his opinions and his passions will have a reciprocal influence on each other; and the former will be objects to which the latter will attach themselves. The diversity in the faculties of men, from which the rights of property originate, is not less an insuperable obstacle to a uniformity of interests. The protection of these faculties is the first object of government. From the protection of different and unequal faculties of acquiring property, the possession of different degrees and kinds of property immediately results; and from the influence of these on the sentiments and views of the respective proprietors, ensues a division of the society into different interests and parties.

The latent causes of faction are thus sown in the nature of man; and we see them everywhere brought into different degrees of activity, according to the different circumstances of civil society. A zeal for different opinions concerning religion, concerning government, and many other points, as well of speculation as of practice; an attachment to different leaders ambitiously contending for pre-eminence and power; or to persons of other descriptions whose fortunes have been interesting to the human passions, have, in turn, divided mankind into parties, inflamed them with mutual animosity, and rendered them much more disposed to vex and oppress each other than to co-operate for their common good. So strong is this propensity of mankind to fall into mutual animosities, that where no substantial occasion presents itself, the most frivolous and fanciful distinctions have been sufficient to kindle their unfriendly passions and excite their most violent conflicts. But the most common and durable source of factions has been the various and unequal distribution of property. Those who hold and those who are without property have ever formed distinct interests in society. Those who are creditors, and those who are debtors, fall under a like discrimination. A landed interest, a manufacturing interest, a mercantile interest, a moneyed interest, with many lesser interests, grow up of necessity in civilized nations, and divide them into different classes, actuated by different sentiments and views. The regulation of these various and interfering interests forms the principal task of modern legislation, and involves the spirit of party and faction in the necessary and ordinary operations of the government.

No man is allowed to be a judge in his own cause, because his interest would certainly bias his judgment, and, not improbably, corrupt his integrity. With equal, nay with greater reason, a body of men are unfit to be both judges and parties at the same time; yet what are many of the most important acts of legislation, but so many judicial determinations, not indeed concerning the rights of single persons, but concerning the rights of large bodies of citizens? And what are the different classes of legislators but advocates and parties to the causes which they determine? Is a law proposed concerning private debts? It is a question to which the creditors are parties on one side and the debtors on the other. Justice ought to hold the balance between them. Yet the parties are, and must be, themselves the judges; and the most numerous party, or, in other words, the most powerful faction must be expected to prevail. Shall domestic manufactures be encouraged, and in what degree, by restrictions on foreign manufactures? are questions which would be differently decided by the landed and the manufacturing classes, and probably by neither with a sole regard to justice and the public good. The apportionment of taxes on the various descriptions of property is an act which seems to require the most exact impartiality; yet there is, perhaps, no legislative act in which greater opportunity and temptation are given to a predominant party to trample on the rules of justice. Every shilling with which they overburden the inferior number, is a shilling saved to their own pockets.

It is in vain to say that enlightened statesmen will be able to adjust these clashing interests, and render them all subservient to the public good. Enlightened statesmen will not always be at the helm. Nor, in many cases, can such an adjustment be made at all without taking into view indirect and remote considerations, which will rarely prevail over the immediate interest which one party may find in disregarding the rights of another or the good of the whole.

The inference to which we are brought is, that the CAUSES of faction cannot be removed, and that relief is only to be sought in the means of controlling its EFFECTS.

If a faction consists of less than a majority, relief is supplied by the republican principle, which enables the majority to defeat its sinister views by regular vote. It may clog the administration, it may convulse the society; but it will be unable to execute and mask its violence under the forms of the Constitution. When a majority is included in a faction, the form of popular government, on the other hand, enables it to sacrifice to its ruling passion or interest both the public good and the rights of other citizens. To secure the public good and private rights against the danger of such a faction, and at the same time to preserve the spirit and the form of popular government, is then the great object to which our inquiries are directed. Let me add that it is the great desideratum by which this form of government can be rescued from the opprobrium under which it has so long labored, and be recommended to the esteem and adoption of mankind.

By what means is this object attainable? Evidently by one of two only. Either the existence of the same passion or interest in a majority at the same time must be prevented, or the majority, having such coexistent passion or interest, must be rendered, by their number and local situation, unable to concert and carry into effect schemes of oppression. If the impulse and the opportunity be suffered to coincide, we well know that neither moral nor religious motives can be relied on as an adequate control. They are not found to be such on the injustice and violence of individuals, and lose their efficacy in proportion to the number combined together, that is, in proportion as their efficacy becomes needful.

From this view of the subject it may be concluded that a pure democracy, by which I mean a society consisting of a small number of citizens, who assemble and administer the government in person, can admit of no cure for the mischiefs of faction. A common passion or interest will, in almost every case, be felt by a majority of the whole; a communication and concert result from the form of government itself; and there is nothing to check the inducements to sacrifice the weaker party or an obnoxious individual. Hence it is that such democracies have ever been spectacles of turbulence and contention; have ever been found incompatible with personal security or the rights of property; and have in general been as short in their lives as they have been violent in their deaths. Theoretic politicians, who have patronized this species of government, have erroneously supposed that by reducing mankind to a perfect equality in their political rights, they would, at the same time, be perfectly equalized and assimilated in their possessions, their opinions, and their passions.

A republic, by which I mean a government in which the scheme of representation takes place, opens a different prospect, and promises the cure for which we are seeking. Let us examine the points in which it varies from pure democracy, and we shall comprehend both the nature of the cure and the efficacy which it must derive from the Union.

The two great points of difference between a democracy and a republic are: first, the delegation of the government, in the latter, to a small number of citizens elected by the rest; secondly, the greater number of citizens, and greater sphere of country, over which the latter may be extended.

The effect of the first difference is, on the one hand, to refine and enlarge the public views, by passing them through the medium of a chosen body of citizens, whose wisdom may best discern the true interest of their country, and whose patriotism and love of justice will be least likely to sacrifice it to temporary or partial considerations. Under such a regulation, it may well happen that the public voice, pronounced by the representatives of the people, will be more consonant to the public good than if pronounced by the people themselves, convened for the purpose. On the other hand, the effect may be inverted. Men of factious tempers, of local prejudices, or of sinister designs, may, by intrigue, by corruption, or by other means, first obtain the suffrages, and then betray the interests, of the people. The question resulting is, whether small or extensive republics are more favorable to the election of proper guardians of the public weal; and it is clearly decided in favor of the latter by two obvious considerations:

In the first place, it is to be remarked that, however small the republic may be, the representatives must be raised to a certain number, in order to guard against the cabals of a few; and that, however large it may be, they must be limited to a certain number, in order to guard against the confusion of a multitude. Hence, the number of representatives in the two cases not being in proportion to that of the two constituents, and being proportionally greater in the small republic, it follows that, if the proportion of fit characters be not less in the large than in the small republic, the former will present a greater option, and consequently a greater probability of a fit choice.

In the next place, as each representative will be chosen by a greater number of citizens in the large than in the small republic, it will be more difficult for unworthy candidates to practice with success the vicious arts by which elections are too often carried; and the suffrages of the people being more free, will be more likely to centre in men who possess the most attractive merit and the most diffusive and established characters.

It must be confessed that in this, as in most other cases, there is a mean, on both sides of which inconveniences will be found to lie. By enlarging too much the number of electors, you render the representatives too little acquainted with all their local circumstances and lesser interests; as by reducing it too much, you render him unduly attached to these, and too little fit to comprehend and pursue great and national objects. The federal Constitution forms a happy combination in this respect; the great and aggregate interests being referred to the national, the local and particular to the State legislatures.

The other point of difference is, the greater number of citizens and extent of territory which may be brought within the compass of republican than of democratic government; and it is this circumstance principally which renders factious combinations less to be dreaded in the former than in the latter. The smaller the society, the fewer probably will be the distinct parties and interests composing it; the fewer the distinct parties and interests, the more frequently will a majority be found of the same party; and the smaller the number of individuals composing a majority, and the smaller the compass within which they are placed, the more easily will they concert and execute their plans of oppression. Extend the sphere, and you take in a greater variety of parties and interests; you make it less probable that a majority of the whole will have a common motive to invade the rights of other citizens; or if such a common motive exists, it will be more difficult for all who feel it to discover their own strength, and to act in unison with each other. Besides other impediments, it may be remarked that, where there is a consciousness of unjust or dishonorable purposes, communication is always checked by distrust in proportion to the number whose concurrence is necessary.

Hence, it clearly appears, that the same advantage which a republic has over a democracy, in controlling the effects of faction, is enjoyed by a large over a small republic,—is enjoyed by the Union over the States composing it. Does the advantage consist in the substitution of representatives whose enlightened views and virtuous sentiments render them superior to local prejudices and schemes of injustice? It will not be denied that the representation of the Union will be most likely to possess these requisite endowments. Does it consist in the greater security afforded by a greater variety of parties, against the event of any one party being able to outnumber and oppress the rest? In an equal degree does the increased variety of parties comprised within the

Union, increase this security. Does it, in fine, consist in the greater obstacles opposed to the concert and accomplishment of the secret wishes of an unjust and interested majority? Here, again, the extent of the Union gives it the most palpable advantage.

The influence of factious leaders may kindle a flame within their particular States, but will be unable to spread a general conflagration through the other States. A religious sect may degenerate into a political faction in a part of the Confederacy; but the variety of sects dispersed over the entire face of it must secure the national councils against any danger from that source. A rage for paper money, for an abolition of debts, for an equal division of property, or for any other improper or wicked project, will be less apt to pervade the whole body of the Union than a particular member of it; in the same proportion as such a malady is more likely to taint a particular county or district, than an entire State.

In the extent and proper structure of the Union, therefore, we behold a republican remedy for the diseases most incident to republican government. And according to the degree of pleasure and pride we feel in being republicans, ought to be our zeal in cherishing the spirit and supporting the character of Federalists.

PUBLIUS.

Appendix B

John Quincy Adams,
Lectures on Rhetoric and Oratory

FROM LECTURE II: "OBJECTIONS AGAINST ELOQUENCE CONSIDERED"

I will conclude with urging upon your reflections the last great consideration, which I mentioned, as giving its keenest edge to the argument for devoting every faculty of the mind to the acquisition of eloquence; a consideration, arising from the peculiar situation and circumstances of our own country, and naturally connecting my present subject, the vindication of the science, with that, which will next claim your attention; I mean its origin and history.

Should a philosophical theorist, reasoning a priori, undertake to point out the state of things and of human society, which must naturally produce the highest exertions of the power of speech, he would recur to those important particulars which actually existed in the Grecian commonwealths. The most strenuous energies of the human mind, would he say, are always employed, where they are instigated by the stimulus of the highest rewards. The art of speaking must be most eagerly sought, where it is found to be most useful. It must be most useful, where it is capable of producing the greatest effects; and that can be in no other state of things, than where the power of persuasion operates upon the will, and prompts the actions of other men. The only birth place of eloquence therefore must be a free state. Under arbitrary governments, where the lot is cast upon one man to command, and upon all the rest to obey; where the despot, like the Roman centurion, has only to say to one man, go, and he goeth, and to another, come, and he cometh;

persuasion is of no av[a]il. Between authority and obedience there can be no deliberation; and wheresoever submission is the principle of government in a nation, eloquence can never arise. Eloquence is the child of liberty, and can descend from no other stock. And where will she find her most instructive school? Will it not be in a country, where the same spirit of liberty, which marks the relations between the individuals of the same community, is diffused over those more complicated and important relations between different communities. Where the independence of the man is corroborated and invigorated by the independence of the state? Where the same power of persuasion, which influences the will of the citizens at home, has the means of operating upon the will and the conduct of sovereign societies? Should it happen then, that a number of independent communities, founded upon the principles of civil and political liberty, were so reciprocally situated, as to have a great and continual intercourse with each other, and many momentous common interests, occasional as well as permanent, there above all the others will be the spot, where eloquence will spring to light; will flourish; will rise to the highest perfection, of which human art or science is susceptible.

The experience of mankind has proved exactly conformable to this theory. The Grecian commonwealths furnish the earliest examples in history of confederated states with free governments; and there also the art of oratory was first practised, the science of rhetoric first invented; and both were raised to a pitch of unrivalled excellence and glory.

From this powerful concurrence of philosophical speculation with historical proof, there are several important inferences, which ought to be pressed with peculiar energy upon the consideration of all youthful Americans; and more especially of those, who are distinguished by the liberal discipline of a classical education, and enjoy the advantages of intellectual cultivation. They cannot fail to remark, that their own nation is at this time precisely under the same circumstances, which were so propitious to the advancement of rhetoric and oratory among the Greeks. Like them, we are divided into a number of separate commonwealths, all founded upon the principles of the most enlarged social and civil liberty. Like them, we are united in certain great national interests, and connected by a confederation, differing indeed in many essential particulars from theirs, but perhaps in a still higher degree favorable to the influence and exertion of eloquence. Our institutions, from the smallest municipal associations to the great national bond, which links this continent in union, are republican. Their vital principle is liberty. Persuasion, or the influence of reason and of feeling, is the great if not the only instrument, whose operation can affect the acts of all our corporate bodies; of towns, cities, counties, states, and of the whole confederated empire. Here then eloquence is recommended by the most elevated usefulness, and encouraged by the promise of the most precious rewards.

Finally, let us observe how much it tends to exalt and ennoble our ideas of this art, to find it both in speculation and experience, thus grappled, as with hooks of steel, to the soul of liberty. So dear, and so justly dear to us are the blessings of freedom, that if no other advantage could be ascribed to the powers of speech, than that they are her inseparable companions, that alone would be an unanswerable argument for us to cherish them with more than a mother's affection. Let then the frosty rigor of the logician tell you, that eloquence is an insidious appeal to the passions of men. Let the ghastly form of despotism groan from his hollow lungs and bloodless heart, that eloquence is the instrument of turbulence and the weapon of action. Nay, let the severe and honest moralist himself pronounce in the dream of abstraction, that truth and virtue need not the aid of foreign ornament. Answer; silence them all. Answer; silence them forever, by recurring to this great and overpowering truth. Say, that by the eternal constitution of things it was ordained, that liberty should be the parent of eloquence; that eloquence should be the last stay and support of liberty; that with her she is ever destined to live, to flourish, and to die. Call up the shades of Demosthenes and Cicero to vouch your words; point to their immortal works, and say, these are not only the sublimest strains of oratory, that ever issued from the uninspired lips of mortal men; they are at the same time the expiring accents of liberty, in the nations, which have shed the brightest lustre on the name of man.

Appendix C
Alexis de Tocqueville, Democracy in America

FROM CHAPTER XII: "POLITICAL ASSOCIATIONS IN THE UNITED STATES"

The most natural privilege of man, next to the right of acting for himself, is that of combining his exertions with those of his fellow-creatures, and of acting in common with them. I am therefore led to conclude that the right of association is almost as inalienable as the right of personal liberty. No legislator can attack it without impairing the very foundations of society. Nevertheless, if the liberty of association is a fruitful source of advantages and prosperity to some nations, it may be perverted or carried to excess by others, and the element of life may be changed into an element of destruction. A comparison of the different methods which associations pursue in those countries in which they are managed with discretion, as well as in those where liberty degenerates into license, may perhaps be thought useful both to governments and to parties.

The greater part of Europeans look upon an association as a weapon which is to be hastily fashioned, and immediately tried in the conflict. A society is formed for discussion, but the idea of impending action prevails in the minds of those who constitute it: it is, in fact, an army; and the time given to parley serves to reckon up the strength and to animate the courage of the host, after which they direct their march against the enemy. Resources which lie within the bounds of the law may suggest themselves to the persons who compose it as means, but never as the only means, of success.

Such, however, is not the manner in which the right of association is understood in the United States. In America the citizens who form the minority associate, in order, in the first place, to show their numerical strength, and so to diminish the moral authority of the majority; and, in the second place, to stimulate competition, and to discover those arguments which are most fitted to act upon the majority; for they always entertain hopes of drawing over their opponents to their own side, and of afterwards disposing of the supreme power in their name. Political associations in the United States are therefore peaceable in their intentions, and strictly legal in the means which they employ; and they assert with perfect truth that they only aim at success by lawful expedients.

The difference which exists between the Americans and ourselves depends on several causes. In Europe there are numerous parties so diametrically opposed to the majority that they can never hope to acquire its support, and at the same time they think that they are sufficiently strong in themselves to struggle and to defend their cause. When a party of this kind forms an association, its object is, not to conquer, but to fight. In America the individuals who hold opinions very much opposed to those of the majority are no sort of impediment to its power, and all other parties hope to win it over to their own principles in the end. The exercise of the right of association becomes dangerous in proportion to the impossibility which excludes great parties from acquiring the majority. In a country like the United States, in which the differences of opinion are mere differences of hue, the right of association may remain unrestrained without evil consequences. The inexperience of many of the European nations in the enjoyment of liberty leads them only to look upon the liberty of association as a right of attacking the Government. The first notion which presents itself to a party, as well as to an individual, when it has acquired a consciousness of its own strength, is that of violence: the notion of persuasion arises at a later period and is only derived from experience. The English, who are divided into parties which differ most essentially from each other, rarely abuse the right of association, because they have long been accustomed to exercise it. In France the passion for war is so intense that there is no undertaking so mad, or so injurious to the welfare of the State, that a man does not consider himself honored in defending it, at the risk of his life.

But perhaps the most powerful of the causes which tend to mitigate the excesses of political association in the United States is Universal Suffrage. In countries in which universal suffrage exists the majority is never doubtful, because neither party can pretend to represent that portion of the community which has not voted. The associations which are formed are aware, as well as the nation at large, that they do not represent the majority: this is, indeed, a condition inseparable from their existence; for if they did represent the preponderating power, they would change the law instead of soliciting its reform. The consequence of this is that the moral influence of the Government which they attack is very much increased, and their own power is very much enfeebled.

In Europe there are few associations which do not affect to represent the majority, or which do not believe that they represent it. This conviction or this pretension tends to augment their force amazingly, and contributes no less to legalize their measures. Violence may seem to be excusable in defence of the cause of oppressed right. Thus it is, in the vast labyrinth of human laws, that extreme liberty sometimes corrects the abuses of license, and that extreme democracy obviates the dangers of democratic government. In Europe, associations consider themselves, in some degree, as the legislative and executive councils of the people, which is unable to speak for itself. In America, where they only represent a minority of the nation, they argue and they petition.

The means which the associations of Europe employ are in accordance with the end which they propose to obtain. As the principal aim of these bodies is to act, and not to debate, to fight rather than to persuade, they are naturally led to adopt a form of organization which differs from the ordinary customs of civil bodies, and which assumes the habits and the maxims of military life. They centralize the direction of their resources as much as possible, and they intrust the power of the whole party to a very small number of leaders.

The members of these associations respond to a watchword, like soldiers on duty; they profess the doctrine of passive obedience; say rather, that in uniting together they at once abjure the exercise of their own judgment and free will; and the tyrannical control which these societies exercise is often far more insupportable than the authority possessed over society by the Government which they attack. Their moral force is much diminished by these excesses, and they lose the powerful interest which is always excited by a struggle between oppressors and the oppressed. The man who in given cases consents to obey his fellows with servility, and who submits his activity and even his opinions to their control, can have no claim to rank as a free citizen.

The Americans have also established certain forms of government which are applied to their associations, but these are invariably borrowed from the forms of the civil administration. The independence of each individual is formally recognized; the tendency of the members of the association points, as it does in the body of the community, towards the same end, but they are not obliged to follow the same track. No one abjures the exercise of his reason and his free will; but every one exerts that reason and that will for the benefit of a common undertaking.

Respect for the Law in the United States

Respect of the Americans for the law—Parental affection which they entertain for it—Personal interest of everyone to increase the authority of the law.

It is not always feasible to consult the whole people, either directly or indirectly, in the formation of the law; but it cannot be denied that, when such a measure is possible the authority of the law is very much augmented. This popular origin, which impairs the excellence and the wisdom of legislation, contributes prodigiously to increase its power. There is an amazing strength in the expression of the determination of a whole people, and when it declares itself the imagination of those who are most inclined to contest it is overawed by its authority. The truth of this fact is very well known by parties, and they consequently strive to make out a majority whenever they can. If they have not the greater number of voters on their side, they assert that the true majority abstained from voting; and if they are foiled even there, they have recourse to the body of those persons who had no votes to give.

In the United States, except slaves, servants, and paupers in the receipt of relief from the townships, there is no class of persons who do not exercise the elective franchise, and who do not indirectly contribute to make the laws. Those who design to attack the laws must consequently either modify the opinion of the nation or trample upon its decision.

A second reason, which is still more weighty, may be further adduced; in the United States everyone is personally interested in enforcing the obedience of the whole community to the law; for as the minority may shortly rally the majority to its principles, it is interested in professing that respect for the decrees of the legislator which it may soon have occasion to claim for its own. However irksome an enactment may be, the citizen of the United States complies with it, not only because it is the work of the majority, but because it originates in his own authority, and he regards it as a contract to which he is himself a party.

In the United States, then, that numerous and turbulent multitude does not exist which always looks upon the law as its natural enemy, and accordingly surveys it with fear and with distrust. It is impossible, on the other hand, not to perceive that all classes display the utmost reliance upon the legislation of their country, and that they are attached to it by a kind of parental affection.

I am wrong, however, in saying all classes; for as in America the European scale of authority is inverted, the wealthy are there placed in a position analogous to that of the poor in the Old World, and it is the opulent classes which frequently look upon the law with suspicion. I have already observed that the advantage of democracy is not, as has been sometimes asserted, that it protects the interests of the whole community, but simply that it protects those of the majority. In the United States, where the poor rule, the rich have always some reason to dread the abuses of their power. This natural anxiety of the rich may produce a sullen dissatisfaction, but society is not disturbed by it; for the same reason which induces the rich to withhold their confidence in the legislative authority makes them obey its mandates; their wealth, which prevents them from making the law, prevents them from withstanding it. Amongst civilized nations revolts are rarely excited, except by such persons as have nothing to lose by them; and if the laws of a democracy are not always worthy of respect, at least they always obtain it; for those who usually infringe the laws have no excuse for not complying with the enactments they have themselves made, and by which they are themselves benefited, whilst the citizens whose interests might be promoted by the infraction of them are induced, by their character and their stations, to submit to the decisions of the legislature, whatever they may be. Besides which, the people in America obeys the law not only because it emanates from the popular authority, but because that authority may modify it in any points which may prove vexatory; a law is observed because it is a self-imposed evil in the first place, and an evil of transient duration in the second.

FROM CHAPTER XIV: "PUBLIC SPIRIT IN THE UNITED STATES"

Patriotism of instinct—Patriotism of reflection—Their different characteristics—Nations ought to strive to acquire the second when the first has disappeared—Efforts of the Americans to it—Interest of the individual intimately connected with that of the country.

There is one sort of patriotic attachment which principally arises from that instinctive, disinterested, and undefinable feeling which connects the affections of man with his birthplace. This natural fondness is united to a taste for ancient customs, and to a reverence for ancestral traditions of the past; those who cherish it love their country as they love the mansions of their fathers. They enjoy the tranquillity which it affords them; they cling to the peaceful habits which they have contracted within its bosom; they are attached to the reminiscences which it awakens, and they are even pleased by the state of obedience in which they are placed. This patriotism is sometimes stimulated by religious enthusiasm, and then it is capable of making the most prodigious efforts. It is in itself a kind of religion; it does not reason, but it acts from the impulse of faith and of sentiment. By some nations the monarch has been regarded as a personification of the country; and the fervor of patriotism being converted into the fervor of loyalty, they took a sympathetic pride in his conquests, and gloried in his power. At one time, under the ancient monarchy, the French felt a sort of satisfaction in the sense of their dependence upon the arbitrary pleasure of their king, and they were wont to say with pride, "We are the subjects of the most powerful king in the world."

But, like all instinctive passions, this kind of patriotism is more apt to prompt transient exertion than to supply the motives of continuous endeavor. It may save the State in critical circumstances, but it will not unfrequently allow the nation to decline in the midst of peace. Whilst the manners of a people are simple and its faith unshaken, whilst society is steadily based upon traditional institutions whose legitimacy has never been contested, this instinctive patriotism is wont to endure.

But there is another species of attachment to a country which is more rational than the one we have been describing. It is perhaps less generous and less ardent, but it is more fruitful and more lasting; it is coeval with the spread of knowledge, it is nurtured by the laws, it grows by the exercise of civil rights, and, in the end, it is confounded with the personal interest of the citizen. A man comprehends the influence which the prosperity of his country has upon his own welfare; he is aware that the laws authorize him to contribute his assistance to that prosperity, and he labors to promote it as a portion of his interest in the first place, and as a portion of his right in the second.

But epochs sometimes occur, in the course of the existence of a nation, at which the ancient customs of a people are changed, public morality destroyed, religious belief disturbed, and the spell of tradition broken, whilst the diffusion of knowledge is yet imperfect, and the civil rights of the community are ill secured, or confined within very narrow limits. The country then assumes a dim and dubious shape in the eyes of the citizens; they no longer behold it in the soil which they inhabit, for that soil is to them a dull inanimate clod; nor in the usages of their forefathers, which they have been taught to look upon as a debasing yoke; nor in religion, for of that they doubt; nor in the laws, which do not originate in their own authority; nor in the legislator, whom they fear and despise. The country is lost to their senses, they can neither discover it under its own nor under borrowed features, and they entrench themselves within the dull precincts of a narrow egotism. They are emancipated from prejudice without having acknowledged the empire of reason; they are neither animated by the instinctive patriotism of monarchical subjects nor by the thinking patriotism of republican citizens; but they have stopped halfway between the two, in the midst of confusion and of distress.

In this predicament, to retreat is impossible; for a people cannot restore the vivacity of its earlier times, any more than a man can return to the innocence and the bloom of childhood; such things may be regretted, but they cannot be renewed. The only thing, then, which remains to be done is to proceed, and to accelerate the union of private with public interests, since the period of disinterested patriotism is gone by forever.

I am certainly very far from averring that, in order to obtain this result, the exercise of political rights should be immediately granted to all the members of the community. But I maintain that the most powerful, and perhaps the only, means of interesting men in the welfare of their country which we still possess is to make them partakers in the Government. At the present time civic zeal seems to me to be inseparable from the exercise of political rights; and I hold that the number of citizens will be found to augment or to decrease in Europe in proportion as those rights are extended.

In the United States the inhabitants were thrown but as yesterday upon the soil which they now occupy, and they brought neither customs nor traditions with them there; they meet each other for the first time with no previous acquaintance; in short, the instinctive love of their country can scarcely exist in their minds; but everyone takes as zealous an interest in the affairs of his township, his county, and of the whole State, as if they were his own, because everyone, in his sphere, takes an active part in the government of society.

The lower orders in the United States are alive to the perception of the influence exercised by the general prosperity upon their own welfare; and simple as this observation is, it is one which is but too rarely made by the people. But in America the people regards this prosperity as the result of its own exertions; the citizen looks upon the fortune of the public as his private interest, and he co-operates in its success, not so much from a sense of pride or of duty, as from what I shall venture to term cupidity.

It is unnecessary to study the institutions and the history of the Americans in order to discover the truth of this remark, for their manners render it sufficiently evident. As the American participates in all that is done in his country, he thinks himself obliged to defend whatever may be censured; for it is not only his country which is attacked upon these occasions, but it is himself. The consequence is, that his national pride resorts to a thousand artifices, and to all the petty tricks of individual vanity.

Nothing is more embarrassing in the ordinary intercourse of life than this irritable patriotism of the Americans. A stranger may be very well inclined to praise many of the institutions of their country, but he begs permission to blame some of the peculiarities which he observes—a permission which is, however, inexorably refused. America is therefore a free country, in which, lest anybody should be hurt by your remarks, you are not allowed to speak freely of private individuals, or of the State, of the citizens or of the authorities, of public or of private undertakings, or, in short, of anything at all, except it be of the climate and the soil; and even then Americans will be found ready to defend either the one or the other, as if they had been contrived by the inhabitants of the country.

In our times option must be made between the patriotism of all and the government of a few; for the force and activity which the first confers are irreconcilable with the guarantees of tranquillity which the second furnishes.

Appendix D

Abraham Lincoln, First Inaugural Address,
March 4, 1861

Fellow-citizens of the United States:

In compliance with a custom as old as the government itself, I appear before you to address you briefly, and to take, in your presence, the oath prescribed by the Constitution of the United States, to be taken by the President "before he enters on the execution of this office."

I do not consider it necessary at present for me to discuss those matters of administration about which there is no special anxiety or excitement.

Apprehension seems to exist among the people of the Southern States, that by the accession of a Republican Administration, their property, and their peace, and personal security, are to be endangered. There has never been any reasonable cause for such apprehension. Indeed, the most ample evidence to the contrary has all the while existed, and been open to their inspection. It is found in nearly all the published speeches of him who now addresses you. I do but quote from one of those speeches when I declare that "I have no purpose, directly or indirectly, to interfere with the institution of slavery in the States where it exists. I believe I have no lawful right to do so, and I have no inclination to do so." Those who nominated and elected me did so with full knowledge that I had made this, and many similar declarations, and had never recanted them. And more than this, they placed in the platform, for my acceptance, and as a law to themselves, and to me, the clear and emphatic resolution which I now read:

Resolved, That the maintenance inviolate of the rights of the States, and especially the right of each State to order and control its own domestic

177

institutions according to its own judgment exclusively, is essential to that balance of power on which the perfection and endurance of our political fabric depend; and we denounce the lawless invasion by armed force of the soil of any State or Territory, no matter what pretext, as among the gravest of crimes.

I now reiterate these sentiments; and in doing so, I only press upon the public attention the most conclusive evidence of which the case is susceptible, that the property, peace and security of no section are to be in any wise endangered by the now incoming Administration. I add too, that all the protection which, consistently with the Constitution and the laws, can be given, will be cheerfully given to all the States when lawfully demanded, for whatever cause—as cheerfully to one section as to another.

There is much controversy about the delivering up of fugitives from service or labor. The clause I now read is as plainly written in the Constitution as any other of its provisions:

"No person held to service or labor in one State, under the laws thereof, escaping into another, shall, in consequence of any law or regulation therein, be discharged from such service or labor, but shall be delivered up on claim of the party to whom such service or labor may be due."

It is scarcely questioned that this provision was intended by those who made it, for the reclaiming of what we call fugitive slaves; and the intention of the law-giver is the law. All members of Congress swear their support to the whole Constitution—to this provision as much as to any other. To the proposition, then, that slaves whose cases come within the terms of this clause, "shall be delivered," their oaths are unanimous. Now, if they would make the effort in good temper, could they not, with nearly equal unanimity, frame and pass a law, by means of which to keep good that unanimous oath?

There is some difference of opinion whether this clause should be enforced by national or by state authority; but surely that difference is not a very material one. If the slave is to be surrendered, it can be of but little consequence to him, or to others, by which authority it is done. And should any one, in any case, be content that his oath shall go unkept, on a merely unsubstantial controversy as to how it shall be kept?

Again, in any law upon this subject, ought not all the safeguards of liberty known in civilized and humane jurisprudence to be introduced, so that a free man be not, in any case, surrendered as a slave? And might it not be well, at the same time to provide by law for the enforcement of that clause in the Constitution which guarantees that "the citizens of each State shall be entitled to all privileges and immunities of citizens in the several States"?

I take the official oath to-day, with no mental reservations, and with no purpose to construe the Constitution or laws, by any hypercritical rules. And while I do not choose now to specify particular acts of Congress as proper to be enforced, I do suggest that it will be much safer for all, both in official and private stations, to conform to, and abide by, all those acts which stand unrepealed, than to violate any of them, trusting to find impunity in having them held to be unconstitutional.

It is seventy-two years since the first inauguration of a President under our national Constitution. During that period fifteen different and greatly distinguished citizens, have, in succession, administered the executive branch of the government. They have conducted it through many perils; and, generally, with great success. Yet, with all this scope for [of] precedent, I now enter upon the same task for the brief constitutional term of four years, under great and peculiar difficulty. A disruption of the Federal Union, heretofore only menaced, is now formidably attempted.

I hold, that in contemplation of universal law, and of the Constitution, the Union of these States is perpetual. Perpetuity is implied, if not expressed, in the fundamental law of all national governments. It is safe to assert that no government proper, ever had a provision in its organic law for its own termination. Continue to execute all the express provisions of our national Constitution, and the Union will endure forever—it being impossible to destroy it, except by some action not provided for in the instrument itself.

Again, if the United States be not a government proper, but an association of States in the nature of contract merely, can it, as a contract, be peaceably unmade, by less than all the parties who made it? One party to a contract may violate it—break it, so to speak; but does it not require all to lawfully rescind it?

Descending from these general principles, we find the proposition that, in legal contemplation, the Union is perpetual, confirmed by the history of the Union itself. The Union is much older than the Constitution. It was formed in fact, by the Articles of Association in 1774. It was matured and continued by the Declaration of Independence in 1776. It was further matured and the faith of all the then thirteen States expressly plighted and engaged that it should be perpetual, by the Articles of Confederation in 1778. And finally, in 1787, one of the declared objects for ordaining and establishing the Constitution, was "to form a more perfect Union." But if [the] destruction of the Union, by one, or by a part only, of the States, be lawfully possible, the Union is less perfect than before the Constitution, having lost the vital element of perpetuity.

It follows from these views that no State, upon its own mere motion, can lawfully get out of the Union,—that resolves and ordinances to that effect are legally void, and that acts of violence, within any State or States, against the authority of the United States, are insurrectionary or revolutionary, according to circumstances.

I therefore consider that in view of the Constitution and the laws, the Union is unbroken; and to the extent of my ability I shall take care, as the Constitution itself expressly enjoins upon me, that the laws of the Union be faithfully executed in all the States. Doing this I deem to be only a simple duty on my part; and I shall perform it, so far as practicable, unless my rightful masters, the American people, shall withhold the requisite means, or in some authoritative manner, direct the contrary. I trust this will not be regarded as a menace, but only as the declared purpose of the Union that will constitutionally defend and maintain itself.

In doing this there needs to be no bloodshed or violence; and there shall be none, unless it be forced upon the national authority. The power confided to me will be used to hold, occupy, and possess the property and places belonging to the government, and to collect the duties and imposts; but beyond what may be necessary for these objects, there will be no invasion—no using of force against or among the people anywhere. Where hostility to the United States in any interior locality, shall be so great and so universal, as to prevent competent resident citizens from holding the Federal offices, there will be no attempt to force obnoxious strangers among the people for that object. While the strict legal right may exist in the government to enforce the exercise of these offices, the attempt to do so would be so irritating, and so nearly impracticable with all, that I deem it better to forego, for the time, the uses of such offices.

The mails, unless repelled, will continue to be furnished in all parts of the Union. So far as possible, the people everywhere shall have that sense of perfect security which is most favorable to calm thought and reflection. The course here indicated will be followed, unless current events and experience shall show a modification or change to be proper; and in every case and exigency my best discretion will be exercised according to circumstances actually existing, and with a view and a hope of a peaceful solution of the national troubles, and the restoration of fraternal sympathies and affections.

That there are persons in one section or another who seek to destroy the Union at all events, and are glad of any pretext to do it, I will neither affirm nor deny; but if there be such, I need address no word to them. To those, however, who really love the Union may I not speak?

Before entering upon so grave a matter as the destruction of our national fabric, with all its benefits, its memories, and its hopes, would it not be wise to ascertain precisely why we do it? Will you hazard so desperate a step, while there is any possibility that any portion of the ills you fly from have no real existence? Will you, while the certain ills you fly to, are greater than all the real ones you fly from? Will you risk the commission of so fearful a mistake?

All profess to be content in the Union, if all constitutional rights can be maintained. Is it true, then, that any right, plainly written in the Constitution, has been denied? I think not. Happily the human mind is so constituted, that no party can reach to the audacity of doing this. Think, if you can, of a single instance in which a plainly written provision of the Constitution has ever been denied. If by the mere force of numbers, a majority should deprive a minority of any clearly written constitutional right, it might, in a moral point of view, justify revolution—certainly would, if such right were a vital one. But such is not our case. All the vital rights of minorities, and of individuals, are so plainly assured to them, by affirmations and negations, guaranties and prohibitions, in the Constitution, that controversies never arise concerning them. But no organic law can ever be framed with a provision specifically applicable to every question which may occur in practical administration. No foresight can anticipate, nor any document of reasonable length contain express provisions for all possible questions. Shall fugitives from labor be surrendered by national or by State authority? The Constitution does not expressly say. May Congress prohibit slavery in the territories? The Constitution does not expressly say. Must Congress protect slavery in the territories? The Constitution does not expressly say.

From questions of this class spring all our constitutional controversies, and we divide upon them into majorities and minorities. If the minority will not acquiesce, the majority must, or the government must cease. There is no other alternative; for continuing the government, is acquiescence on one side or the other. If a minority, in such case, will secede rather than acquiesce, they make a precedent which, in turn, will divide and ruin them; for a minority of their own will secede from them whenever a majority refuses to be controlled by such minority. For instance, why may not any portion of a new confederacy, a year or two hence, arbitrarily secede again, precisely as portions of the present Union now claim to secede from it? All who cherish disunion sentiments, are now being educated to the exact temper of doing this.

Is there such perfect identity of interests among the States to compose a new Union, as to produce harmony only, and prevent renewed secession?

Plainly, the central idea of secession, is the essence of anarchy. A majority, held in restraint by constitutional checks and limitations, and always changing easily with deliberate changes of popular opinions and sentiments, is the only true sovereign of a free people. Whoever rejects it, does, of necessity, fly to anarchy or to despotism. Unanimity is impossible; the rule of a minority, as a permanent arrangement, is wholly inadmissible; so that, rejecting the majority principle, anarchy or despotism in some form is all that is left.

I do not forget the position assumed by some, that constitutional questions are to be decided by the Supreme Court; nor do I deny that such decisions must be binding in any case, upon the parties to a suit, as to the object of that suit, while they are also entitled to very high respect and consideration in all parallel cases by all other departments of the government. And while it is obviously possible that such decision may be erroneous in any given case, still the evil effect following it, being limited to that particular case, with the chance that it may be over-ruled, and never become a precedent for other cases, can better be borne than could the evils of a different practice. At the same time, the candid citizen must confess that if the policy of the government upon vital questions, affecting the whole people, is to be irrevocably fixed by decisions of the Supreme Court, the instant they are made, in ordinary litigation between parties, in personal actions, the people will have ceased to be their own rulers, having to that extent practically resigned their government into the hands of that eminent tribunal. Nor is there in this view any assault upon the court or the judges. It is a duty from which they may not shrink, to decide cases properly brought before them; and it is no fault of theirs if others seek to turn their decisions to political purposes.

One section of our country believes slavery is right, and ought to be extended, while the other believes it is wrong, and ought not to be extended. This is the only substantial dispute. The fugitive slave clause of the Constitution, and the law for the suppression of the foreign slave trade, are each as well enforced, perhaps, as any law can ever be in a community where the moral sense of the people imperfectly supports the law itself. The great body of the people abide by the dry legal obligation in both cases, and a few break over in each. This, I think, cannot be perfectly cured, and it would be worse in both cases after the separation of the sections, than before. The foreign slave trade, now imperfectly suppressed, would be ultimately revived without restriction, in one section; while fugitive slaves, now only partially surrendered, would not be surrendered at all, by the other.

Physically speaking, we cannot separate. We can not remove our respective sections from each other, nor build an impassable wall between them. A husband and wife may be divorced, and go out of the presence, and beyond the reach of each other; but the different parts of our country cannot do this. They cannot but remain face to face; and intercourse, either amicable or hostile, must continue between them. Is it possible, then, to make that intercourse more advantageous or more satisfactory, after separation than before? Can aliens make treaties easier than friends can make laws? Can treaties be more faithfully enforced between aliens than laws can among friends? Suppose you go to war, you cannot fight always; and when, after much loss on both sides, and no gain on either, you cease fighting, the identical old questions, as to terms of intercourse, are again upon you.

This country, with its institutions, belongs to the people who inhabit it. Whenever they shall grow weary of the existing Government, they can exercise their constitutional right of amending it, or their revolutionary right to dismember or overthrow it. I cannot be ignorant of the fact that many worthy and patriotic citizens are desirous of having the national Constitution amended. While I make no recommendation of amendments, I fully recognize the rightful authority of the people over the whole subject to be exercised in either of the modes prescribed in the instrument itself; and I should, under existing circumstances, favor rather than oppose a fair opportunity being afforded the people to act upon it.

I will venture to add that to me the Convention mode seems preferable, in that it allows amendments to originate with the people themselves, instead of only permitting them to take or reject propositions, originated by others, not especially chosen for the purpose, and which might not be precisely such as they would wish to either accept or refuse. I understand a proposed amendment to the Constitution, which amendment, however, I have not seen, has passed Congress, to the effect that the federal government shall never interfere with the domestic institutions of the States, including that of persons held to service. To avoid misconstruction of what I have said, I depart from my purpose not to speak of particular amendments, so far as to say that holding such a provision to now be implied constitutional law, I have no objection to its being made express and irrevocable.

The Chief Magistrate derives all his authority from the people, and they have referred none upon him to fix terms for the separation of the States. The people themselves can do this if also they choose; but the executive, as such, has nothing to do with it. His duty is to administer the present government, as it came to his hands, and to transmit it, unimpaired by him, to his successor.

Why should there not be a patient confidence in the ultimate justice of the people? Is there any better or equal hope, in the world? In our present differences, is either party without faith of being in the right? If the Almighty Ruler of nations, with his eternal truth and justice, be on your side of the North, or on yours of the South, that truth, and that justice, will surely prevail, by the judgment of this great tribunal of the American people.

By the frame of the government under which we live, this same people have wisely given their public servants but little power for mischief; and have, with equal wisdom, provided for the return of that little to their own hands at very short intervals.

While the people retain their virtue and vigilance, no administration, by any extreme of wickedness or folly, can very seriously injure the government in the short space of four years.

My countrymen, one and all, think calmly and well, upon this whole subject. Nothing valuable can be lost by taking time. If there be an object to hurry any of you, in hot haste, to a step which you would never take deliberately, that object will be frustrated by taking time; but no good object can be frustrated by it. Such of you as are now dissatisfied still have the old Constitution unimpaired, and, on the sensitive point, the laws of your own framing under it; while the new administration will have no immediate power, if it would, to change either. If it were admitted that you who are dissatisfied, hold the right side in the dispute, there still is no single good reason for precipitate action. Intelligence, patriotism, Christianity, and a firm reliance on Him, who has never yet forsaken this favored land, are still competent to adjust, in the best way, all our present difficulty.

In your hands, my dissatisfied fellow countrymen, and not in mine, is the momentous issue of civil war. The government will not assail you. You can have no conflict without being yourselves the aggressors. You have no oath registered in Heaven to destroy the government, while I shall have the most solemn one to "preserve, protect, and defend it."

I am loath to close. We are not enemies, but friends. We must not be enemies. Though passion may have strained, it must not break our bonds of affection. The mystic chords of memory, stretching from every battlefield, and patriot grave, to every living heart and hearthstone, all over this broad land, will yet swell the chorus of the Union, when again touched, as surely they will be, by the better angels of our nature.

Appendix E

Abraham Lincoln, Second Inaugural Address,
March 4, 1865

At this second appearing to take the oath of the presidential office, there is less occasion for an extended address than there was at the first. Then a statement, somewhat in detail, of a course to be pursued, seemed fitting and proper. Now, at the expiration of four years, during which public declarations have been constantly called forth on every point and phase of the great contest which still absorbs the attention, and engrosses the energies of the nation, little that is new could be presented. The progress of our arms, upon which all else chiefly depends, is as well known to the public as to myself; and it is, I trust, reasonably satisfactory and encouraging to all. With high hope for the future, no prediction in regard to it is ventured.

On the occasion corresponding to this four years ago, all thoughts were anxiously directed to an impending civil war. All dreaded it—all sought to avert it. While the inaugeral [*sic*] address was being delivered from this place, devoted altogether to saving the Union without war, insurgent agents were in the city seeking to destroy it without war—seeking to dissole [*sic*] the Union, and divide effects, by negotiation. Both parties deprecated war; but one of them would make war rather than let the nation survive; and the other would accept war rather than let it perish. And the war came.

One eighth of the whole population were colored slaves, not distributed generally over the Union, but localized in the Southern part of it. These slaves constituted a peculiar and powerful interest. All knew that this interest was, somehow, the cause of the war. To strengthen, perpetuate, and extend this interest was the object for which the insurgents would rend the Union, even by war; while the government claimed no right to do more than to restrict the territorial enlargement of it. Neither party expected for the war, the magnitude, or the duration, which it has already attained. Neither anticipated that the cause of the conflict might cease with, or even before, the conflict itself should cease. Each looked for an easier triumph, and a result less fundamental and astounding. Both read the same Bible, and pray to the same God; and each invokes His aid against the other. It may seem strange that any men should dare to ask a just God's assistance in wringing their bread from the sweat of other men's faces; but let us judge not that we be not judged. The prayers of both could not be answered; that of neither has been answered fully. The Almighty has his own purposes. "Woe unto the world because of offences! for it must needs be that offences come; but woe to that man by whom the offence cometh!" If we shall suppose that American Slavery is one of those offences which, in the providence of God, must needs come, but which, having continued through His appointed time, He now wills to remove, and that He gives to both North and South, this terrible war, as the woe due to those by whom the offence came, shall we discern therein any departure from those divine attributes which the believers in a Living God always ascribe to Him? Fondly do we hope—fervently do we pray—that this mighty scourge of war may speedily pass away. Yet, if God wills that it continue, until all the wealth piled by the bond-man's two hundred and fifty years of unrequited toil shall be sunk, and until every drop of blood drawn with the lash, shall be paid by another drawn with the sword, as was said three thousand years ago, so still it must be said "the judgments of the Lord, are true and righteous altogether."

With malice toward none; with charity for all; with firmness in the right, as God gives us to see the right, let us strive on to finish the work we are in; to bind up the nation's wounds; to care for him who shall have borne the battle, and for his widow, and his orphan—to do all which may achieve and cherish a just and lasting peace, among ourselves, and with all nations.

Notes

CHAPTER 1

1. Much ink has been spilled, not always wisely, parsing the difference between a "republic" and a "democracy." In the usage of ancient Greece and Rome, a democracy was a small city in which every citizen voted on almost every issue. Clearly the United States is not such a nation. But neither are we quite like the Roman Republic, in which the common people voted only for a slate of elected leaders who decided everything else. However, this is a purely academic distinction in the twenty-first century, as there has not been a direct, Athenian democracy in the world for two thousand years and the broader term "democracy" can refer to a wide variety of government systems that combine multiparty elections, written constitutions, and adherence to the rule of law.

2. Thomas B. Griffith, "The Hard Work of Understanding the Constitution" (address at Brigham Young University, Provo, Utah, September 18, 2012), https://speeches.byu.edu/talks/thomas-b-griffith_the-hard-work-of-understanding-the-constitution.

3. "Partisanship and Political Animosity in 2016," Pew Research Report, June 22, 2016, 5–6, 29, 53.

4. "Calamus #5" in Walt Whitman and Jason Stacy, *Leaves of Grass, 1860: The 150th Anniversary Facsimile Edition* (Iowa City: University of Iowa Press, 2011), 349.

5. Anthony Everett, *The Rise of Athens* (New York: Random House, 2016), 101–2.

6. Walt Whitman, *Complete Poetry and Collected Prose: Leaves of Grass* (New York: Library of America, 1996), 646.

CHAPTER 2

1. Alexis de Tocqueville and Arthur Goldhammer, *Democracy in America* (New York: Library of America, 2004), 352.

2. From the Revolution in 1789 until 1804, France was a republic based on revolutionary principles; from 1804 to 1814, it was an empire ruled by Napoleon; from 1815 to 1830, it was a restored monarchy under Kings Louis XVIII and Charles X (minus 110 days in which Napoleon returned to power); in 1830, a second revolution deposed Charles X and installed his cousin, Louis-Philippe, as a constitutional monarch who ruled until he was forced out by another revolution in 1848; in 1848, Napoleon's nephew, Napoleon III, was elected president of the Second Republic; three years later, in 1851, Napoleon III tired of republican rule and declared himself emperor of the Second French Empire. During this entire time, the only peaceful transfer of power occurred in 1824, when Charles X came to the throne upon the death of his brother, Louis XVIII.

3. Tocqueville and Goldhammer, *Democracy in America*, 331.

4. Tocqueville and Goldhammer, *Democracy in America*, 278.

5. Tocqueville and Goldhammer, *Democracy in America*, 279.

6. Tocqueville and Goldhammer, *Democracy in America*, 352.

7. David Hamlin, *The Nazi-Skokie Conflict: A Civil Liberties Battle* (Boston: Beacon Press, 1980), 53.

8. Emma Beswick, "The EU Countries That Will Punish You for Disrespecting Their Flags," *Euronews*, September 11, 2017, http://www.euronews.com/2017/11/09/which-country-has-the-harshest-punishments-for-disrespecting-flags-and-national (accessed May 12, 2018).

9. "Germany Starts Enforcing Hate Speech Law," *BBC News*, January 1, 2018, http://www.bbc.com/news/technology-42510868 (accessed May 12, 2018).

10. "The Islamic Veil across Europe," *BBC News*, January 31, 2017, http://www.bbc.com/news/world-europe-13038095 (accessed May 12, 2018).

11. See Robert Justin Goldstein, *Burning the Flag: The Great 1989–1990 American Flag Desecration Controversy* (Kent, OH: Kent State University Press), 1996.

12. "Global Support for Principle of Free Expression, but Opposition to Some Forms of Speech," Pew Research Center, November 18, 2015, http://www.pewglobal.org/2015/11/18/global-support-for-principle-of-free-expression-but-opposition-to-some-forms-of-speech.

13. Tocqueville and Goldhammer, *Democracy in America*, 271.

14. Tocqueville and Goldhammer, *Democracy in America*, 221.

15. Amy Gutmann and Dennis F. Thompson, *Democracy and Disagreement* (Cambridge, MA: Belknap Press of Harvard University Press, 1996), 14.

16. Gutmann and Thompson, *Democracy and Disagreement*, 16.

17. Tocqueville and Goldhammer, *Democracy in America*, 221.

18. In 1937, the third democratically elected president of Finland, Pehr Svinhufvud, lost his reelection bid to become the first head of state outside the United States to relinquish power after an election. During the nineteenth century, three

other American presidents lost reelection bids: Adams's son John Quincy Adams, who lost to Andrew Jackson in 1828; Grover Cleveland, who lost to Benjamin Harrison in 1884; and Benjamin Harrison, who lost to Grover Cleveland in 1888.

19. Tocqueville and Goldhammer, *Democracy in America*, 276.

20. "A Time of Testing," *Arkansas Gazette*, September 1, 1957; "Support Your School Board," *Arkansas Democrat*, September 2, 1957; "The Crisis Mr. Faubus Made," *Arkansas Gazette*, September 4, 1957; "What Now in Our School Trouble?" *Arkansas Democrat*, September 5, 1957; "Governor Faubus Got His Answer," *Arkansas Gazette*, September 15, 1957.

21. Josh Gottheimer, *Ripples of Hope: Great American Civil Rights Speeches* (New York: Basic Civitas Books, 2003), 224–25.

22. R. Bentley Anderson, "Prelates, Protest, and Public Opinion: Catholic Opposition to Desegregation, 1947–1955," *Journal of Church and State* 46, no. 3 (2004): 617–44; Erica Frankenberg and Rebecca Jacobsen, "Trends School Integration Polls," *Public Opinion Quarterly* 75, no. 4 (2011): 790.

23. Jean E. Smith, *Eisenhower in War and Peace* (New York: Random House, 2013), 726.

24. Thomas Jefferson, Adrienne Koch, and William Peden, *The Life and Selected Writings of Thomas Jefferson* (New York: Modern Library, 2004), 319.

25. Jason A. Scorza, *Strong Liberalism: Habits of Mind for Democratic Citizenship* (Medford, MA: Tufts University Press, 2008), 135, 146.

26. Fareed Zakaria, *The Future of Freedom: Illiberal Democracy at Home and Abroad* (New York: Norton, 2007), 17.

27. Zakaria, *The Future of Freedom*, 89–118.

28. Tocqueville and Goldhammer, *Democracy in America*, 493.

29. Tocqueville and Goldhammer, *Democracy in America*, 299.

CHAPTER 3

1. Of the eleven states that ultimately seceded and formed the Confederate States of America, only Virginia allowed Lincoln on the 1860 presidential ballot.

2. Abraham Lincoln, *Speeches and Writings, 1859–1865*, ed. Don E. Fehrenbacher (New York: Library of America, 1989), 215, 221.

3. At the time of his inauguration, eight slave states remained in the Union. Four of these states—Missouri, Kentucky, Maryland, and Delaware—stayed in the Union throughout the Civil War, as did the portion of Virginia that became West Virginia and revoked secession. The rest of Virginia, along with Arkansas, North Carolina, and Tennessee, all ended up joining the seven states that had seceded before Lincoln's inauguration.

4. Lincoln, *Speeches and Writings*, 220.

5. Lincoln, *Speeches and Writings*, 217.

6. Steven Pinker, *The Better Angels of Our Nature: Why Violence Has Declined* (New York: Penguin Books, 2012), 482–670.

7. William Flesch, *Comeuppance: Costly Signaling, Altruistic Punishment, and Other Biological Components of Fiction* (Cambridge, MA: Harvard University Press, 2009), 31–45.

8. Most organisms overestimate and overreact to threats. This phenomenon is often referred to as the "smoke detector principle," a term coined by psychologist Randolph Nesse. Nesse points out that we regularly evacuate buildings when a smoke detector goes off, even though it is almost never actually a fire, because the results of evacuating are trivial compared to the catastrophic result of dying in a fire. The same logic causes organisms to overreact to potential threats in their environment as a way to make sure they react correctly when the threat is real. See Randolph Nesse, "The Smoke Detector Principle: Natural Selection and the Regulation of Defensive Responses," *Annals of the New York Academy of Sciences* 935 (2001): 75–85.

9. John M. Cooper, "Political Animals and Civic Friendship," in *Friendship: A Philosophical Reader*, ed. Neera K. Badhwar (Ithaca, NY: Cornell University Press, 1993), 319.

10. Aristotle, *The Ethics of Aristotle: The Nichomachean Ethics*, trans. James A. K. Thomson, ed. Hugh Tredennick (Harmondsworth, UK: Penguin, 1976), 215.

11. Sibyl A. Schwarzenbach, "On Civic Friendship," *Ethics* 107, no. 1 (1996): 109.

12. Adlai E. Stevenson, *Major Campaign Speeches of Adlai E. Stevenson, 1952* (New York: Random House, 1953), 319.

13. Robert Neelly Bellah, "Civil Religion in America," *Journal of the American Academy of Arts and Sciences* 96, no. 1 (winter 1967): 13.

14. Alexis de Tocqueville and Arthur Goldhammer, *Democracy in America* (New York: Library of America, 2004), 458–59.

15. "NPR/PBS NewsHour/Marist Poll, November 2017," Marist Poll, http://maristpoll.marist.edu/nprpbs-newshourmarist-poll-results-november-2017 (accessed May 25, 2018).

16. Quoted in Perry Bacon Jr., "Democrats Are Wrong about Republicans. Republicans Are Wrong about Democrats," *FiveThirtyEight*, June 26, 2018, https://fivethirtyeight.com/features/democrats-are-wrong-about-republicans-republicans-are-wrong-about-democrats.

17. Roy Morris, *The Long Pursuit: Abraham Lincoln's Thirty-Year Struggle with Stephen Douglas for the Heart and Soul of America* (Lincoln: University of Nebraska Press, 2010), xi–xii.

18. Morris, *The Long Pursuit*, 24.

19. Douglas R. Egerton, *Year of Meteors: Stephen Douglas, Abraham Lincoln, and the Election That Brought on the Civil War* (New York: Bloomsbury Press, 2010), 203.

20. Egerton, *Year of Meteors*, 3.

CHAPTER 4

1. Steven Levitsky and Daniel Ziblatt, *How Democracies Die: What History Tells Us about Our Future* (London: Viking, 2018), 102.

2. See the "Methodology" section of the 2017 *Economist* Democracy Index at https://www.eiu.com/topic/democracy-index (accessed May 30, 2018).

3. Lilliana Mason, *Uncivil Agreement: How Politics Became Our Identity* (Chicago: University of Chicago Press, 2018), 6.

4. George Washington, *Writings*, ed. Bernard Bailyn (New York: Library of America, 1997), 969–70.

5. *The Debate on the Constitution: Federalist and Anti-Federalist Speeches, Articles, and Letters during the Struggle over Ratification: Part 1: September 1787 to February 1788* (New York: Library of America, 1993), 410.

6. Edward J. Larson, *A Magnificent Catastrophe: The Tumultuous Election of 1800, America's First Presidential Campaign* (New York: Free Press, 2008), 39.

7. *Hartford Courant*, September 15, 1800.

8. Gordon S. Wood, *Empire of Liberty: A History of the Early Republic, 1789–1815*, Oxford History of the United States (Oxford: Oxford University Press, 2009), 247.

9. Alexander Hamilton, *Writings*, ed. Joanne B. Freeman (New York: Library of America, 2010), 924.

10. Susan Dunn, *Jefferson's Second Revolution: The Election Crisis of 1800 and the Triumph of Republicanism* (Boston: Houghton Mifflin, 2004), 208–89.

11. Dunn, *Jefferson's Second Revolution*, 214.

12. Maurice Duverger and David Wagoner, *Party Politics and Pressure Groups: A Comparative Introduction* (New York: Thomas Y. Crowell, 1972), 27.

13. Cass R. Sunstein, *#republic: Divided Democracy in the Age of Social Media* (Princeton, NJ: Princeton University Press, 2018), 10.

14. "Just 11% of Americans say they would be unhappy at the prospect of a family member marrying someone of a different race, and only 7% say the same about a marriage to someone born and raised outside of the U.S." "Political Polarization in the American Public," Pew Research Center, June 2014, 49.

15. Lilliana Mason, "Ideologues without Issues: The Polarizing Consequences of Ideological Identities," *Public Opinion Quarterly* 82, no. S1 (April 2018): 291.

16. Mason, *Uncivil Agreement*, 127.

17. Abigail Geiger, "For Many Voters, It's Not Which Presidential Candidate They're for but Which They're Against," Pew Research Center, September 2, 2016, http://www.pewresearch.org/fact-tank/2016/09/02/for-many-voters-its-not -which-presidential-candidate-theyre-for-but-which-theyre-against (retrieved May 18, 2018).

18. A. I. Abramowitz and S. W. Webster, "Negative Partisanship: Why Americans Dislike Parties but Behave like Rabid Partisans," *Political Psychology* 39 (2018): 119.

19. Thucydides, *Thucydides History of the Peloponnesian War*, ed. Richard Crawley (London: J. M. Dent & Sons, 1910), 224–25 (3:282).

20. A. Adams to T. Jefferson, July 1, 1804, in John Adams and Lester J. Cappon, *The Adams-Jefferson Letters: The Complete Correspondence between Thomas Jefferson and Abigail and John Adams* (Chapel Hill: University of North Carolina Press, 1987), 271–74.

21. Jefferson to Adams, January 21, 1812, in Adams and Cappon, *The Adams-Jefferson Letters*, 290–92.

22. Adams to Jefferson, July 15, 1813, in Adams and Cappon, *The Adams-Jefferson Letters*, 356.

23. Jefferson to Adams, June 15, 1813, in Adams and Cappon, *The Adams-Jefferson Letters*, 331.

24. Jefferson to Adams, June 15, 1813, in Adams and Cappon, *The Adams-Jefferson Letters*, 333.

25. Adams to Jefferson, June 30, 1813, in Adams and Cappon, *The Adams-Jefferson Letters*, 347.

26. Jefferson to Adams, October 28, 1813, in Adams and Cappon, *The Adams-Jefferson Letters*, 391.

27. Merrill D. Peterson, *Adams and Jefferson: A Revolutionary Dialogue* (Oxford: Oxford University Press, 1980), 109.

28. Adams to Jefferson, June 10, 1813, in Adams and Cappon, *The Adams-Jefferson Letters*, 327.

29. Jefferson to Adams, June 15, 1813, in Adams and Cappon, *The Adams-Jefferson Letters*, 331.

30. Adams to Jefferson, June 30, 1813, in Adams and Cappon, *The Adams-Jefferson Letters*, 348.

31. Peterson, *Adams and Jefferson*, 105.

32. Adams and Cappon, *The Adams-Jefferson Letters*, 284.

CHAPTER 5

1. Charles Sumner, *The Crime against Kansas: The Apologies for the Crime, the True Remedy, Speech of Hon. Charles Sumner, in the Senate of the United States, 19th and 20th May, 1856* (Boston: John P. Jewett & Company, 1856), 9.

2. See William E. Gienapp, "The Crime against Sumner: The Caning of Charles Sumner and the Rise of the Republican Party," *Civil War History* 25, no. 3 (1979): 218–45.

3. Stephen Puleo, *The Caning: The Assault That Drove America to Civil War* (Yardley, PA: Westholme, 2012), 118–24.

4. Puleo, *The Caning*, 173–74.

5. For recent work on the social benefits of third-party punishment, see Jillian J. Jordan et al., "Third-Party Punishment as a Costly Signal of Trustworthiness," *Nature* 530, no. 7591 (2016): 473–76.

6. Marion M. Miller, *Slavery from 1790 to 1857* (New York: Current Literature Publishing Company, 1913), 363.

7. Puleo, *The Caning*, 71.

8. Steven Pinker, *How the Mind Works* (New York: Norton, 1999), 525–26.

9. Tim Kreider, "Isn't It Outrageous?" *New York Times*, September 6, 2015.

10. Kreider, "Isn't It Outrageous?"

11. Jeffrey M. Berry and Sarah Sobieraj, *The Outrage Industry: Political Opinion Media and the New Incivility* (Oxford: Oxford University Press, 2014), 7.

12. Berry and Sobieraj, *The Outrage Industry*. Descriptions of each of these indicators, along with the specific content examined, can be found in the "Methods Appendix" (241–55).

13. Berry and Sobieraj, *The Outrage Industry*, 13.

14. Berry and Sobieraj, *The Outrage Industry*, 130.

15. Berry and Sobieraj, *The Outrage Industry*, 130–31.

16. Terri Apter, *Passing Judgment: Praise and Blame in Everyday Life* (New York: W. W. Norton, 2018), 226–27.

17. Timothy Snyder, *The Road to Unfreedom: Russia, Europe, America* (New York: Tim Duggan Books, 2018), 227–29.

18. Snyder, *The Road to Unfreedom*, 228.

19. Madeleine Korbel Albright and William Woodward, *Fascism: A Warning* (New York: Harper, 2018), 115.

20. Berry and Sobieraj, *The Outrage Industry*, 50.

21. Berry and Sobieraj, *The Outrage Industry*, 47.

22. Amy Gutmann and Dennis Thompson, *The Spirit of Compromise: Why Governing Demands It and Campaigning Undermines It* (Princeton, NJ: Princeton University Press, 2012), 204.

23. Berry and Sobieraj, *The Outrage Industry*, 223.

24. David Brooks, "Ryan's Biggest Mistake," *New York Times*, August 24, 2012, A25.

25. Brooks, "Ryan's Biggest Mistake," A25.

26. Jon Meacham, *The Soul of America: The Battle for Our Better Angels* (New York: Random House, 2018), 230.

27. Frank Newport, "Americans Favor Compromise to Get Things Done in Washington," Gallup Survey, October 9, 2017, http://news.gallup.com/poll/220265/americans-favor-compromise-things-done-washington.aspx (accessed June 2, 2018). "Fifty-four percent of Americans want political leaders in Washington to compromise to get things done. This far outpaces the 18% who would prefer that leaders stick to their beliefs even if little gets done, while the views of 28% fall somewhere in between."

CHAPTER 6

1. See Crispin Sartwell, "Fight with Your Friends about Politics," *The Atlantic*, August 12, 2014, https://www.theatlantic.com/politics/archive/2014/08/against-consensus/375684 (accessed June 4, 2018).

2. "How to Distinguish a Flatterer from a Friend," in Plutarch and Robin Waterfield, *Essays* (London: Penguin Books, 1992), 70.

3. Richard Stengel, *You're Too Kind: A Brief History of Flattery* (New York: Simon & Shuster, 2002), 95.

4. Elaine Chan and Jaideep Sengupta, "Insincere Flattery Actually Works: A Dual Attitudes Perspective," *JMR: Journal of Marketing Research* 47, no. 1 (2010): 122–33.

5. Ralph W. Emerson, *Essays by Ralph Waldo Emerson: First and Second Series Complete in One Volume* (New York: Perennial Library, 1951), 143.

6. Emerson, *Essays*, 150.

7. Emerson, *Essays*, 419.

8. Jason A. Scorza, *Strong Liberalism: Habits of Mind for Democratic Citizenship* (Medford, MA: Tufts University Press, 2008), 114–15.

9. Duncan Cramer, "Effect of the Destructive Disagreement Belief on Satisfaction with One's Closest Friend," *Journal of Psychology* 139, no. 1 (2005): 57–66.

10. See Jim A. Kuypers, *Partisan Journalism: A History of Media Bias in the United States* (Lanham, MD: Rowman & Littlefield, 2013), 15–33.

11. "News Use across Social Media Platforms 2017," Pew Research Center, September 2017.

12. Cass R. Sunstein, *#republic: Divided Democracy in the Age of Social Media* (Princeton, NJ: Princeton University Press, 2018), 9.

13. "Frum, Cocktail Parties, and the Threat of Doubt," Julian Sanchez, March 26, 2010, http://www.juliansanchez.com/2010/03/26/frum-cocktail-parties-and -the-threat-of-doubt (accessed May 8, 2018).

14. Craig Gibson and Trudi Jacobson, "Habits of Mind in an Uncertain Information World," *Reference & User Services Quarterly* 57, no. 3 (2018): 185.

15. Reinhard H. Luthin, *American Demagogues: The Twentieth Century* (Boston: Beacon Press, 1954), 3.

16. Michael Signer, *Demagogue: The Fight to Save Democracy from Its Worst Enemies* (New York: Palgrave Macmillan, 2009), 57.

17. Bernard Bailyn, ed., *The Debate on the Constitution: Federalist and Anti-Federalist Speeches, Articles, and Letters during the Struggle over Ratification: Part 1: September 1787 to February 1788* (New York: Literary Classics of the United States, 1993), 221.

18. James Fenimore Cooper, *The American Democrat* (Indianapolis: Liberty Fund, 1981), 121.

19. Cooper, *The American Democrat*, 121.

20. Cooper, *The American Democrat*, 122.

21. Cooper, *The American Democrat*, 124.

22. Cooper, *The American Democrat*, 122.

23. Andrés Miguel Rondón, "In Venezuela, We Couldn't Stop Chávez. Don't Make the Same Mistakes We Did," *Washington Post*, January 17, 2017.

24. Long was assassinated in September 1935, before *It Can't Happen Here* was published but after most of it had been written.

CHAPTER 7

1. John Quincy Adams, *Lectures on Rhetoric and Oratory* (New York: Russell & Russell, 1962), volume 1, 68.

2. Adams, *Lectures*, 70.

3. Adams, *Lectures*, 71.

4. Aeschylus, *The Oresteia: Agamemnon, The Libation Bearers, The Eumenides,* trans. Robert Fagles (New York: Penguin Books, 1977), 260, line 652.

5. Aeschylus, *The Oresteia,* 266, lines 792–99.

6. Aristotle, W. R. Roberts, and Ingram Bywater, *The Rhetoric and Poetics of Aristotle* (New York: Modern Library, 1984), 24–25.

7. Aristotle, Roberts, and Bywater, *The Rhetoric and Poetics of Aristotle,* 91.

8. Jonathan Haidt, *The Righteous Mind: Why Good People Are Divided by Politics and Religion* (New York: Vintage Books, 2012).

9. Alexander Edwards Coppock, "Positive, Small, Homogeneous, and Durable: Political Persuasion in Response to Information" (PhD diss., Columbia University, 2016), 41–42.

10. Coppock, "Positive, Small, Homogeneous, and Durable," x.

11. Haidt, *The Righteous Mind,* 106–7.

12. H. L. Roediger III and K. A. DeSoto, "Forgetting the Presidents," *Science* 346, no. 6213 (2014): 1106–9.

13. Henry L. Roediger and K. DeSoto, "Recognizing the Presidents: Was Alexander Hamilton President?" *Psychological Science* 27, no. 5 (2016): 644–50.

14. Ari Hoogenboom, *Outlawing the Spoils: A History of the Civil Service Reform Movement, 1865–1883* (Urbana: University of Illinois Press, 1968), 153.

15. Hoogenboom, *Outlawing the Spoils,* 167.

CHAPTER 8

1. The term "prisoner's dilemma" comes from the imaginary scenario that inspired the game: Two people commit a crime, are arrested, and are questioned separately by the police. Both are offered the same deal: confess and implicate your partner, and you will receive a light sentence. In this sense, "defecting" means implicating your partner, and "cooperating" means denying the charge and hoping that your partner does too.

2. Robert Axelrod, *The Evolution of Cooperation* (New York: Basic Books, 1984), 33.

3. Axelrod, *The Evolution of Cooperation,* 36.

4. Axelrod, *The Evolution of Cooperation,* 39.

5. Axelrod, *The Evolution of Cooperation,* 112.

6. Axelrod, *The Evolution of Cooperation,* 120–23.

7. Anatol Rapoport, *Fights, Games, and Debates* (Ann Arbor: University of Michigan Press, 1960).

8. Daniel C. Dennett, *Intuition Pumps and Other Tools for Thinking* (London: Penguin Books, 2014), 33.

9. Rapoport, *Fights, Games, and Debates,* 292.

10. Rapoport, *Fights, Games, and Debates,* 302.

11. Rapoport, *Fights, Games, and Debates,* 287.

12. Rapoport, *Fights, Games, and Debates,* 309.

13. Dennett, *Intuition Pumps and Other Tools for Thinking,* 34.

14. Amy Mitchell et al., "Distinguishing between Factual and Opinion Statements in the News," Pew Research Center, June 18, 2018, http://www.journalism .org/2018/06/18/distinguishing-between-factual-and-opinion-statements-in -the-news. The five factual statements were (1) "Spending on Social Security, Medicare, and Medicaid makes up the largest portion of the US federal budget"; (2) "ISIS lost a significant portion of its territory in Iraq"; (3) "Health care costs per person in the US are the highest in the developed world"; (4) "Immigrants who are in the US illegally have some rights under the Constitution"; and (5) "President Barack Obama was born in the United States." The five opinion statements were (1) "Immigrants who are in the US illegally are a very big problem for the country today"; (2) "Government is almost always wasteful and inefficient"; (3) "Democracy is the greatest form of government"; (4) "Abortion should be legal in most cases"; and (5) "Increasing the federal minimum wage to $15 an hour is essential for the health of democracy."

15. Mitchell et al., "Distinguishing between Factual and Opinion Statements," 6.

16. Mitchell et al., "Distinguishing between Factual and Opinion Statements," 3.

17. The phrase comes from the title of Laurence H. Tribe's book *Abortion: The Clash of Absolutes* (New York: Norton, 1990).

18. Abraham Lincoln, *Speeches and Writings, 1859–1865*, edited by Don E. Fehrenbacher (New York: Library of America, 1989), 708.

19. Lincoln, *Speeches and Writings*, 709.

CHAPTER 9

1. See Michael Austin, *Useful Fictions: Evolution, Anxiety, and the Origins of Literature* (Lincoln: University of Nebraska Press, 2011), 20–27.

2. Ezra Klein, "The Green Lantern Theory of the Presidency, Explained," *Vox*, May 20, 2014, https://www.vox.com/2014/5/20/5732208/the-green-lantern-theory -of-the-presidency-explained.

3. Ellen J. Langer, "The Illusion of Control," *Journal of Personality and Social Psychology* 32, no. 2 (1975): 311–28.

4. Raymond S. Nickerson, "Confirmation Bias: A Ubiquitous Phenomenon in Many Guises," *Review of General Psychology* 2, no. 2 (June 1998): 175–220.

5. P. C. Wason, "Reasoning about a Rule," *Quarterly Journal of Experimental Psychology* 20, no. 3 (1968): 273–81.

6. I did exactly this, in fact, and the result was a top-ten list that included Berlioz, Chopin, Schumann, Liszt, Wagner, Verdi, Bruckner, Puccini, Tchaikovsky, and Brahms. There is plenty to argue with in such a list, and I would certainly make a strong case for Mahler and Dvorak. But it is not an entirely unreasonable group, and it is certainly more accurate than a random list of names.

7. Drew Fudenberg and David K. Levine, "Recency, Consistent Learning, and Nash Equilibrium," *Proceedings of the National Academy of Sciences of the United States*

of America 111 (Supplement 3) (July 22, 2014): 10826–29; Drew Fudenberg and Alexander Peysakhovich, "Recency, Records, and Recaps: Learning and Nonequilibrium Behavior in a Simple Decision Problem," *ACM Transactions on Economics and Computation* 4, no. 4 (2016): 1–18; Dirk D. Steiner, Jeffrey S. Rain, and Neal Schmitt, "Immediate and Delayed Primacy and Recency Effects in Performance Evaluation," *Journal of Applied Psychology* 74, no. 1 (1989): 136–42.

8. Eli Pariser, *The Filter Bubble: What the Internet Is Hiding from You* (New York: Penguin Press, 2011), 1–10.

9. Daniel Kahneman, *Thinking, Fast and Slow* (New York: Farrar, Straus and Giroux, 2011), 427–28.

10. Ron Hansen, *Exiles* (New York: Farrar, Straus and Giroux, 2009), 99.

11. Kahneman, *Thinking, Fast and Slow*, 367.

12. Kahneman, *Thinking, Fast and Slow*, 139.

13. Paul Slovic, Melissa L. Finucane, Ellen Peters, and Donald G. MacGregor, "Risk as Analysis and Risk as Feelings: Some Thoughts about Affect, Reason, Risk, and Rationality," *Risk Analysis: An International Journal* 24, no. 2 (April 2004): 321.

14. Kahneman, *Thinking, Fast and Slow*, 169.

15. Francis Bacon and Fulton H. Anderson, *The New Organon* (Indianapolis: Bobbs-Merrill, 1960), 47.

16. Bacon and Anderson, *The New Organon*, 51.

17. Bacon and Anderson, *The New Organon*, 50.

18. Bacon and Anderson, *The New Organon*, 50.

19. Bacon and Anderson, *The New Organon*, 52–53.

20. Bacon and Anderson, *The New Organon*, 52.

CHAPTER 10

1. Abraham Lincoln, *Speeches and Writings, 1859–1865*, edited by Don E. Fehrenbacher (New York: Library of America, 1989), 686–87.

2. Matthew S. Holland, *Bonds of Affection: Civic Charity and the Making of America—Winthrop, Jefferson, and Lincoln* (Washington, DC: Georgetown University Press, 2007), 223.

3. Lincoln, *Speeches and Writings*, 687.

4. Lincoln, *Speeches and Writings*, 687.

5. The way Lincoln used Gettysburg to reframe America's founding documents is the subject of Gary Wills's Pulitzer Prize–winning book *Lincoln at Gettysburg: The Words That Remade America* (New York: Simon & Schuster, 1992).

6. 1 Corinthians 13.

7. Holland, *Bonds of Affection*, 13.

8. Martin L. King and James M. Washington, *A Testament of Hope: The Essential Writings and Speeches of Martin Luther King, Jr.* (New York: HarperOne, 2006), 208–16.

9. Abraham Lincoln, *Speeches and Writings*, 426.

10. King and Washington, *A Testament of Hope*, 209.

11. Immaculée Ilibagiza, Steve Erwin, and Wayne W. Dyer, *Left to Tell: Discovering God amidst the Rwandan Holocaust* (Carlsbad, CA: Hay House Publishing, 2006), xix.

12. Miroslav Volf, *Exclusion and Embrace: A Theological Exploration of Identity, Otherness, and Reconciliation* (Nashville, TN: Abingdon, 1996), 111.

13. Volf, *Exclusion and Embrace*, 147.

Bibliography

Abramowitz, A. I., and S. W. Webster. "Negative Partisanship: Why Americans Dislike Parties but Behave like Rabid Partisans." *Political Psychology* 39 (2018): 119–35.

Adams, John Quincy. *Lectures on Rhetoric and Oratory*. New York: Russell & Russell, 1962.

Aeschylus. *The Oresteia: Agamemnon, The Libation Bearers, The Eumenides*. Translated by Robert Fagles. New York: Penguin Books, 1977.

Albright, Madeleine Korbel, and William Woodward. *Fascism: A Warning*. New York: Harper, 2018.

Anderson, R. Bentley. "Prelates, Protest, and Public Opinion: Catholic Opposition to Desegregation, 1947–1955." *Journal of Church and State* 46, no. 3 (2004): 617–44.

Apter, Terri. *Passing Judgment: Praise and Blame in Everyday Life*. New York: W. W. Norton, 2018.

Aristotle. *The Ethics of Aristotle: The Nichomachean Ethics*. Translated by James A. K. Thomson, edited by Hugh Tredennick. Harmondsworth, UK: Penguin, 1976.

Aristotle, W. R. Roberts, and Ingram Bywater. *The Rhetoric and Poetics of Aristotle*. New York: Modern Library, 1984.

Austin, Michael. *That's Not What They Meant: Reclaiming the Founding Fathers from America's Right Wing*. Amherst, NY: Prometheus Books, 2012.

———. *Useful Fictions: Evolution, Anxiety, and the Origins of Literature*. Lincoln: University of Nebraska Press, 2011.

Axelrod, Robert. *The Evolution of Cooperation*. New York: Basic Books, 1984.

Bacon, Francis, and Fulton H. Anderson. *The New Organon*. Indianapolis: Bobbs-Merrill, 1960.

Badhwar, Neera K. *Friendship: A Philosophical Reader.* Ithaca, NY: Cornell University Press, 1993.

Bailyn, Bernard, ed. *The Debate on the Constitution: Federalist and Anti-Federalist Speeches, Articles, and Letters during the Struggle over Ratification: Part 1: September 1787 to February 1788.* New York: Literary Classics of the United States, 1993.

Bellah, Robert Neely. "Civil Religion in America." *Journal of the American Academy of Arts and Sciences* 96, no. 1 (winter 1967): 1–21.

Berry, Jeffrey M., and Sarah Sobieraj. *The Outrage Industry: Political Opinion Media and the New Incivility.* Oxford: Oxford University Press, 2014.

Brooks, David. "Ryan's Biggest Mistake." *New York Times*, August 24, 2012, A25.

Cappon, Lester J., ed. *The Adams-Jefferson Letters: The Complete Correspondence between Thomas Jefferson and Abigail and John Adams.* Chapel Hill: University of North Carolina Press, 1987.

Chan, Elaine, and Jaideep Sengupta. "Insincere Flattery Actually Works: A Dual Attitudes Perspective." *JMR: Journal of Marketing Research* 47, no. 1 (2010): 122–33.

Cooper, James Fenimore. *The American Democrat.* Indianapolis: Liberty Fund, 1981.

Cooper, John M. "Political Animals and Civic Friendship." *In Friendship: A Philosophical Reader*, edited by Neera K. Badhwar. Ithaca, NY: Cornell University Press, 1993.

Coppock, Alexander Edwards. "Positive, Small, Homogeneous, and Durable: Political Persuasion in Response to Information." PhD diss., Columbia University, 2016.

Cramer, Duncan. "Effect of the Destructive Disagreement Belief on Satisfaction with One's Closest Friend." *Journal of Psychology* 139, no. 1 (2005): 57–66.

Dennett, Daniel C. *Intuition Pumps and Other Tools for Thinking.* London: Penguin Books, 2014.

Dunn, Susan. *Jefferson's Second Revolution: The Election Crisis of 1800 and the Triumph of Republicanism.* Boston: Houghton Mifflin, 2004.

Duverger, Maurice, and David Wagoner. *Party Politics and Pressure Groups: A Comparative Introduction.* New York: Thomas Y. Crowell, 1972.

Egerton, Douglas R. *Year of Meteors: Stephen Douglas, Abraham Lincoln, and the Election That Brought on the Civil War.* New York: Bloomsbury Press, 2010.

Emerson, Ralph W. *Essays by Ralph Waldo Emerson: First and Second Series Complete in One Volume.* New York: Perennial Library, 1951.

Everett, Anthony. *The Rise of Athens.* New York: Random House, 2016.

Flesch, William. *Comeuppance: Costly Signaling, Altruistic Punishment, and Other Biological Components of Fiction.* Cambridge, MA: Harvard University Press, 2009.

Frankenberg, Erica, and Rebecca Jacobsen. "Trends School Integration Polls." *Public Opinion Quarterly* 75, no. 4 (2011): 788–811.

Fudenberg, Drew, and David K. Levine. "Recency, Consistent Learning, and Nash Equilibrium." *Proceedings of the National Academy of Sciences of the United States of America* 111 (Supplement 3) (July 22, 2014): 10826–29.

Fudenberg, Drew, and Alexander Peysakhovich. "Recency, Records, and Recaps: Learning and Nonequilibrium Behavior in a Simple Decision Problem." *ACM Transactions on Economics and Computation* 4, no. 4 (2016): 1–18.

Gibson, Craig, and Trudi Jacobson. "Habits of Mind in an Uncertain Information World." *Reference & User Services Quarterly* 57, no. 3 (2018): 183–92.

Gienapp, William E. "The Crime against Sumner: The Caning of Charles Sumner and the Rise of the Republican Party." *Civil War History* 25, no. 3 (1979): 218–45.

Goldstein, Robert Justin. *Burning the Flag: The Great 1989–1990 American Flag Desecration Controversy.* Kent, OH: Kent State University Press, 1996.

Gottheimer, Josh. *Ripples of Hope: Great American Civil Rights Speeches.* New York: Basic Civitas Books, 2003.

Griffith, Thomas B. "The Hard Work of Understanding the Constitution." Address at Brigham Young University, Provo, Utah, September 18, 2012. https://speeches .byu.edu/talks/thomas-b-griffith_the-hard-work-of-understanding-the-constitution.

Gutmann, Amy, and Dennis F. Thompson. *Democracy and Disagreement.* Cambridge, MA: Belknap Press of Harvard University Press, 1996.

———. *The Spirit of Compromise: Why Governing Demands It and Campaigning Undermines It.* Princeton, NJ: Princeton University Press, 2012.

Haidt, Jonathan. *The Righteous Mind: Why Good People Are Divided by Politics and Religion.* New York: Vintage Books, 2012.

Hamilton, Alexander. *Writings.* Edited by Joanne B. Freeman. New York: Library of America, 2010.

Hamlin, David. *The Nazi-Skokie Conflict: A Civil Liberties Battle.* Boston: Beacon Press, 1980.

Hansen, Ron. *Exiles.* New York: Farrar, Straus and Giroux, 2009.

Holland, Matthew S. *Bonds of Affection: Civic Charity and the Making of America—Winthrop, Jefferson, and Lincoln.* Washington, DC: Georgetown University Press, 2007.

Hoogenboom, Ari. *Outlawing the Spoils: A History of the Civil Service Reform Movement, 1865–1883.* Urbana: University of Illinois Press, 1968.

Ilibagiza, Immaculée, Steve Erwin, and Wayne W. Dyer. *Left to Tell: Discovering God amidst the Rwandan Holocaust.* Carlsbad, CA: Hay House Publishing, 2006.

Jefferson, Thomas, Adrienne Koch, and William Peden. *The Life and Selected Writings of Thomas Jefferson.* New York: Modern Library, 2004.

Jordan, Jillian J., Moshe Hoffman, Paul Bloom, and David G. Rand. "Third-Party Punishment as a Costly Signal of Trustworthiness." *Nature* 530, no. 7591 (2016): 473–76.

Kahneman, Daniel. *Thinking, Fast and Slow.* New York: Farrar, Straus and Giroux, 2011.

King, Martin L., and James M. Washington. *A Testament of Hope: The Essential Writings and Speeches of Martin Luther King, Jr.* New York: HarperOne, 2006.

Kreider, Tim. "Isn't It Outrageous?" *New York Times.* September 6, 2015.

Kuypers, Jim A. *Partisan Journalism: A History of Media Bias in the United States.* Lanham, MD: Rowman & Littlefield, 2013.

Langer, Ellen J. "The Illusion of Control." *Journal of Personality and Social Psychology* 32, no. 2 (1975): 311–28.

Larson, Edward J. *A Magnificent Catastrophe: The Tumultuous Election of 1800, America's First Presidential Campaign.* New York: Free Press, 2008.

Levitsky, Steven, and Daniel Ziblatt. *How Democracies Die: What History Tells Us about Our Future.* London: Viking, 2018.

Lincoln, Abraham. *Speeches and Writings, 1859–1865.* Edited by Don E. Fehrenbacher. New York: Library of America, 1989.

Luthin, Reinhard H. *American Demagogues: The Twentieth Century.* Boston: Beacon Press, 1954.

Mason, Lilliana. "Ideologues without Issues: The Polarizing Consequences of Ideological Identities." *Public Opinion Quarterly* 82, no. S1 (April 2018): 280–301.

———. *Uncivil Agreement: How Politics Became Our Identity.* Chicago: University of Chicago Press, 2018.

Meacham, Jon. *The Soul of America: The Battle for Our Better Angels.* New York: Random House, 2018.

Miller, Marion M. *Slavery from 1790 to 1857.* New York: Current Literature Publishing Company, 1913.

Morris, Roy. *The Long Pursuit: Abraham Lincoln's Thirty-Year Struggle with Stephen Douglas for the Heart and Soul of America.* Lincoln: University of Nebraska Press, 2010.

Nesse, Randolph. "The Smoke Detector Principle: Natural Selection and the Regulation of Defensive Responses." *Annals of the New York Academy of Sciences* 935 (2001): 75–85.

Nickerson, Raymond S. "Confirmation Bias: A Ubiquitous Phenomenon in Many Guises." *Review of General Psychology* 2, no. 2 (June 1998): 175–220.

Pariser, Eli. *The Filter Bubble: What the Internet Is Hiding from You.* New York: Penguin Press, 2011.

Peterson, Merrill D. *Adams and Jefferson: A Revolutionary Dialogue.* Oxford: Oxford University Press, 1980.

Pinker, Steven. *The Better Angels of Our Nature: Why Violence Has Declined.* New York: Penguin Books, 2012.

———. *How the Mind Works.* New York: Norton, 1999.

Plutarch and Robin Waterfield. *Essays.* London: Penguin Books, 1992.

Puleo, Stephen. *The Caning: The Assault That Drove America to Civil War.* Yardley, PA: Westholme, 2012.

Rapoport, Anatol. *Fights, Games, and Debates.* Ann Arbor: University of Michigan Press, 1960.

Roediger, H. L., III, and K. A. DeSoto. "Forgetting the Presidents." *Science* 346, no. 6213 (2014): 1106–9.

Roediger, Henry L., and K. DeSoto. "Recognizing the Presidents: Was Alexander Hamilton President?" *Psychological Science* 27, no. 5 (2016): 644–50.

Schwarzenbach, Sibyl A. "On Civic Friendship." *Ethics* 107, no. 1 (1996): 109.

Scorza, Jason A. *Strong Liberalism: Habits of Mind for Democratic Citizenship.* Medford, MA: Tufts University Press, 2008.

Signer, Michael. *Demagogue: The Fight to Save Democracy from Its Worst Enemies.* New York: Palgrave Macmillan, 2009.

Slovic, Paul, Melissa L. Finucane, Ellen Peters, and Donald G. MacGregor. "Risk as Analysis and Risk as Feelings: Some Thoughts about Affect, Reason, Risk, and Rationality." *Risk Analysis: An International Journal* 24, no. 2 (April 2004): 311–22.

Smith, Jean E. *Eisenhower in War and Peace*. New York: Random House, 2013.

Snyder, Timothy. *The Road to Unfreedom: Russia, Europe, America*. New York: Tim Duggan Books, 2018.

Steiner, Dirk D., Jeffrey S. Rain, and Neal Schmitt. "Immediate and Delayed Primacy and Recency Effects in Performance Evaluation." *Journal of Applied Psychology* 74, no. 1 (1989): 136–42.

Stengel, Richard. *You're Too Kind: A Brief History of Flattery*. New York: Simon & Shuster, 2002.

Stevenson, Adlai E. *Major Campaign Speeches of Adlai E. Stevenson, 1952*. New York: Random House, 1953.

Sumner, Charles. *The Crime against Kansas: The Apologies for the Crime, the True Remedy, Speech of Hon. Charles Sumner, in the Senate of the United States, 19th and 20th May, 1856*. Boston: John P. Jewett & Company, 1856.

Sunstein, Cass R. *#republic: Divided Democracy in the Age of Social Media*. Princeton, NJ: Princeton University Press, 2018.

Thucydides. *Thucydides History of the Peloponnesian War*. Edited by Richard Crawley. London: J. M. Dent & Sons, 1910.

Tocqueville, Alexis de, and Arthur Goldhammer. *Democracy in America*. New York: Library of America, 2004.

Tribe, Laurence H. *Abortion: The Clash of Absolutes*. New York: Norton, 1990.

Volf, Miroslav. *Exclusion and Embrace: A Theological Exploration of Identity, Otherness, and Reconciliation*. Nashville, TN: Abingdon, 1996.

Washington, George. *Writings*. Edited by Bernard Bailyn. New York: Library of America, 1997.

Wason, P. C. "Reasoning about a Rule." *Quarterly Journal of Experimental Psychology* 20, no. 3 (1968): 273–81.

Whitman, Walt. *Complete Poetry and Collected Prose: Leaves of Grass*. New York: Library of America, 1996.

Whitman, Walt, and Jason Stacy. *Leaves of Grass, 1860: The 150th Anniversary Facsimile Edition*. Iowa City: University of Iowa Press, 2011.

Wills, Gary. *Lincoln at Gettysburg: The Words That Remade America*. New York: Simon & Schuster, 1992.

Wood, Gordon S. *Empire of Liberty: A History of the Early Republic, 1789–1815*. Oxford History of the United States. Oxford: Oxford University Press, 2009.

Zakaria, Fareed. *The Future of Freedom: Illiberal Democracy at Home and Abroad*. New York: Norton, 2007.

Index

abortion, 115–16
accessibility, 134, 135
ACLU. *See* American Civil Liberties
    Union
Adams, John, 4, 21–22; and Jefferson,
    48–50, 55–60, 89, 90
Adams, John Quincy, 4, 40, 56, 89–90,
    189n18; lectures on rhetoric, 90,
    165–67
Adams and Jefferson (Peterson), 59
adversaries, external, 67–70
Aeschylus, 89, 91–94
affect heuristic, 138–39, 140
affection, 5–6, 29, 76–77
affinity networks, 80
African Americans, 151
Agamemnon, 91–92
agape, 147
"agreeing to disagree," 107–24
agreement, universal, 76
Albright, Madeline, 70
Alcibiades, 82
Alien and Sedition Acts, 49, 56, 57
Alighieri, Dante, 45–46, 76
All in the Family (TV show), 26

alliances: political, 80; strategic, 36
altruism, 110
"altruistic punishment," 34
ambition, 24–25
American Civil Liberties Union
    (ACLU), 16–17
The American Democrat (Cooper), 84–85
anarchy, 23
anchoring heuristic, 136–38, 140
animosity, partisan, 52
Apollo, 92, 93
"appeal to pity," 138
Apter, Terri, 67
arguments: agreeing to disagree,
    107–24; benefits of, 108; and civic
    friendship, 6; clarifying what is being
    argued, 116, 120–24; with friends,
    xi, 57–60, 75; in good faith, 125–41;
    meaningful, 96–97
argumentum ad misericordiam, 138
aristocracy, 37
aristoi, 6–7, 37
Aristophanes, 26
Aristotle, 6, 35–38, 83, 94
Arthur, Chester, 102–5

About the Author

Michael Austin received his BA and MA in English from Brigham Young University and his PhD in English literature from the University of California, Santa Barbara. He is the author or editor of ten books and more than fifty articles, book chapters, and reviews. His books include *New Testaments* (a study of biblical typology in the seventeenth and eighteenth centuries); *That's Not What They Meant!* (an analysis of the debates of America's Founding Fathers); and *Useful Fictions* (an exploration of the connections between cognitive psychology and literature that was named a *Choice* outstanding academic title for 2011). His composition textbook, *Reading the World: Ideas That Matter*, is used in more than two hundred colleges and universities worldwide. He is currently provost and executive vice president for academic affairs at the University of Evansville in Evansville, Indiana.